# WHY DO CATHOLICS
# EAT FISH ON FRIDAY?

## THE CATHOLIC ORIGIN TO
## JUST ABOUT EVERYTHING

# WHY DO CATHOLICS EAT FISH ON FRIDAY?

## THE CATHOLIC ORIGIN TO JUST ABOUT EVERYTHING

MICHAEL P. FOLEY

WHY DO CATHOLICS EAT FISH ON FRIDAY?:
THE CATHOLIC ORIGIN TO JUST ABOUT EVERYTHING
Copyright © Michael P. Foley, 2005.

First published 2005 by
PALGRAVE MACMILLAN™
175 Fifth Avenue, New York, N.Y. 10010 and
Houndmills, Basingstoke, Hampshire, England RG21 6XS.
Companies and representatives throughout the world.

PALGRAVE MACMILLAN is the global academic imprint of the Palgrave
Macmillan division of St. Martin's Press, LLC and of Palgrave Macmillan
Ltd. Macmillan® is a registered trademark in the United States, United
Kingdom and other countries. Palgrave is a registered trademark in the
European Union and other countries.

ISBN 1-4039-6967-1 paperback

Library of Congress Cataloging-in-Publication Data
Foley, Michael P., 1970-
    Why do Catholics eat fish on Friday?: the Catholic origin to just about
everything/by Michael P. Foley.
        p.   cm
    Includes bibliographical references and index.
    ISBN 1-4039-6967-1
    1. Catholic Church—Miscellanea.   I. Title.
BX1754.F597    2005
282—dc22

                                                                2005047524

A catalogue record for this book is available from the British Library.

Design by Letra Libre, Inc.

First edition: Pub Month Year
20  19  18  17  16  15  14  13  12  11
Printed in the United States of America

*This volume is dedicated to the Irish Presentation sisters of Our Lady of Lourdes Elementary School in Montclair, California, and to my parents, James and Lucille, whose loving practice of their faith sowed in me a keen interest in all things Catholic.*

# Contents

*Acknowledgments*                                                                ix
*Introduction*                                                                    1

### Part I: La Dolce Vita

1.  Making the Time                                                               7
2.  Holidays and Festivities                                                     11
3.  Manners and Dining Etiquette                                                 21
4.  Food and Drink                                                               27

### Part II: That's Entertainment

5.  The Arts                                                                      39
6.  Music and Theater                                                            53
7.  Sports and Games                                                             67

### Part III: The Tree of Knowledge

8.  Flowers and Plants                                                           75
9.  Insects, Animals, and Other Natural Phenomena                                89
10. Science                                                                      97
11. Inventions                                                                  105
12. Education and Superstition                                                  113

### Part IV: The Body Politic

13. American Places                                                             123
14. International, National, and State Symbols                                   131
15. Law                                                                         137

## Part V: Our Mother Tongue

16. Words, Words, Words—Catholic, Anti-Catholic,
    and Post-Catholic                                           145

17. Biblical Names and Expressions                              169

*Index*                                                           0

# Acknowledgments

I would like to thank Dr. Thomas E. Woods, Jr., who graciously let me see an advanced copy of his book *How the Catholic Church Built Western Civilization* (Regnery, 2005), and Professor Charles Rice at the University of Notre Dame Law School for the valuable data he provided on the Christian origins of Western law.

# INTRODUCTION

✠

What is *Why Do Catholics Eat Fish on Friday?* and why is it worth reading? As its title suggests, this volume presents the Catholic origins of many of the things in our lives that we currently tend to regard as secular or nonreligious. Rather than offer an overview of recognizably religious phenomena, *Why Do Catholics Eat Fish on Friday?* revels in the kinds of things that the average person would be surprised to learn have a Catholic meaning behind them, such as the Marian devotion that led to Groundhog Day or the three Catholic saints implicitly honored in the Hawaiian state flag. A number of these phenomena came about through bizarre twists of history, such as the convergence of pagan, Catholic, and anti-Catholic customs that shape our contemporary observance of Halloween. Others are the result of a long process of secularization, such as the transformation of the pretzel from a pious Lenten reward to a Super Bowl Sunday snack. And still others reflect shifting meanings in nomenclature, such as the devolution of the word *gossip* from honorable godparent to chatty detractor. Regardless of the means, however, *Why Do Catholics Eat Fish on Friday?* endeavors to unearth and present the forgotten Catholic genealogies of the world we know.

And there is much to present. From the custom of saying "goodbye" to the drinking of cappuccino, from the flowers in our garden to the way we label the levels of a building, from the music we hear to the insults we give, Catholic belief has left an indelible yet often unrecognized mark on the present-day world. This is true even in the United States. Though its founding may be better explained in terms of the Protestant Reformation or the secular Enlightenment and though the impact of Catholicism is more palpable in other countries and languages, the United States still resonates with the influence of Catholic ways, a fact that may be adduced not only from the cities, counties, and streets named after Catholic saints, feasts, and even sacraments, but from the very holidays—secular as well as sacred—it keeps. That is why much of this book lingers on the Catholic story in America, for while St. Patrick's conversion of Ireland or the grand cathedrals of Europe are common knowledge to all, many American Catholics remain unaware of the Catholic footprints on their own shores.

That the Catholic faith has played a vast and significant role in shaping Western sensibility as a whole, even in the face of erosive abandonment or outright suppression, should come as no great surprise. In addition to the extrinsic accidents of history that witnessed the Church filling the educational, cultural, and social void left by a declining Roman Empire, there is something intrinsic to Catholicism that lends to it a vibrant dynamism. Academics and wags have lately taken to calling this phenomenon the Catholic sacramental imagination, that capacity to "see the Holy lurking in creation."[1] "As Catholics," writes the sociologist Andrew Greeley, "we find our houses and our world haunted by a sense that the objects, events, and persons of daily life are revelations of grace." Greeley's observation about the Catholic propensity to see the cosmos as "enchanted" is nothing new but one that stretches back to the early days of the Church, which saw the created universe as a "book" that when read properly disclosed nothing less than its divine author.

This is not to say that every facet of the Catholic imagination is the epitome of taste and decorum: the word *gaudy* comes from rosary beads and *maudlin* from medieval portrayals of St. Mary Magdalene. This is not to say that the Catholic imagination always hits the bull's-eye of orthodox belief: hence a number of Catholic-related superstitions. It is not even to deny that Catholic practices have sometimes caused some well-deserved backlash: terms like *pontificating* and *jesuitical* stem from abuses, real and perceived, of ecclesiastical power.

Nevertheless, for the Catholic the world remains something that, in the words of Gerard Manley Hopkins, "is charged with the grandeur of God." At the heart of the Catholic faith lies the conviction that the world is an intelligible whole, and that it is intelligible precisely because a supremely intelligible and intelligent God is continually making it, preserving it, and manifesting Himself through it. And man, mortal and fallen though he be, is still capable of knowing this intelligibility: first because he is made in the image of God, but also because he knows through the sanctifying gift of faith that all of creation elegantly points to its Creator. Seen in this light, the names that Catholics devised for the natural world around them (such as "marigolds" for the Virgin Mary's gold or "John Dory" for the fish that St. Peter, the *Janitor* of heaven, supposedly caught in Matthew 17:26) are simple reminders of God's goodness in their daily lives and testaments to the communion of His saints, ever present and ever ready to respond in holy friendship. Seen in this light, the intense reality of the Gospel that is refracted and reflected in all of the created order is made manifest in the lowly labels we use, the holidays we keep, and the simple rituals we perfunctorily perform.

It is the enduring value of these subtle mnemonic devices, in fact, that has inspired me to compose this book. *Why Do Catholics Eat Fish on Friday?* was born out of a curiosity about the origins of what we now consider mundane, but it was nourished by an increasing realization that our linguistic and cultural world bears the traces of Catholicism's incarnational, sacramental gratitude to God. This is obvious in the religious objects, devotions, and actions that permeate the life of the practicing Catholic, but what intrigued me is how it can also become obvious in the secular realm if only one knows what to look for. The sight of a rosary, for example, obviously evokes for many a fond recollection of the Blessed Virgin Mary, but once you learn how lily of the valley is also a title of Our Lady you will never look at that flower the same way again. The solemn reading or chanting of the Gospel at Mass can inspire and enlighten, but once you remember how opera was developed by the Jesuits as a teaching aid to reeducate lapsed Catholics, it will put a new perspective on your appreciation of the fine arts. True, many of the things mentioned in this book have lost their original meaning, so they may no longer serve the same salutary purpose they once did. However, once their original significance is relearned, they may once again function as the charming pedagogues they once were. It is to reacquaint us with our enchanted, Catholic world through the aid of these forgotten mementos that this book is written, and it is to those who delight in seeing the world in a grain of sand and Heaven in a wildflower that it is presented.

*Michael P. Foley*
*January 25, 2005*

# Part I

# *La Dolce Vita*

1

# MAKING THE TIME

✠

> *But when the fulness of the time was come, God sent his Son,*
> *made of a woman, made under the law: That he might redeem*
> *them who were under the law: that we might receive the adoption*
> *of sons.*
>
> —Galatians 4:4–5[1]

One of the more distinguishing characteristics of Christianity is its notion of time—or at least of what happens *in* time. While classical philosophy abstracts from the spatial and the temporal in order to arrive at the eternal, and while Eastern religions, with their various doctrines on reincarnation, generally conceive of time as cyclical, Christianity is grounded in Judaism's realization that the God of eternity has definitively entered into the particularity of history. This belief crescendos in the Christian doctrine of the Incarnation, when, in the "fullness of time," the Word through whom all things were made became flesh (John 1:3,14); and it anticipates the final consummation of time, when God will be all in all (I Corinthians 15:28).

The Christian stress laid on divine revelation's entry into a specific and real point of time can be seen in the care that St. Luke gives to identifying the precise historical moment in which St. John the Baptist began his preaching (Luke 3:1). And it may also be seen in more mundane areas as well, from the way we count our years to the way we measure our day. In former ages this influence was much more palpable: when the liturgical calendar exercised the imagination more than the secular, late August would be known as **Bartholomew-tide** (in honor of the St. Bartholomew's feast day, August 24) and an Indian summer would be called **St. Martin's summer** (warm weather around November 11, St. Martin's Day). Below are a few of the lingering ways in which Catholic Christianity continues to affect our perception of time.

**B.C. and A.D.** While the ancient Romans counted the passage of the years from the founding of their city (*ab urbe condita,* or A.U.C.) and while Jewish calendars begin with the creation of the world (*anno mundi,* or A.M.), it is the Christian chronology—the starting point of which is the birth of Jesus Christ—that has come to hold sway around the world. Several competing Christian timetables had been in use for a while when in the sixth century Pope John I commissioned a Scythian monk named Dionysius Exiguus to provide a viable calendar for liturgical use. Synthesizing some of the existent calendars, Dionysius took as his *terminus a quo* the Incarnation of Our Lord, but he made one crucial error, calculating that Christ was born in the year 753 A.U.C. when in fact the latest he could have been born was 750 A.U.C. Several medieval scholars caught the mistake, but Dionysius' calendar endured nonetheless, leaving us with the anomaly that Christ was born three to six years "before Christ."

Regardless of the blunder, the idea of a "Christian era" appropriately reflects the Catholic sense that the advent of the God-man has ushered in a new dispensation of time. The terms **B.C.** ("Before Christ") and **A.D.** (*anno Domini,* or "year of the Lord") thus have a theological as well as a practical significance, though they are slowly being replaced in scholarly circles with **B.C.E.** and **C.E.**, "Before the Common Era" and "Common Era," respectively. While these politically correct terms are somewhat overstated (the Christian era, for instance, is not held in common with traditional Chinese and Muslim cultures), it is interesting to note that the A.D. dating has never been the sole means of annual measuring in Christendom. Until the fourteenth century Spain retained a chronology that began with the Roman conquest of that land, while the Greek Orthodox world did not adapt Dionysius' chronology until the fifteenth century. Instead of the Era of the Incarnation, France in the eleventh century toyed with an **Era of the Passion**, which began around the year A.D. 33.[2] Yet another convention accepted the Dionysian dating but used a different name. Instead of A.D., some old records show the abbreviation **An. Sal. Rep.**, *Anno Salutis Reparatae,* "in the year of salvation regained." To this day, *An. Sal. Rep.* occasionally makes a surprise appearance, as on a University of Notre Dame campus statue honoring its founder, Father Edward Sorin.

**Calendar.** Not just the counting of years but the reckoning of the year itself has been influenced by the Church. Since the first century B.C., the West had relied on the Julian calendar, named after Julius Caesar and devised by the Alexandrian astronomer Sosigenes. The calendar, however, was flawed, losing eleven minutes a year, and so after over fifteen hundred years of use, ten whole days had been "lost." To correct the error, Pope Gregory XIII ordered the calendar to be revised: ten days in 1582 were to be skipped (October 5 for that year would become October 15), and leap years were to occur only ninety seven times in four hundred years.[3] Though the Gregorian calendar successfully brought a closer alignment of our marking of time to the actual solar year, it was initially resisted by Protestant and Eastern Orthodox countries. Britain, for example, did not adopt the calendar until 1752, while to this day several Eastern Orthodox communities reject it as a virtually heretical invention of the papacy.

**Sunday and the Weekend.** Taking Saturday and Sunday off from work is a relatively recent phenomenon, but the anchor of the weekend, Sunday, is a quintessentially Christian day that goes back to Apostolic times. In flagrant violation of Roman law (which forbade unauthorized religious assemblies), the first Christians gathered to offer the Eucharistic sacrifice early Sunday morning, the day on which Christ rose from the dead. As Pope Benedict XVI explains in one of his earlier writings, observing the Lord's Day even under threat of death was not for them "a case of choosing between *one* law and *another,* but of choosing between the meaning that sustains life and a meaningless life."[4] Given the paramount importance of the Lord's Day in Christian life and thought, it is not surprising that its observance even anticipated our modern weekend in some respects. As early as the fourth century, many masters would release their slaves from work on Saturday so that they could better prepare for Sunday, the day on which no distinction was made between free man and slave.[5] (For more on the impact of Sunday, see p. 39.)

**The Eighth Day.** Sunday, incidentally, is also sometimes called in early Christian literature the "eighth day" of the week, since Jesus Christ rose from the dead the day after the seventh day (Saturday, or the Sabbath). By counting the days in this way the Church Fathers did not wish to change the structure of the week but to highlight the mystical significance of the number eight in the Bible, which is used throughout to symbolize eternal life and resurrection, a new beginning and a consummated end. (St. Peter, for example, suggests that the eight souls who were saved in Noah's ark foreshadows Christian salvation in baptism (I Peter 3:20, 21)). The meaning of the number eight is manifested in Christian art and design in a number of ways, such as the octagonal shape of baptismal fonts in many traditional churches. It is also from this mystical reckoning of time that there come various expressions about an eight-day week such as the Beatles' song, "Eight Days a Week."

**Clocks.** Though various kinds of sundials, water clocks, and even rudimentary mechanical clocks existed long before the Middle Ages, the invention of the first successful mechanical pendulum clock is credited to the man who would become Pope Sylvester II. Gerbert of Aurillac (ca. 940–1003) was a talented scholar who studied mathematics and natural science under Arab teachers in Spain before ascending the See of Peter as the first French pontiff. In addition to inventing the clock, Gerbert is also said to have introduced the use of Arabic numbers into Europe.[6]

Though it is difficult to say with certainty whether or not Pope Sylvester II invented the clock, it is relatively certain that the medieval development of timekeeping devices was prompted by the daily prayer of monastic life. Monks, nuns, and priests prayed the Divine Office eight times a day (see p. 55), and clocks became instrumental in helping them keep that schedule, primarily by ringing a bell at the appointed hour. (Indeed, the oldest surviving clock in Great Britain has a bell with no hands at all.) Hence Dante, when describing the mellifluous praise that the holy teachers of the Church sing to God in heaven, writes that they are:

> Like a clock that calls us at the hour
> In which the Bride of God, on waking,
> Sings Matins to her Bridegroom. . . .
> Chiming the sounds with notes so sweet that those
> With spirit well-disposed feel their love grow.[7]

The historic connection between bells for the Divine Office and chronometers has even given us our word "clock," which comes from the German *glocke,* or bell.

2

# HOLIDAYS AND FESTIVITIES

✠

*This is a holy day to the Lord our God: do not mourn, nor weep . . . Go, eat fat meats, and drink sweet wine, and send portions to them that have not prepared for themselves: because it is the holy day of the Lord, and be not sad: for the joy of the Lord is our strength.*

—Nehemiah 8:9, 10

Holidays are solemn and public reminders of important truths, virtues, or events that inspire and define a church, people, or polity. Yet as the prophet Nehemiah proclaimed, holidays also bring joy to the heart, punctuating as they do the monotony of time. (St. Augustine, the great Church Father writing in the fifth century, was quite frank about the purpose of holidays, speculating that God and the Church instituted different feasts to relieve man's boredom.) Though keeping annual holidays is a custom that long predates Christianity, our current list of American civic holidays remains influenced by the Catholic liturgical year, down to the word we still use (*holiday* obviously being a contraction of "holy day"). And other forms of public merriment betray a Catholic note of celebration as well: the word *fair* is derived from the ecclesiastical Latin, *feria,* a generic weekday feast, while the word *carnival,* as we shall see below, comes from Catholic pre-Lenten festivities.

In some respects this enduring influence is surprising, given historic anti-Catholic sentiment in some English and American circles. **Guy Fawkes**

**Day** on November 5, for example, commemorates a failed plot by several English Catholics to blow up Parliament in 1605. After the plot was foiled, the British government declared November 5 "a holiday for ever in . . . detestation of the Papists."[1] The anniversary, despite George Washington's admonitions, continued to be celebrated in some parts of the United States (where it was known as "Pope's Day") into the late nineteenth and early twentieth centuries.

Nevertheless, several Catholic customs survived in muted form or were transplanted by later waves of immigration, and so it is those secular holidays that can claim some Catholic derivation, which we present below. Before we do so, however, we will take a quick look at two examples of how the season of Lent has impacted our vocabulary.

## FESTIVITIES

**First the Carnival . . .** Today the word *carnival* evokes images of amusement parks, Ferris wheels, and side shows, but it originally referred to a much more religiously centered time of feasting and merrymaking. Prior to the season of Lent (and prior to the age of refrigeration), Christians would slowly begin to abstain from the cheese, dairy, and meat products that they would be giving up completely during the "Great Fast." This voluntary period of fasting, known as pre-Lent, began in the Roman Catholic calendar three Sundays before Ash Wednesday and would culminate around the Sunday before Lent (Quinquagesima Sunday) with abstinence from meat. Quinquagesima Sunday was thus called *Dominica Carnevala, carnevala* coming from the Latin for "removal" (*levare*) of "meat" (*caro/carnis*), though many would instead come to think of the term as a saying goodbye (*vale*) to meat (*carne*).[2] Of course, this farewell party need not be gloomy, and so the voluntary process of pious asceticism also gave rise, ironically, to the pre-Lenten excesses and glittering pageantry we associate with Mardi Gras in New Orleans or the *carnevales* in Brazil and Venice, Italy.

**. . . Then the Quarantine.** The holy season of Lent, incidentally, began in part as a time of atonement for public penitents, persons who had committed notorious and scandalous sins and were thus formally required by the Church to do public acts of penance. Beginning on Ash Wednesday, the penitents could not bathe, shave, wear shoes, talk to others, remain with their families, or sleep on a comfortable mattress, nor were they allowed to receive any of the sacraments until they were formally absolved of their sins on Holy Thursday by the bishop and allowed to return to their normal lives. This period of exclusion, because it roughly lasted forty days, was called a *quarantine* (from the medieval Latin *quarentena*), a term eventually extended by physicians to include the controlled isolation of those whose infirmities had more to do with the body than with the soul. The term *quarantine* was first used in its current medical sense in Venice during the Plague.

## HOLIDAYS

**Groundhog Day, February 2.** February 2 in the Roman Catholic calendar is "Candlemas," the Feast of the Purification of the Blessed Virgin Mary, which commemorates Mary's solemn presentation of her Son in the Holy Temple forty days after his birth. It was on this occasion that the aged prophet Simeon took the infant Jesus in his hands and declared him to be a "light for the revelation of the gentiles" (Luke 2:32). Simeon's prophecy and the focus on light eventually led to a folk belief that the weather on February 2 had a particularly keen prognostic value. If the sun shone for the greater part of the day, there would be, it was claimed, forty more days of winter, but if the skies were cloudy and gray, there would be an early spring. The Germans amended this lore by bringing into the equation either the badger or the hedgehog (not to mention their shadows); yet when they emigrated to Pennsylvania in colonial times, they could find no such creatures around. Instead they saw plenty of what the Native Americans in the area called a *wojak,* or woodchuck. Since the Indians considered the groundhog to be a wise animal, it seemed only natural to appoint the furry fellow—as Phil the Groundhog in Punxsutawney, Pennsylvania, is now called—"Seer of Seers, Sage of Sages, Prognosticator of Prognosticators and Weather Prophet Extraordinary."[3]

**St. Valentine's Day, February 14.** This popular holiday for lovers and sweethearts takes its name from St. Valentine, a Catholic priest who was martyred on February 14, 270, in the persecution of Emperor Claudius II. The anniversary of a celibate saint's violent death may seem an odd occasion for the amorous selection of a mate, so it may not come as a surprise to learn that the association is more coincidental than historical. In pagan Rome, February 15 was the feast of the *Lupercalia* in honor of the pastoral god Lupercus. The night before the feast, young people used to declare their love for each other or propose marriage. They also used to pledge their companionship and affection to a prospective spouse for the next twelve months with a view toward marriage. (From this custom comes the original meaning of being someone's "Valentine.") Medieval authors "baptized" this pagan observance by telling stories about Father Valentine as a matchmaker for Christian couples. According to one of these stories, the custom of sending cards on Valentine's Day hearkens back to a note that Valentine wrote to his jailer's daughter (whom he had miraculously cured of blindness) shortly before his execution, a note that he signed with the words, "Your Valentine."[4]

**Easter Sunday.** Easter is the great celebration of the bodily resurrection of Jesus Christ from the dead, and it remains a deeply religious holiday. On this note it is interesting to observe that even the secular customs associated with the day have their origins in Catholic devotional practice. While antedating Christianity as a spring symbol of new life, the **egg** took on new meaning as a token of Christ's resurrection from the hard shell of his stone tomb (eggs were also savored during Eastertide because the traditional Lenten fast prohibited their consumption). The wearing of new **Easter clothes** stems from the ancient practice of newly baptized Christians wearing a white garment from the moment of their baptism during the Easter Vigil on Holy Saturday until the following Sunday eight days later. After a while, even the faithful who were not neophytes adopted the custom by wearing something new to symbolize the new life brought by the death and resurrection of Christ. Hence an old Irish saying: "For Christmas, food and drink; for Easter, new clothes."[5]

It was also customary in some areas for the faithful, bedecked in their Easter finery, to take part in a religious procession after the Easter morning Mass. A crucifix or the Paschal candle would often lead the way, and while the entourage would make several stops in order to pray or sing hymns, a good part of the time would be spent in light banter. This Easter walk was secularized after the Reformation and survives today as the **Easter Parade**, the extravagant spectacle that takes place on New York's City Fifth Avenue and in other areas of the country every year.[6]

**Mother's Day, Second Sunday in May.** Contrary to the often-heard claim that Mother's Day is a self-serving invention of the greeting card industry, Mother's Day was instituted by a devout Methodist and celebrated first in a Christian church. Mrs. Ana Jarvis, a schoolteacher from Philadelphia, convinced her mother's parish in Grafton, West Virginia, to observe Mother's Day on the second anniversary of her mother's death. The year was 1907, and the Sunday on which the anniversary happened to fall was the second Sunday in May. Within a matter of a few years the holiday swept across the nation; by the time President Woodrow Wilson declared it a national holiday in 1914, it was already being observed in almost every state in the union.[7] Mrs. Jarvis promoted the holiday with the hope that it would encourage children to appreciate their mothers while they were still alive. As the holiday became more commercialized, however, she grew increasingly disenchanted with it and even tried to stop its observance. Shortly before her sad demise in a sanatorium, she told a reporter that she regretted starting Mother's Day at all.

Interestingly enough, a quasi-liturgical commemoration of mothers is not unprecedented in Catholic life. December 8, the Feast of the Immaculate Conception, is celebrated as Mother's Day in Spain, while in England *Laetare* Sunday in Lent was known as "Mothering Sunday," the day on which servants and apprentices were released in order to visit their "mother churches" (that is, their home parishes) and, by extension, their mothers. (To this day it is possible to buy simnel cakes, the traditional gift for one's mother on Mothering Sunday, in Great Britain.)[8] But there may also be another tenuous link between Catholicism and the current Mother's Day holiday. Though Ana Jarvis was almost certainly not drawing from any Catholic sources, it has been speculated that the extraordinary popularity of Mother's Day stems in part from its replacing devotion to the Blessed Virgin Mary. May is traditionally the month of Mary and was the locus for many kinds of Marian devotions, such as the crowning of the May Queen. Such adoration of the Mother of God became the object of attack during the Protestant Reformation, with one of the subsequent results being the absence in many Protestant churches of any solemn or liturgical veneration of a feminine figure. *Sans* devotion to Mary and other female saints, Christianity arguably lost a certain sentimental warmth associated with motherhood. Having a Mother's Day on the second Sunday in May could thus very well be a secular way of filling a void left by the suppression of a Catholic Marian devotion.

**Columbus Day, October 12 (generally observed on the second Monday in October).** A most American holiday has a most American Catholic origin. Though there had been sporadic celebrations of Columbus' discovery of America from 1792 on, it was thanks in large part to the Knights of Columbus' vigorous lobbying of state legislatures in the 1900s that the anniversary became a legal holiday in most states and eventually a federal holiday. The Knights of Columbus are the Catholic Church's largest lay organization, founded by Father Michael McGivney in 1882 at St. Mary's Church in New Haven, Connecticut. Though they were instituted as a fraternal benefits organization with their own insurance system (today they have assets for their members and families exceeding 52 billion dollars)[9] the Knights were also keen to dispel prejudice against Catholic participation in U.S. civic society. To meet this goal, the Knights fostered patriotism within their ranks (their "Fourth Degree" of membership is specifically for patriotic events), while to the broader public they emphasized America's debt to Catholic figures. Not coincidentally, this fraternity founded by an Irish priest was named not after St. Patrick but after Columbus, the ostensibly devout Catholic discoverer of America (see p. 124 for more on the Catholic use of Columbus and p. 152 for more on the anti-Catholic). The Knights, incidentally, are also largely responsible for the clause "under God" in the Pledge of Allegiance.[10]

**Halloween, October 31.** Controversy continues to swirl around one of America's most popular holidays, with various groups denouncing or defending Halloween as darkly pagan, harmlessly secular, liturgically Catholic, or historically anti-Catholic. In a sense they are all right, for Halloween today is a combination of all these strains.

Halloween began as the Celtic festival of *Samhain* (the Lord of the dead in Celtic mythology). It was believed that on the night before the feast, the gates of the underworld were opened and that ghosts, demons, and witches were allowed to roam freely. In response to this otherworldly menace, the Celts followed the principle "if you can't beat 'em, join 'em" and disguised themselves as various kinds of ghouls to escape harm. (From this practice comes our custom of Halloween **masquerading**). And in addition to blending in with the infernal, the Celts also tried to appease evil spirits by offering them food and wine.

After the Catholic faith came to Celtic lands, the old Druidic festival came to be associated with the night before All Saints' Day and was thus called **All Hallows' Eve** (a name that gives us the modern appellation of Halloween), even though the establishment of All Saints' Day on November 1 was a complete coincidence. Church officials were gradually able to wean the Celts from their sacrifices, replacing the food offerings to the gods with "soul cakes" that would be made on Halloween and offered to the poor in memory of the faithful departed. (This was centuries before the Western Church instituted November 2 as All Souls' Day, the day commemorating the souls suffering in Purgatory; see p. 124.) The original intention of distributing soul cakes was doubly charitable, ensuring that the poor would be fed on this day, in exchange for which the poor would pray for the donor's dead. Eventually, however, **souling** became more frolicsome as groups of young men and boys began going from house to house and asking for food, money, or ale instead of cakes. The Church, incidentally, also transformed the nature of *masquerading* during this time from the evasion of evil spirits to the emulation of Christian saints. Large processions in honor of all the saints were held in England and Ireland on the vigil of the feast, with participants either carrying relics of the saints or dressing up as angels and saints.

The Irish also put a unique spin on the feast with their story about a deceased scamp named Jack. Jack had been kicked out of heaven because he was not good enough and out of hell because he kept playing tricks on the devil. It was thus arranged that Jack would roam the earth with only a lantern to guide him until the Last Judgment, when God would finally be able to decide what to do with him. Hence the ubiquitous Halloween **jack-o'-lantern**, which in Ireland is made out of the potato and in America out of the more commodious pumpkin.

The Protestant Reformation all but eliminated Halloween, since most Protestant churches removed the Feast of All Saints from their calendar. In England, however, many of the old Catholic customs were transferred to Guy Fawkes Day, which was only six days later (see the introduction to this chapter). Instead of "souling," for example, boys in England and later America would beg for lumps of coal on the night before the holiday in order to burn effigies of Guy Fawkes or the pope. After the Irish emigrated to the United States in the nineteenth century, bringing with them their old Halloween customs, the coal-begging of Guy Fawkes Day gradually elided back into the souling of October 31. It is from this combination of Irish Catholic and British anti-Catholic observances that our modern custom of **trick-or-treating** has emerged.[11]

**Thanksgiving Day, Fourth Thursday in November.** Thanksgiving is a quintessentially American holiday, famously begun by the pilgrims as a three-day feast in the autumn of 1621 to give thanks to their Creator for surviving their first year in the New World. The act of giving thanks is nothing new to Catholic worship; indeed, every Mass is an act of infinite thanksgiving. Moreover, Catholics in Europe observed a number of festivals that coincided with the completion of various crop cycles in order to give thanks for the harvest. One of the greatest of these thanksgiving festivals was the Feast of St. Martin of Tours (Martinmas) on November 11, and one of its principal components was a large goose dinner. According to one popular legend, when the people of Tours tried to make the holy monk Martin their bishop, he tried to hide but was betrayed by honking geese. Whatever the real reason for the association, not even the Reformation could persuade Protestant regions like Holland from abandoning the custom of eating "Martin's goose" on November 11, and so when the pilgrims stayed there prior to their departure to America, they became acquainted with this tradition. It was only natural for them, then, to want geese for their own Thanksgiving celebration in Plymouth. They were able to find several wild geese, but because they could not catch enough, they supplemented their banquet with a strange bird unique to the North American continent: the turkey. It was in this way that the Martinmas goose became the Thanksgiving turkey.[12]

**Christmas, December 25.** Though Christmas is obviously still regarded as a Christian holiday (despite its rampant commercialization), it should also be remembered that it is a deeply Catholic feast. To this day, the anniversary of Our Lord's birth is named after the Catholic Masses offered during it, Christmas being a contraction of "Christ's Mass." (Formerly, such appellations were not unusual: see Candlemas and Martinmas in the *Groundhog Day* and *Thanksgiving Day* entries, respectively.) Christmas, however, not only has a Catholic name, but in some parts of the United States it was regarded as a predominantly Catholic holiday. In New England, Puritans virtually outlawed the celebration of this "papist" feast, requiring employees to work and students to attend school on December 25, all under penalty of dismissal or expulsion. Factory owners would even open their plants earlier than usual on Christmas Day to make sure that Catholics could not attend a morning Mass.

Christmas symbols these days are also apt to lose their religious significance. **Christmas trees**, for example, are either treated as secular adornments for office buildings or equated with the pagan yule customs of pre-Christian Germany. Both assessments are incorrect. The Christmas tree has an entirely medieval Catholic origin, being a combination of two phenomena: a pyramid of candles representing Christ's ancestors called a *Weinachtspyramide* in German and the so-called **Paradise tree**. In the Eastern churches, December 24 is the Feast of Adam and Eve, and though this holiday is not in the Latin calendar, Church officials nevertheless allowed Roman Catholics to observe it. In the Middle Ages mystery plays that were staged on this day included a Paradise tree, a tree representing both the Tree of the Knowledge of Good and Evil as well as the Tree of Life from the Garden of Eden (Genesis 2:9). To symbolize both of these Edenic arbors, the Paradise tree was decorated with apples to represent the forbidden fruit and sweets to represent the Tree of Life. When the mystery plays were suppressed in the fifteenth century, the faithful moved the Paradise trees from the stage to their homes. The apples were later substituted for other round objects (such as shiny red balls) while a Star of Bethlehem and lights from the *Weinachtspyramide* were added, but the symbolism remained essentially the same. Thus, our modern Christmas tree is actually the medieval Paradise tree, a reminder of the reason why God became man in the first place and a foretaste of the sweet Tree from which Our Lord's birth would once again enable us to taste.[13]

Two other seemingly secular customs bear mention: Christmas lights and decking the halls with boughs of holly. The custom of **putting lights in the window** was begun by Catholics in Ireland during the times of persecution, when Mass was outlawed by the British and had to be held in secret. Faithful Irish believers would place a candle in the window on Christmas Eve as a sign to any priest who happened by that this home was a safe haven in which Mass could be offered. When interrogated by the British about the meaning of this practice, the Irish replied that the lights were an invitation for Joseph and Mary to stay the night. Unthreatened by this supposed superstition, the British left them alone.[14] For the Christmas appeal of **holly**, see p. 75.

**Boxing Day, December 26.** The day after Christmas is known in Canada, the United Kingdom, and other areas of the English-speaking world as Boxing Day, the day on which the collection or poor boxes of the church were opened and their contents distributed to the needy. (Nowadays it is also the time to offer annual gifts to one's servants, personal or civil, such as postal and sanitation workers.) In the Roman Catholic calendar, December 26 is the feast of St. Stephen, the first martyr and one of the first seven deacons ordained by the Church (Acts 6:1–5). As a deacon, Stephen was responsible for distributing the Church's wealth to all of its members, especially the lowly, and it is in imitation of his care for the poor that the various Boxing Day customs originated. The philanthropic focus of the day also explains the meaning of the Christmas hymn, "Good King Wenceslaus," an actual historical saint from Bohemia who, according to the song, traipsed through the deep snow to feed a poor man "on the Feast of Stephen."

# 3

# MANNERS AND DINING ETIQUETTE

✠

> *Far more important than any mere dictum of etiquette is the fundamental code of honor, without strict observance of which no man, no matter how "polished," can be considered a gentleman.... He is the descendant of the knight, the crusader; he is the defender of the defenseless and the champion of justice—or he is not a gentleman.*
>
> —Emily Post[1]

During the Middle Ages, Catholic Christianity was not only the principal preservative of Western civilization, but it also acted as a stimulus for new forms of civility that still survive today—this despite the fact that the so-called Dark Ages were not exactly renowned for their refinement. As Emily Post attests, it was the rise of Christian knighthood during the Crusades that led to a rebirth of Western etiquette.[2] But there is more here than an historical causality at play. Manners reflect both a sense of self-respect and a regard for the welfare of others, and so it is not surprising that a religion which teaches that man is made in the image of God should encourage a courteous disposition toward oneself and one's neighbor. As one early sixteenth-century author put it, "Courtesy came from heaven, when Gabriel did Our Lady greet, and Elizabeth with her did meet. All virtues are enclosed in courtesy, and all vices in rudeness."[3] In the following chapter we will examine some of the concrete manifestations of this charitable propriety.

**Chivalry.** The ideal of medieval knighthood not only resuscitated the idea of etiquette; it directly or indirectly precipitated a number of specific acts of courtesy. Chivalry began as an attempt by the Church to curb the anarchy and bloodshed of constant feudal conflicts in the eleventh century. The so-called **Truce of God** limited violence by prohibiting, on pain of excommunication, armed engagement every Thursday through Sunday and during the holy seasons of Advent and Lent. The **Crusades**, in turn, added a sacred purpose to this restraint by channeling warfare into the defense of Christian lands from aggressive Islamic forces. One of the key duties of the knight who upheld this new code of chivalry was the protection of the weak and oppressed: when a knight was consecrated or "dubbed," for instance, it was so that he would become a defender of "churches, widows, orphans, and all those serving God."[4] This was obviously the instantiation of an important biblical theme (Judas Maccabeus, the Old Testament prototype of the medieval knight, is described in II Maccabees 2:38 as providing for the widow and orphan), and so was the care extended to another group: women.

Though the chivalrous regard for the welfare of women would later become subject to all sorts of romantic distortions (hence the parodies of love-stricken knights in the works of Chaucer and Cervantes), even here there lies the kernel of a uniquely Christian insight. When St. Paul tells husbands to love their wives as Christ loved the Church (Ephesians 5:25), he is essentially telling them to put the welfare of their spouses high above their own, even to the point of death. Today the concept of **"ladies first"** is more often than not condemned as quaint or chauvinist, but when it is properly understood and practiced it reflects this Christlike conversion of male power and aggression to the selfless service of others. It presupposes that if a Christian man is designed to rule, he is to exercise that rule paradoxically by serving, just as Christ exercised his lordship paradoxically by humbly washing the feet of his apostles (John 13:4–16). This insight is well-reflected in the famous medieval legend of the Holy Grail as told by Chrétien de Troyes. When Perceval the knight is about to part from his mother, she enjoins him with these powerful words: "Should you encounter, near or far, a lady in need of aid, or a maiden in distress, make yourself ready to assist them if they ask for your help, for it is the most honourable thing to do. He who fails to honour ladies finds his own honour dead inside him."[5]

Over time, several customs developed from this transformed understanding of male honor. Simple gestures such as **opening doors** or **pulling out a chair** for a lady bespoke a gentleman's humble respect for women and a recognition of his responsibilities. Particularly noteworthy in this regard is the practice of **tipping one's hat to a lady**. Given that a man's hat is a traditional symbol of his rank and authority, the gesture is essentially a ritual acknowledgment of the fact that his position is in some crucial respects ordered to the service and regard of women.[6]

**Goodbye.** Wishing someone "goodbye" when parting is more pious than one might have imagined, since it is an Old English variation of "God be with you." In that respect, the parting salutation is no different than the Spanish *via con Dios* and *adios* or the French *adieu*.

**"God bless you."** According to the ancient author Pliny (ca. A.D. 77), the custom of saluting someone who sneezes was well-established by the time of Tiberius Caesar, the Roman emperor during the earthly life of Jesus. However, the particular formula, "God bless you" (or *Gesundheit* in German) may have begun during the time of Pope St. Gregory the Great (A.D. 600) in response to a plague sweeping Rome, the initial symptom of which was a sneeze. A similar explanation has been given for covering one's mouth when one yawns, which initially began as the sign of the cross over one's mouth.[7]

**The Table Knife.** Table knives were invented independently of Christianity, though the shape of the current knife is owed to the remarkable French statesman and prelate, Cardinal Armand-Jean du Plessig Richelieu (1585–1642). According to the story, this urbane prince of the Church was disgusted by the sight of his dining companions picking their teeth with their knife-tips, so he ordered his chief steward to file off the points of his household knives. Soon other French hosts and hostesses, also aghast at the teeth-picking habit, began ordering knives like the ones Richelieu had designed. Richelieu's knives were square-tipped, but over time the tip became round, giving us its current configuration.[8]

**Discreet Behavior.** As Richelieu's disdain makes plain, table etiquette became an intrinsic part of Christian courtliness. Medieval manuals warned their readers not to pick their nose, teeth, and nails at table, not to rush at the cheese or throw their bones on the floor, not to make noises when they ate, and not to spit on or over the table.[9] In *The Canterbury Tales* we see a similar appreciation of refinement in Chaucer's description of the Prioress:

> At meat her manners were well taught withal;
> No morsel from her lips did she let fall,
> Nor dipped her fingers in the sauce too deep.[10]

But good manners extended beyond the banquet hall. Admonitions of a more general nature included laughing moderately, reverencing one's betters, sharing with one's fellows, and breaking wind silently.[11] Such advice is commendable, though it also bears witness to the kind of uncouth behavior that was no doubt prevalent.

**Discreet Language.** In an age when self-expression and authenticity have replaced the restraint that is born from a selfless desire not to offend or cause discomfort, the idea of not discussing certain matters in public is easily dismissed. Yet it was only a generation ago that the television show *I Love Lucy* refrained from using the word *pregnant* on the air to describe Lucille Ball's obvious condition. Judiciously avoiding certain topics for the sake of decorum and decency has been the hallmark of the civilized in all times and places, to say nothing of Christian comportment. The epistles of St. Paul, for instance, evince an appreciation of not only truthful but appropriate conversation. The same can be seen in medieval etiquette books, which cautioned against excessive or crude speech. During the Renaissance writers like Erasmus (1466–1536) offered boys appropriate expressions to use in polite company for bodily functions.[12] Indeed, the producers of *I Love Lucy* could have benefited from Catholic sensibilities: an old euphemism for pregnancy is "Our Lady's bands."[13]

**George Washington's Rules of Civility.** A good combination of discreet word and deed is also one of the more famous examples of early American etiquette. George Washington lived by 110 aphorisms that he had written down as a youth and had called *The Rules of Civility and Decent Behavior in Company and Conversation.* Washington was so fastidious in his observance of these rules that when he was president, a foreign diplomat's wife marveled at his "perfect good breeding and a correct knowledge of even the etiquette of a court." Later historians have revealed the surprising source of Washington's inspiration, a 1595 set of maxims written by French Jesuits and entitled, *Decency of Conversation among Men.* As educators of the wealthy and powerful, the Jesuits had taken a keen interest in courtly manners. *Decency* was one of their more popular works: originally written in French, it was later translated into Latin and several modern languages before it somehow found its way to Virginia,[14] where a teenaged Washington, possibly unaware of its popish origins, took it to heart.

**Breakfast and Dinner.** The customary times of and terms for our dining habits also bear the traces of a Catholic stamp. As can be seen from the two words that comprise it, **breakfast** is the morning act of breaking the fast; indeed, the word was once used to denote any act of eating after a fast of some time. Such an understanding makes sense in light of the Church's tradition for receiving the Eucharist, which required that the communicant refrain from food and drink (even water) from midnight of the night before. (Though hard evidence is wanting, we also wonder if these ascetical practices were not the inspiration for the **midnight snack**.) Similarly, **dinner** which was once the name not for the evening meal but for the principal meal held at midday comes from the late Latin *disjejunare,* "to cease fasting."[15] This also makes sense, especially during times of solemn fasting, when, as we are about to see, only one meal a day would be taken.

**Twelve o'Clock and the Noonday Meal.** *Nona* in Latin refers to the ninth hour of the day—that is to say, three o'clock in the afternoon. Starting in the eighth century, it was the earliest time that one could eat something during the Great Fast of Lent (in an earlier age, one would have waited until evening). Gradually, however, the three o'clock rule was softened, so that by the fourteenth century it was common to have one's "noonday" meal in the middle of the day, at twelve o'clock in the afternoon. The custom took, even on non-fast days.[16]

**Collation.** The word *collation,* meaning a light meal, also comes from a medieval Lenten practice. Originally, only one meal per day was allowed during the Great Fast. Benedictine monks in the ninth century, however, altered this practice on account of the amount of heavy labor they did in the fields. In addition to their principal meal, they were allowed to have a small amount of drink along with a small piece of bread while they listened to the daily reading of Abbot Cassian's fourth-century *Collationes* ("collected instructions"). Over time the meaning of the word was transferred from the prayers they heard to the meal itself.[17]

**Begging.** Since we have been highlighting the Catholic influence on manners, it is only fair to mention the Catholic influence on a practice deemed by many to be most unmannerly. Lambert the Stammerer—or le Bègue, in French—was a twelfth-century priest from Liège who founded two lay "mendicant" orders, which survived solely on alms. Both the male order (the Beghards) and the female (the Beguines) spread quickly throughout Europe, though they were eventually denounced by a number of popes and councils. Before being suppressed, however, the alms-seeking activity of the Beghards became synonymous with their names. Thus the French word for stuttering became the English word, *begging.*[18]

# 4

# FOOD AND DRINK

✠

*Not that which goeth into the mouth defileth a man: but what*
*cometh out of the mouth, this defileth a man.*

—*Matthew 15:11*

Unlike Judaism and Islam, Christianity is a major Western religion with no
specific and strict dietary code. Since the moment an angel showed St. Peter
every manner of clean and unclean food crawling about on a large tablecloth
and instructed him to "arise, kill, and eat" (Acts 10:13), Christians have attached no intrinsic religious significance to what they consume or imbibe
(except, of course, for the Eucharist). This does not mean, however, that
Christian groups over the years have done nothing to supplement the New
Testament's gastronomic generalizations. In the nineteenth century, the popular Presbyterian minister Sylvester Graham thought that rich and spicy foods
led to inordinate sexual desire and as a result invented what is known today
as the graham cracker, a deliberately bland yet nutritious alternative to
morally dangerous cuisine. Similarly, after the Seventh Day Adventist Dr.
John Harvey Kellogg designed corn flakes to increase health and decrease
lust, his brother Will took the idea and founded the W. K. Kellogg Company,
thus making corn flakes the breakfast staple that they are today.

The Catholic approach, on the other hand, reflects a sacramental sense of
"eating and drinking to the glory of God" (I Corinthians 10:13). Catholics
have traditionally created and enjoyed food that reminds them of a sacred

mystery or season, an important historical event, or the life of a saint, thus having the meal function as a *sacramentum,* or sacred sign, of something holy. And though there is a good deal of diversity among the many different kinds of ethnic Catholic foods, they all may be said to reflect the basic sacramental principle in which the physical traits of a particular food somehow betoken the spiritual traits of this or that supernatural truth. It is as if the joy of the feast day or of the mystery of redemption has trickled down into the very morsels we eat at the table.

There are, of course, literally thousands of such dishes from around the world, a good number of which can be found in the Catholic cookbooks currently in print (see Works Consulted). In this chapter, however, we will focus on the foods and drinks in America that both Catholic and non-Catholic typically enjoy, often without realizing their deeper Catholic significance.

## FOOD

**Cheeses.** As we will see in later chapters, monastic influence on Western civilization was deep and vast, extending into technology, commerce, and education. One of the areas on which the monks of the Middle Ages left an indelible mark was the production of cheese. Since everything a monk does is a part of his unceasing prayer to God, cheeses produced in the monastery were of the highest quality, earning for themselves a reputation beyond the cloister. Even to this day cheesemakers in France often place a cheery, red-cheeked monk on their label as a symbol of their commitment to excellence and tradition, and many cheese varietals, such as **Saint-Agur**, **Saint-Albray**, **Saint-Christophe**, **Saint-Marcellin**, **Saint-Nectaire**, and **Sainte Maure**, bear the names of Catholic saints as a matter of course.

The monastic leaders in fine cheese have been the Benedictines, whose daily diet traditionally places a high premium on dairy products. In France, the Benedictines have made delicious cheese varieties such as **Abbaye de Belloc** and **Maroilles**, the latter of which celebrated its one thousandth anniversary with a Mass held in its honor. In Germany, monks lent their name not only to the city of **Munster** (German for monastery) but to the eponymous soft aromatic cheese.[1]

But Benedictines are not the only monks who produce fine *fromage*. About two hundred years ago Trappists in Entrammes, France, invented a tangy solid cheese and named it after their abbey, *Notre Dame du Port du Salut,* "Our Lady of the Port of Salvation." The abbey was built after the persecution of the French Revolution by monks who had learned the art of making cheese while in exile. Though it sold the rights to its secret formula in 1959, the abbey's S.A.F.R. abbreviation (short for Société Anonyme des

Fermiers Réunis, or Anonymous Society of Reunited Cheesemakers), is still printed on the wheels of every **Port Salut** cheese.[2] In America, the Trappist flair for fine cheese continues at Kentucky's Abbey of Gethsemani, the former home of the famous author Thomas Merton (for more on Merton, see p. 46).

**Croissant.** This flaky and buttery pastry commemorates one of the most crucial battles in European history. The Battle of Vienna in 1683 pitted a beleaguered city, at the time the eastern outpost of Western Christendom, against a much larger and superior army from the Ottoman Empire led by the formidable strategist, Kara Mustapha. If Vienna had fallen, the Turks would have quite possibly taken the rest of Western Europe. However, the king of Poland, John Sobieski, staged a spectacular counterattack with a coalition of troops from various Catholic countries, thus saving Europe from Ottoman rule and essentially ending Ottoman aggression in the region.

According to one legend, the Turks had also tried to tunnel under the city's walls in the early morning. A baker heard them and notified the Viennese troops, who staged a counterattack of their own. After the battle, the baker was rewarded with a patent to produce a bread commemorating the victory over the Turks, whose flag bore a crescent, the symbol of Islam. The result: the *croissant,* which is French for crescent.[3] Regardless of whether the baker's story is true, culinary historians generally agree that the croissant symbolizes the defeat of the Islamic forces at Vienna in 1683.

**Eggs Benedict.** This meal of poached eggs placed on a slice of ham on toast with a covering of hollandaise sauce is reputed to take its name from Pope Benedict XIII, who usually had it for breakfast during his six-year reign from 1724 to 1730. Interestingly, the delicious and decadent dish contrasts sharply with the pontiff's overall personal austerity as well as his efforts to crack down on luxury in the Vatican.[4]

**Fish on Friday.** For centuries Roman Catholics have abstained from eating "flesh meat," such as beef, pork, or poultry, on Friday. Moving beyond the somewhat far-fetched theory that Friday abstinence was a medieval invention designed to help the fishing industry of the time, this weekly act of abstinence is, according to canon law, a sign of penance on the day of Our Lord's crucifixion. It also aptly symbolizes a rejection of "carnality." There is a certain theological appropriateness to abstaining from the meat of an animal whose blood has been shed on the day in which the blood of the God-man was shed, the absence of the former reminding us paradoxically of the latter. Fish would be an exception to this rule because of its symbolic association with Christ and the Eucharist.

Because Friday abstinence from flesh meat was mandatory for most Roman Catholics prior to the Second Vatican Council (1962–1965), restaurants were quick to offer appropriate fare for the day. Even McDonald's added the Filet-o-Fish sandwich to its menus in 1962 after Louis Groen, owner of the chain's Cincinnati franchises, noticed that his restaurants experienced a sharp drop in sales every Friday.[5] And even today, restaurant menus on any given Friday in the United States continue to be influenced by the old custom. For example, it is still common to see on Friday a seafood dish as the special of the day or clam chowder as the *soup du jour*. Technically speaking, Roman Catholics are still required to abstain from meat on Fridays unless they replace it with some other act of penance or good work (such as the Stations of the Cross), or unless their local bishop has officially decreed an alternative.[6] Most Catholics, clergy as well as laity, are oddly unaware of this obligation, though they do at least know that the Fridays during Lent are days of abstinence.

**Hot Cross Buns.** The steaming buns formerly sold on the streets of Old England, as the nursery rhyme tells us, for "one a penny, two a penny," began as an act of charity on one day of the year. The legend is that Father Rocliff, the priest in charge of distributing bread to the poor at St. Alban's Abbey in Hertfordshire, decided on Good Friday in 1361 to decorate buns with a cross in honor of the day. The custom spread throughout the country and endured well into the nineteenth century. So esteemed was this Good Friday food that it was even believed a hot cross bun would never grow moldy.[7]

**Mincemeat Pie.** It is difficult to say who invented mincemeat pie and why, but one thing is certain: over time, these pies came to be intimately linked with the English Catholic celebration of Christmas. During the Middle Ages these pies were made in the shape of a rectangle to resemble the manger in Bethlehem, with a hump in the middle to signify the infant Jesus. So closely associated was Catholicism with these pies that when the Puritans tried to abolish the celebration of Christmas in the seventeenth century, they also forbade mincemeat pies. From that point on the pies have been made in a circular shape.[8]

**Mole.** Mole (pronounced *moe-lay*) is a spicy Mexican sauce served with meat or poultry. Though Native Americans had been making a similar sauce for centuries, it is thanks to the cook of a convent in the city of Puebla (the capital of the Mexican state of Puebla de los Angeles) that we have mole today. Maria del Perpetuo Socorro (named after Our Lady of Perpetual Help) was preparing Sunday dinner for Archbishop Manuel Fernández de Santa Cruz when she decided to add unsweetened chocolate, peanuts, sesame seeds, and cinnamon in order to accommodate their guest's delicate palate.[9]

***Pączki.*** As we mentioned earlier, there are hundreds of "ethnic" dishes that have developed out of the Catholic liturgical year, many of them in response to Lent. Of the many culinary candidates worthy of mention, *pączki* is particularly interesting, first because it is relatively well known in several regions of the United States and second because it has a rather peculiar and zealous group of devotees, including its own lobby, the National Pączki Promotional Board. *Pączki* (pronounced *paunch-key*) is a Polish pastry similar to a jelly donut that is traditionally eaten in the weeks immediately prior to Lent. As with many pre-Lenten foods, the idea of making *pączki* was to get rid of all the perishable dairy products in the home before Lent began, since the old Lenten fast, which was much stricter than it is now, once prohibited eating anything that came from an animal (see **Carnival** on p. 12 for another example of this trend). Hence the old custom in many American Catholic parishes of **pancake breakfasts** on the Sunday before Ash Wednesday (Quinquagesima Sunday) and hence *pączki,* introduced to these shores by Polish immigrants and now eaten by Americans of all creeds.[10]

**Pasta.** Over the years, the Italians have developed several different shapes of pasta that now bear Catholic names. The most notoriously named is *strozzapreti,* or "priest-chokers." Stories abound about the origin of this colorful cognomen, though one recurring theory is that in the days when priests ate for free in Italian restaurants, restaurateurs served the pasta to priests as a cheap first course to fill them up. Today the pasta is occasionally used as an anti-clerical symbol, as when Catholic dissidents, atheists, and agnostics staged an "anti-Jubilee" luncheon in Rome during the Great Jubilee Year of 2000–2001 and served *strozzapreti* as the main course.[11]

**Pretzel.** The pretzel was *the* Lenten treat of ancient Christianity. In the 400s, when the Great Fast of Lent included total abstinence from all meat and dairy products, Roman Christians made a simple bread out of flour, water, and salt. And to remind themselves that Lent was a time of prayer, they shaped the bread in the form of praying arms. (Long before Christians folded their hands in prayer, they prayed with their arms crossed in front of them, as Byzantine Christians still do today). The result was called *bracellae,* Latin for "little arms." From this word comes the German *brezel* or *prezel* and our pretzel.[12]

**Stollen.** This popular bread, baked in Germany since the Middle Ages, is more than just a generic Christmas treat. The deliberately conspicuous folds of the dough are meant to remind us of the swaddling clothes in which Mary wrapped her newborn Son.[13]

**Tempura.** European cuisine is not the only cooking to be affected by Catholicism. The beloved Japanese dish tempura actually comes from the ancient Catholic observance of the Ember Days. Occurring as they did four times a year, the Ember Days corresponded to the four natural seasons and fell on the Wednesday, Friday, and Saturday of a specified week. Since the time of the early Church, it was mandatory to fast and abstain from meat on these days. In the sixteenth century, when Spanish and Portuguese missionaries settled in Nagasaki, Japan, they sought ways of making tasty meatless meals for the Ember Days and started to deep-fry shrimp. The idea caught on with the Japanese, who applied the process to a number of different seafoods and vegetables.[14] Even the name for this delicious food denotes the Catholic Embertides: "tempura" and "ember" both come from the Latin term, *Quatuor Tempora*, "the four seasons."

## DRINK

*Do not still drink water, but use a little wine for thy stomach's sake, and thy frequent infirmities.*

—I Timothy 5:23

Though it is thanks to Protestant pastors like Eliza Craig that we have Kentucky bourbon,[15] the perfecting of alcoholic beverages seems to be an area in which Catholics especially excel. Wine has long been cherished in Catholic life as constitutive of the sacrament of the Eucharist and for its convivial role in gladdening the heart of man (Psalm 103:15). *The Rule of St. Benedict*—the founding document of Western monasticism—grants to each monk a pint of wine a day, and takes it away from him if he is late for grace. It was the monasteries of the Old World that took an early lead in the viticulture and wine trade of the Middle Ages: the Cistercians, for example, whose motto was *Cruce et Aratro* (By the Cross and the Plough), transformed much of the European landscape with their vineyards and fields. And it was Catholic missionaries who first brought the wine grape to the New World: the Franciscan friar Blessed Junipero Serra is credited with starting California's wine industry after planting a vineyard next to the first mission he founded with vines brought to Mexico centuries earlier by the Jesuits.[16]

Other strong drinks, however, have also made their way to the tables of Catholic homes. This section presents a list of some of the wines and spirits influenced or created by Catholic hands, followed by a very Catholic cup of coffee.

*Châteauneuf-du-Pape.* There are numerous wine labels that can claim some kind of monastic or Catholic connection, such as Italy's *Feudo Monaci* (Fiefdom of the Monks) or the dozens and dozens of winemakers and vineyards in France, Germany, and the United States that bear the name of a saint. For the sake of brevity we will focus on only one, since it hearkens to one of the more unusual—and lamentable—chapters in Catholic history. Châteauneuf-du-Pape refers to the well-known wines from the Rhône valley in France, but the name, which means "the Pope's new castle," denotes the ruins of a palace built during the Babylonian Captivity (1305–1377), the period during which the papacy was located not in Rome but in Avignon, France. The castle, begun by Clement V and finished by Clement VI, was to be the summer residence of the Avignon pontiffs, and it was during that time that vines were introduced to the area. The new castle was eventually burned during the religious wars in 1552 and most of it destroyed during World War II.[17]

**Dom Pérignon and Champagne.** Monks not only contributed to the art of viniculture, they were also pioneers in the development of sparkling wine. Dom Pérignon, cellarmaster of the Benedictine Abbey of Hautvillers in the region of Champagne, France, discovered the process that led to the *méthode champenoise*. Pérignon was the first to make stronger wine containers that could withstand the pressure of carbon dioxide released during fermentation, thus trapping the gas and creating sparkling wine. According to one tradition, when Pérignon tasted the first successful fruits of his experiment, he called out to his fellow monks and said, "Brothers, come quickly: I am drinking stars!" Champagne, France, still honors the humble monk with a wine festival held each year in Hautvillers and, of course, the eponymous brand of fine champagne.[18]

**Christian Brothers Brandy.** From wine and sparkling wine it is a small step to brandy, or "burnt wine," as it was originally known. The largest brandy distiller in the United States and most likely the world is that of the La Salle Fathers or Christian Brothers, an order founded in the seventeenth century in France by St. Jean-Baptiste de La Salle. Today the Christian Brothers winery in California's Napa Valley is one of the most important in the region, while its Mont La Salle Vineyards not only controls more vineyard land than any other Napa group, but owns six wineries, including the reputable Beringer Brothers.[19]

**Chartreuse.** One of the world's most distinctive liqueurs is chartreuse, which takes its name from the Carthusian Charterhouse in Voiron, France, and continues to be made by the order there and in Tarragona, Spain. The still-secret formula, known by only three monks in the cloister, supposedly requires over one hundred thirty herbs, some of which are hand picked from the nearby mountains. The formula was perfected by Father Jérôme Maubec after it was given to the monks by a military officer in 1605. The drink, however, did not go beyond the walls of the cloister until 1848, when a group of admiring French army officers publicized its virtues. Today two kinds of chartreuse are made, a strong green liqueur and a yellow that is sweeter and less alcoholic.[20]

**Benedictine D.O.M.** Dom Bernardo Vincelli, a brother of the Benedictine monastery in Fécamp, France, is said to have invented this popular liqueur in order "to fortify and restore the weary monks."[21] Benedictine monks continued to produce their liqueur until their monastery was destroyed during the French Revolution. Eventually a M. Alexandre Le Grand obtained the formula and founded the secular concern that produces the liqueur today. Regardless of the divorce from its religious roots, however, every true bottle of Benedictine still bears the inscription "D.O.M.," an abbreviation of *Deo Optimo et Maximo,* "To God, Most Good and Most Great." According to E. Frank Henriques, the fact that two of the world's great liqueurs, Chartreuse and Benedictine, originate from the cloister proves the veracity of Matthew 6:33, "that all things are added unto those" who "seek first the kingdom of God."[22]

**Rompope.** In the Mexican city of Puebla de los Angeles, colonial-era nuns from the Santa Clara convent made a vanilla liqueur called rompope. Sometimes described as "Mexican eggnog," rompope is made with yolk, sugar, milk, cinnamon, and rum or brandy. It is produced commercially according to the old formula as **Santa Clara Rompope,** though it can also be made at home.

**Frangelico.** This popular hazelnut liqueur is named not after the fifteenth-century Florentine painter, but after a seventeenth-century monk who lived as a hermit in the Piedmont region of northern Italy. Apparently the monk used his solitude in part to experiment with local herbs, nuts, and berries until he came up with the liqueur we enjoy today. Frangelico is not produced by any religious order, though it comes in a brown bottle shaped like a monk with a real cincture around its glass waist.[23]

**Whiskey.** Though it is difficult to say for certain, it is believed that monks coming home from pilgrimage abroad were the first to introduce the knowledge of distillation to Ireland, where they set up distilleries in their monasteries for medicinal purposes. A fifteenth-century Irish manuscript, for example, prescribes the following cure for paralysis of the tongue: "rub the tongue and wash frequently with whiskey."[24] Apparently the Irish liked this cure quite a bit and, thanks to the subsequent cultivation of **Irish whiskey,** have never been caught with paralyzed tongues since. And though historians are not certain, it is also conjectured that the knowledge of making whiskey was then carried to Scotland, giving rise to the development of **Scotch.**[25] In any event, there certainly is a connection between whiskey and the Roman continental patrimony of alcohol. The Latin term for distilled spirits is *aqua vitae,* or "water of life," which in Gaelic is rendered *uisce beathe*—"whiskey" for short.

**The Jägermeister Label.** Though this strong German liqueur, first made in 1935, bears no direct relation to Catholic thought or practice, its unique label does. Jägermeister literally means "master of the hunt," and so its label features a stag with a cross between its antlers, an allusion to the conversion of the patron saint of hunters, St. Hubert (656–727). Hubert was a Frankish nobleman who irreverently decided to go hunting on Good Friday. While he was chasing a deer through the forest, the animal turned around, revealing a glowing cross between its large antlers. The stunned hunter fell to his knees and heard a voice say to him, "Hubert, unless thou turnest to the Lord and leadest a holy life, thou shalt quickly go down to hell." Hubert heeded the warning, eventually becoming a wise and holy bishop of Maastricht, Germany.[26]

**Beer.** Beer was invented long before Christianity, but many of the beers we enjoy today owe their existence to the medieval monasteries that preserved and developed the art of brewing. Because of its nutritional value, beer was nicknamed "liquid bread" in the Middle Ages and was allotted to monks during Lent to compensate for the stringent fast they observed. This was especially the case in Munich, Germany, where the Paulaner Monastery produced a strong Lenten beer that they named after the Savior, *Salvator.* To this day Bavarian breweries produce their own special beers in Lent for *Starkbierzeit,* "Strong Beer Season." The beer known worldwide as **Bock** hearkens to this tradition, though today bock beer or *bockbier* is sold year round.[27]

Several monasteries continue to produce their own beer, most notably the Trappist communities that have given the world **Trappist** or **La Trappe** beer. The more famous of these are the half a dozen or so abbeys in Belgium that have the legal right to produce and trade La Trappe, abbeys such as **Chimay**, **Rochefort**, **Orval**, **Westvleteren**, and **Westmalle**. The beers made within these cloisters are among the finest in the world.

**Cappuccino.** Lest the preceding list give the impression that Catholics are incurable dipsomaniacs, mention should also be made of a gustatory triumph that, like the croissant, emerged from the Battle of Vienna. Blessed Marco D'Aviano was a Capuchin monk, a powerful preacher of repentance, and a priest whose blessings miraculously cured many sick and infirm. According to Pope John Paul II, D'Aviano was also instrumental in promoting unity among the Catholic powers seeking to defend themselves from Ottoman aggression in the seventeenth century.[28] On the eve of the Battle of Vienna in 1683, D'Aviano rallied Catholic and Protestant troops, boosting their morale and helping them gain victory the following day. But D'Aviano is better remembered for what happened afterwards. According to legend, he found sacks of coffee beans that the Turkish forces had left behind in their haste. D'Aviano brewed himself a cup, but finding it too bitter for his taste he added milk and honey, thus turning the coffee brown. The grateful Viennese dubbed the drink, "little Capuchin," or cappuccino, in honor of D'Aviano, whose Capuchin habit was the same color.[29]

Marco D'Aviano was beatified by Pope John Paul II on April 27, 2003, the penultimate step to canonization. As one journalist quipped, however, D'Aviano is "already a saint in the eyes of many."[30]

# Part II

# *That's Entertainment*

# 5

# THE ARTS

✠

*Wherever the arts are nourished through the festive contempla-*
*tion of universal realities . . . there in truth something like a lib-*
*eration occurs: the stepping-out into the open under an endless*
*sky, not only for the creative artist himself but for the beholder*
*as well.*

—Josef Pieper[1]

While most people today tend to see art as an act of pure creation emanating from the artist's inscrutable will, the astute twentieth-century student of
St. Thomas Aquinas, Josef Pieper, boldly makes the opposite claim. True art,
Pieper contends, derives its life "from a hidden root, and this root is a contemplation which is turned toward God and the world so as to affirm them."[2]
It is contemplation, a receptive openness and attentive silence to a reality
greater than oneself, that lies behind all great art. And it is love that deepens
our vision and animates all true contemplation: as the medievals used to say,
*ubi amor, ibi oculus*—where there is love, there are eyes. Finally, it is the
ability to celebrate a feast, to be lost in wonder, gratitude, and delight, that
provides the soil in which the artistic impulse can blossom and thrive.

If Pieper is right, there is little mystery as to why Catholicism has been
such a fertile field for the arts. Simple things like the traditional Catholic celebration of Sunday and holy days, which releases men and women from their
workaday world and liberates them to revel in leisurely acts of gratitude and

joy, have had a profound impact on Western culture. Similarly, if Pieper is right, there is little mystery as to why the West can be said to be experiencing an artistic crisis, for it has lost the sense of genuine leisure, its degradation of Sunday as a day of rest being only one example. And alas, contemporary Catholicism may share some of the blame for this decline. Measures intended to enrich the Catholic observance of Sunday and of holy days by accommodating it to the exigencies of modern life may have actually further weakened it. Saturday vigil Masses are now a convenient way to get one's Sunday obligation "out of the way"; important holy days in the United States have been moved to the nearest Sunday on the assumption that the faithful should not be expected to carve time out of their busy work schedules for Mass; the springboards that precede sacred joy and make it so sweet when its comes—abstinence and fasting—have been substantially reduced in the Church calendar. With this loss of consecrated time and divine leisure comes a shrinking of the horizons and a dehumanization of our existence—never a good thing for art, let alone life.

Fortunately, it was not always so, nor need it be. In this chapter we look at some of the visual arts on which Catholicism, with its contemplative savoring of the divine, has left an indelible mark.

## ARCHITECTURE

*I have loved, O Lord, the beauty of thy house;*
*and the place where thy glory dwelleth.*

—Psalm 25:8

One of the mottos that has come down to us from antiquity is *Bonum, Verum, Pulchrum*—the Good, the True, the Beautiful. According to theologians like St. Thomas Aquinas, these three things are really one and the same, and so it is understandable that a religion that takes such keen interest in truth would likewise be interested in beauty. This is especially the case concerning the place where its central mystery, the Mass, is celebrated. Far more than a communal meal, the Mass is the re-presencing of Christ's sacrifice on the cross and of his resurrection from the dead, which in turn is the culmination of all just sacrifices starting with Abel, the brother of Cain. The Mass as it was traditionally celebrated thus had a cumulative quality to it, incorporating as it did rituals from the Patriarchs, the Passover, and the Levitical code into its sacramental re-presentation of the Last Supper and Passion; at the same time, it had an anticipatory or eschatological quality to it, looking forward to God's altar in heaven and the eternal wedding feast of the Lamb. Similarly, the very structure and design of God's house, the church, traditionally looked "backward" to the splendor of the Tabernacle and Temple of the ancient Hebrews, "in front of itself" at the hierarchical structure of the cosmos now marked by the Cross, and "forward" to the final Judgment and the creation of a new Heaven and a new earth.

No empty aesthetics, then, sacred architecture was a veritable book by which the faithful learned the central mysteries of their faith and were habituated to the recognition and enjoyment of infinite Beauty. Enormous care and love were thus put into the building of Catholic churches, which is why the medieval and Renaissance cathedrals of Europe constitute some of the West's greatest architecture: the cathedrals of Notre Dame de Paris and Notre Dame de Chartres in France, St. Peter's Basilica in Rome, and so on. Of course, the more interesting question for our purposes is to what extent architecture as a whole has been shaped by a Catholic sensibility. Though the complexity of influences on architecture makes it difficult to say, there is an interesting hypothesis by a Spanish scholar from the nineteenth century who contends that the playful sense of elevation in Western architecture (prior, of course, to the advent of skyscrapers, Frank Lloyd Wright, and modernist design) has its roots in the soaring sight of the Church: "Those weather-vanes and spires and turrets impart to our cities, as well as to our fields, a grand religious character never possessed by the buildings of antiquity. Elevated above all earthly objects [for example], the bell tower is like to the finger of Religion, our Divine Mother, who lovingly reminds her numerous children of the great and excellent thoughts of eternity, and the tranquil, smooth road to heaven."[3]

In any event, here are several architectural styles that have been influenced by Catholic life and thought and several "Catholic" architectural terms.

**Romanesque.** *Romanesque* was a term coined in 1818 to describe the remarkable medieval architecture that was inspired by classical Rome and formed by monastic life in the eleventh and twelfth centuries. It was the abbots of the great monasteries of Western Europe who sponsored the adaptation of ancient Roman styles to their communities' worship of God and life in common. Great symmetry and proportion, barrel vaults, and graceful cloisters were among the distinctive elements that brought "about a marvelous richness of expression . . . with a truly noble lucidity in the finest creations."[4] Though Gothic is the most famous architectural byproduct of medieval Catholicism, Romanesque continues to have its admirers. As Gustave Thibon remarks, "Instinctively I have always preferred Romanesque art to Gothic style, for I find in it the most perfect link between the finitude of man and the immensity of God. Gothic spires express a kind of premature thirst for evasion from space and gravity; the Romanesque arch, on the other hand, expresses a kind of consent to the reality of limits, in the motionless expectation of the Infinite."[5]

The Romanesque style went on to influence both sacred and secular architecture and even experienced a brief renaissance in the gates, bridges, and public buildings of Richardsonian Romanesque in the late nineteenth century. And Romanesque churches are an attractive alternative to the bleak theaters-in-the-round and "high-school gymnasium" styles that have dominated sacred architecture over the past generation. Thomas Gordon Smith, a professor of architecture at the University of Notre Dame, has designed a seminary in the Romanesque style of northern Italy for the Fraternity of St. Peter (FSSP) in Denton, Nebraska, which trains seminarians to celebrate the traditional Latin Mass. He has also designed a French Cistercian-style church for Our Lady of Clear Creek Monastery in Hulbert, Oklahoma, a community of Benedictine monks whose spirituality centers on the traditional liturgical year.

**Gothic.** When the cathedrals of the High Middle Ages were being constructed, no one would have thought of calling them "Gothic." An Arian tribe that had played a significant role in destroying Roman civilization in the fifth century, the Goths had no architectural style of which to speak. It was during the Renaissance that neo-classical architects applied the designation to denounce what they deemed barbaric. Though Gothic buildings do indeed depart from several classical principles of ancient Greece and Rome, the characterization is hardly fair. Pointed arches, ribbed and dome vaults, leaf-shaped finials, flying buttresses—all of these coalesced in such a way as to produce a unique and breathtaking effect. The ribbed vaults and flying buttresses in particular enabled medieval builders to reach unprecedented scales of height and to erect walls that seemed to be made almost entirely out of stained glass, a feat that created the most colorful and luminescent interiors the world had ever seen. Further, Gothic churches were designed to be a magnificent fusion of biblical and sacramental teachings from which the faithful could learn their Scripture, their catechism, their path to spiritual perfection, and even the relation of their faith to the seven liberal arts. It seemed as if every inch of a Gothic cathedral, which was covered both inside and out by reliefs, statues, stained glass windows, and paintings, told a story; indeed, this is the source of use of the word *story* for a building level (see p. 44). "Architecture," opines Victor Hugo in *The Hunchback of Notre Dame,* "is the great book of humanity," which is why one of his characters, upon hearing of the printing press, worries that "the book will kill the edifice."[6]

All of these features are reflected in the intricate splendor of medieval Catholic theology, which was likewise carefully and explicitly structured, likewise instructive and erudite, and likewise focused on illumination from without. Catholic thinkers saw a link between geometrical symmetry and the

God who orders "all things in measure and number and weight" (Wisdom11:21); hence the Gothic building was perfectly proportioned. Scholastic theologians "built" their arguments much like a Gothic cathedral—explicitly. Just as a Gothic edifice does not hide its structural support but virtually flaunts it with conspicuous flying buttresses (ridiculed by one detractor as "crutches"), so too do works like St. Thomas Aquinas' *Summa Theologiae* proceed along a conspicuous, tight, and elegant order. And just as medieval schoolmen reflected on the many theological meanings of light, so too did Gothic architects create extraordinary illuminated spaces as a virtual allegory of God's "enlightening the world on high" (Ecclesiasticus [Sirach] 43:10) and of Christ's enlightening "every man that cometh into this world" with faith and knowledge (John 1:9).[7]

At the same time that Gothic architecture is quintessentially medieval, it also has an oddly timeless appeal. Perhaps this explains why the widespread revival of Gothic in the nineteenth century, though motivated in large part by a nostalgia for the Middle Ages, is at home in the modern world, and why the sight of a massive neo-Gothic cathedral like St. Patrick's surrounded by skyscrapers in downtown Manhattan is somehow satisfying. On the other hand, this architectural product of the Age of Faith has also inspired the design of many non-religious buildings such as the British Parliament's Palace of Westminster.

**Baroque.** Another architectural term that began as an insult is Baroque. In medieval philosophy *barocco* denoted a convoluted concept; thus in art it came to signify anything irregular or bizarre. In one respect Baroque architecture marked a return to the more classical principles of architecture that were retrieved during the Renaissance and that had displaced the Gothic; in another, Baroque departed from proportion and moderation with its pronounced use of ornateness and ornamental complexity. (Unlike Gothic, much of this lushness was meaningless and purely decorative.) Baroque architecture became common in Catholic countries and regions like Spain, Portugal, Italy, southern Germany, and Austria, though it also influenced the work of English architects Sir Christopher Wren, the designer of St. Paul's Cathedral in London, and Sir John Vanbrugh.[8] The style was a favorite of Counter-Reformation Catholics who developed it partially in reaction to Protestantism, but *The Catholic Encyclopedia* is generally right to characterize *barocco* as a "debased application to architecture of Renaissance features."[9] For more on Baroque art, see p. 50.

**Trinity Columns.** Many American tourists are puzzled by the presence of large marble or granite columns placed in the central squares or piazzas of Europe and dedicated to the Holy Trinity. Generally constructed in the seventeenth and eighteenth centuries as a public thanksgiving for deliverance from epidemic and disease, these columns are often some of the finest examples of late Baroque art.[10] Though Holy Trinity columns are conspicuous in Vienna and Budapest, one of the most impressive columns (complete with its own chapel inside) is to be found in Olomouc, Czech Republic.

**Mission Style.** Another type of architecture inspired by Catholic tradition is the Spanish Mission style, an adaptation of the Spanish Renaissance to the local conditions of the New World. Though recognizable to most Americans by such features as adobe walls, dark exposed beams, curved dormer windows, and Spanish roof tiles, the style admits of considerable variety from region to region. In the United States, for example, the California Mission style is different from that found in Texas and Florida, while the Santa Fe style, with its distinctive pastel colors, has become a byword unto itself.

The New World missions of first the Jesuits and later the Franciscans were self-sufficient communities that permeated every aspect of life, and so it is appropriate that the style is not to be found with churches alone but also with municipal buildings, office complexes, and private homes as well. The church, however, remains the Mission style's most fetching archetype. Even fast-food chains like Taco Bell capitalize off the signature bell tower, thanks to enduring Hollywood stereotypes of an old Mexican village. Because the Mission church style is beautiful and stately as well as practical and relatively inexpensive to build (at least in comparison to Gothic), it continues to be popular among discriminating Catholics, especially in the Southwest. Notre Dame professor Duncan Stroik, for example, has designed a Mission style chapel for St. Thomas Aquinas College in Ventura, California, a Catholic liberal arts college that bases its curriculum on a close reading of primary texts.

**The Story of the Story.** One of the more interesting byproducts of medieval architecture is our word for the levels of a building. In Romanesque and Gothic architecture it was not uncommon to have allegorical pictures, reliefs, and sculptures on the façade of a church or municipal building. These representations were not ornamental but served an important purpose: they told a story. Since by extension several strata of allegorical representations told several stories, it became custom to indicate the height of a building by how many stories it had.[11]

**Catherine-Wheel Window.** Most Americans would probably refer to a circular window with radiating spokes as a wagon wheel, but formally it is known as a Catherine-wheel window.[12] According to tradition Emperor Maximus II ordered St. Catherine of Alexandria to be killed on a spiked wheel, but divinely sent lightning destroyed the device just as Catherine was mounting the gallows. The story of St. Catherine's wheel has also been applied to a firework (p. 111).

**Lobbies and Lodges.** The waiting rooms of office buildings and the like take their name—and most likely their function—from the monasteries of the Middle Ages. A *lobium* in medieval Latin was a cloistered walkway where it is speculated that illiterate lay folk waited for help from the monks in writing letters and sorting out legal matters. And since the walkway was usually covered with vines, it also led to the word *lodge,* which originally referred to a temporary shelter made out of foliage.[13]

## LITERATURE

*After long years of repression [English Catholic writers] have their full freedom in the arena of literature, and there is more than a promise that when the history of the twentieth century comes to be written many Catholic names will be found in the highest places on the roll of honour.*

—K. M. Warren, 1912[14]

K. M. Warren's prediction about the standing of twentieth-century Catholic authors was prophetic. From Oxford professors to Southern country doctors, the Catholic writers of our time have carried on an impressive tradition of literary achievement dating back to the second century.

**The Autobiography.** The prototype for the first true autobiography is St. Augustine's masterpiece, the *Confessions.* Augustine of Hippo (354–430) was a former heretic, sinner, and teacher of rhetoric who applied his considerable oratorical skills to the telling of his life prior to his ordination to the priesthood and episcopate. The painfully honest recounting of his past is enhanced by an unparalleled psychological analysis of his motives and deeds as well as by his understanding of a life lived well. The work, however, defies our contemporary expectations about autobiography because it is addressed directly to God in prayer: the reader merely "overhears" Augustine making a confession of contrition and praise to his Lord. Further, the *Confessions* ends not with Augustine's condition at the time of writing but with a prolonged reflection on the first fourteen verses of the Genesis account of creation, verses in which Augustine finds the prism that enables him to focus on the enigma of sacred history and of his own life. The highly personal yet universal quality of the work was unheard of in antiquity and went on to inspire a number of other Christian authors through the ages. St. Patrick, the Apostle of Ireland, for example, wrote a work with the same title.

The autobiographical genre was subverted centuries later by Jean-Jacques Rousseau, whose own *Confessions* were a deliberate inversion and contradiction of the themes Augustine had explored.[15] After Rousseau, the autobiography would be incorrigibly associated with a narcissistic revelation of oneself to a voyeuristic readership, with God now removed from the picture. Good Catholic autobiographies, however, continue to be written. Two twentieth-century examples bearing mention are *The Seven Storey Mountain* by Thomas Merton, a talented New York writer who converted and entered a Trappist monastery, and *The Pillar of Fire* by Karl Stern, a Jewish psychiatrist whose conversion was in part due to the Church's courageous efforts in Germany to combat anti-Semitism in the 1930s.

**The Fishing Manual.** Though the title of most famous fishing manual rightly goes to the charming and endearing *Compleat Angler* by the Anglican churchman Izaak Walton, the first manual on angling is reputed to be the *Treatyse of Fysshynge wyth an Angle* by Dame Juliana Berners (fl. 1450), a Catholic prioress and, according to some authorities, the first woman to publish in English. Mother Juliana's small volume is a delight to read, mixing as it does accurate instructions on fly fishing and fly-tying with sagacious advice on living a healthy and happy life (for more on Dame Juliana's treatise, see p. 69).

**The Novel.** One of the twentieth century's finest novelists, **Walker Percy**, once wrote, "I have the strongest feeling that, whatever else the benefits of the Catholic faith, it is of a particularly felicitous use to the novelist. Indeed, if one had to design a religion for novelists, I can think of no better."[16] The novel as a distinct genre of literature is said to have come into its own with the publication of *Don Quixote* by the Catholic author **Miguel de Cervantes** (1547–1616). Moreover, the era in which the novel reached its apogee, the twentieth century, also witnessed a concentration of reputable Catholic novelists. Percy (1916–1990) was not alone; **Robert Hugh Benson** (1871–1914), **Hilaire Belloc** (1870–1953), **G. K. Chesterton** (1874–1936), **Evelyn Waugh** (1903–1966), **Graham Greene** (1904–1991), and **Flannery O'Connor** (1925–1964) were all known for their superb novels. France, on the other hand, was home to **François Mauriac** (1885–1970) and **Georges Bernanos** (1888–1948), while Norway was blessed by **Singrid Undset** (1891–1949), a convert from Lutheranism and the first woman to receive the Nobel Prize in Literature. Even fallen-away Catholics seem to have continued to benefit from their religious formation. **James Joyce** (1882–1941) may have been an apostate, but that did not stop him from generously employing a Catholic repertoire of imagery and symbolism to great effect (for more on Joyce, see p. 166).

Though there are several theories about the vitality of twentieth-century Catholic fiction-writing and its decline following the Second Vatican Council (1962–1965), perhaps the most fundamental ground of inspiration seems to be the way in which traditional Catholic anthropology, liturgy, and sacramentality effect a dilation rather than a constriction of the human capacity to grasp the Beyond. As **Frank Sheed** (1897–1981), another well-regarded Catholic author, once noted, "While the secular novelist sees what's visible, the Catholic novelist sees what's there."[17]

**The Epic.** The grandest genre of narrative was developed in the Golden Ages of antiquity by luminaries such as Homer and Vergil and reached its apex in the English language with John Milton's *Paradise Lost*. Catholic authors, however, have also made impressive contributions to this arena of literature. **Dante Alighieri**'s *Divine Comedy* remains the high watermark of Italian as well as medieval literature, while *The Lord of the Rings* by **J. R. R. Tolkien** (1892–1973) remains the most popular epic fantasy of our own time. (Tolkien was a devout Catholic who converted along with his family when he was eight years old; after his mother died four years later, he and his brothers were cared for by a priest.[18]) Finally, mention should be made of the works of **Abbé Alexis Kagame** (1912–1981), a Rwandan priest, poet, and historian. Abbé Kagame has been described as the man who single-handedly introduced the art of writing, both in French and in his mother tongue Kinyarwanda, to his native country.[19] A prolific author, Kagame's opus magnus is a three-volume Christian epic that consists of 35,000 lines divided into 150 cantos entitled *The Singer of the Lord of Creation*.

**Poetry.** Despite a long and bleak period of persecution, England has been graced with a number of outstanding Catholic poets. **John Dryden** (1631–1700), a convert to Catholicism, was so renowned as an essayist, translator, and poet that the era in which he lived came to be known as the Age of Dryden; one of his most important works, "The Hind and the Panther," allegorically depicts the conflict between the Catholic Church (the Hind) and the Church of England (the Panther). **Alexander Pope** (1688–1744), one of England's greatest poets during the Enlightenment, was the son of a convert who suffered from the penal code against Catholics; he learned Latin and Greek from a local priest and was educated in clandestine Catholic schools. **Francis Thompson** (1859–1907), was an able poet whose works were deeply affected by his Catholicism, the powerful "Hound of Heaven" being a good case in point. **John Henry Newman** (1801–1890), the great theologian and convert from Anglicanism, is rightly regarded as a master of English prose, although his poetry is also deservedly well-regarded. But perhaps the Catholic poet loved most these days is **Gerard Manley Hopkins** (1844–1889), the Jesuit who perfected a vivid and arresting style of poetry he called "inscape." Hopkins was a talented Oxford student who converted to Catholicism and was received into the Church by Newman. As an overzealous novice in the seminary, Hopkins burned all of his poetry, but fortunately for posterity he resumed his writing ten years later.

**Shakespeare?** A curious debate exists as to whether William Shakespeare, the greatest playwright of the English language and the pride of Elizabethan England, was a secret Catholic. Several circumstantial pieces of evidence are proffered in support of this hypothesis, namely, that Shakespeare's family was recusant (they refused to attend the Sunday services of the Church of England, which was legally enforced at the time); Shakespeare was married by a minister who was later exposed as a Catholic priest; Shakespeare's plays betray a nuanced understanding of Catholic beliefs and practices; in the house of Shakespeare's father was found a hidden document mirroring the pamphlets of the English Jesuit martyr Edmund Campion, who was tortured and killed for spreading Catholicism under Queen Elizabeth; and Shakespeare, judging from his writings, was deeply sympathetic with Sir Thomas More, the saint was martyred for the Catholic faith by King Henry VIII (see p. 146). Shakespeare wrote a page and a half of a speech in a play about More's life (the only sample of his handwriting we have), and More is portrayed sympathetically in Shakespeare's last play, *Henry VIII*. There is even evidence that Shakespeare had closely read More's writings and followed them assiduously when composing his own plays.[20]

## PAINTING

*Unbelievers and Rationalists! You ought, like we do, to acknowledge that wherever the Catholic religion is founded and propagated the Fine Arts always succeed and flourish. Although it may be hard for you to hear this, historic truth is always above vain reason.*
—Don Andrés de Salas Y Gilavert[21]

Don Audrés' polemics may be a bit bilious, but they point accurately to a long and congenial rapport between Catholicism and the visual arts. Even before the legalization of Christianity in the fourth century, which made the development of sacred art possible, the faithful had adorned their catacombs with frescos and mosaics depicting Christ, the Mother of God, the saints, and scenes from the Bible. The longing to praise God in art moved out of the catacombs and into the churches the first chance it got, and before long grand basilicas were adorned with sacred images.

The Catholic Church was instrumental in defending as well as promoting art, first from violent Iconoclasts (who merit a separate entry below) and then from equally destructive Protestant Reformers who vandalized church interiors all over Europe in the sixteenth century.[22] There is a theological as well as a pedagogical reason for the steadfast affirmation of sacred art. Theologically, the representation of holy figures attests to both the mystery of the

Incarnation and the communion of saints. No images of God were allowed before the Incarnation and rightly so, because God was a spirit who could not be imagined (Exodus 20:3–5) and whose proper name, YHWH, was not to be uttered by sinful lips.[23] But the astonishing miracle of God becoming man literally changes our perception of and access to the divine: just as God now takes a name we can all say (Jesus), so too does He take on the humanity that we all share. St. Paul thus describes Christ as an image, or *ikon,* of the invisible God (II Corinthians 4:4, Colossians 1:15) made visible, of course, through the medium of his body. Similarly, if Christ is an icon of the Father, then the saints are icons of Christ, reflecting his grace (albeit imperfectly) in each and every age. A picture of a saint, then, is not an idol but an icon of an icon of an icon—a memento third removed of those who now partake of the the Divine Nature in all its glory (II Peter 1:4).

On the other hand, sacred art is a powerful pedagogical tool for educating and inspiring. Pope St. Gregory the Great (d. 604) recognized this early on when he defended the use of images from an overly zealous bishop: "Pictures are used in churches so that those who do not know their letters may at least by looking at the walls read what they cannot read in books."[24] Gregory's remarks have been amply confirmed by experience. In the eighth century, a scene of the Last Judgment painted by the monk Methodius was so powerful that upon seeing it, the king of the Bulgarians immediately converted.[25]

The effect of all this iconographical reflection, it should be added, was not only the defense of sacred art, but the upholding of the essential value of art as a whole. The Church's fidelity to its own tradition of sacred images acted as a rising tide that lifted all artistic boats, a causality that is testified by the rich artistic patrimony of historically Catholic countries such as Italy, France, and Spain.

**Iconoclasm.** *Iconoclasm* refers to a heresy that precipitated two particularly vigorous periods of persecution within the Byzantine Empire, A.D. 726–787 and A.D. 814–842. The Iconoclasts, who were convinced that the use of sacred images was idolatrous, were influenced by Paulicinianism, an earlier heresy characterized by a pronounced hatred of the body and hence of any art that depicted the human form.

Because several consecutive Byzantine emperors were Iconoclasts, the movement was able to wreak great havoc on the Eastern Church. Patriarchs of Constantinople who objected to imperial assaults on the Church's ancient customs were blinded, publicly flogged, paraded through the streets, or beheaded. Accounts of atrocities abound: besides the burning of innumerable and priceless images, the professors of a school in Constantinople that preserved both sacred and secular art were burned alive. The hands of one monk, named Lazaro, were thrust into fire so that he could never hold a brush again.

But the brave monk nevertheless found a way to paint with his mutilated fingers and did so secretly in the crypt of a church.[26]

Though the West was never to experience this level of artistic destruction until the Protestant Reformation in the sixteenth century, the Catholic Church, especially the papacy, can claim some part in the victory over Iconoclasm. During both periods of persecution the East appealed to the See of Peter, and on both occasions the pope defended the ancient use of images. The words of St. Theodore the Studite aptly summarize Byzantine sentiment at the time: "Whatever novelty is brought into the Church by those who wander from the truth must certainly be referred to Peter or to his successor. . . . Save us, chief pastor of the Church under heaven."[27]

**Baroque.** Jokingly defined by one wag as "in-your-face Catholicism," Baroque art was one of the Counter-Reformation's preferred artistic tools against the iconoclastic strains of Protestantism. Baroque art accentuates the corporeal and sensual, partly in order to stress—against Calvinist suspicions of the postlapsarian material world—the goodness of created matter. Hence cherubim are no longer depicted as they were in the Old Testament, as many-eyed and many-winged surreal beings; they are now "cherubs," chubby cupid-like babies with fluffy wings and ruddy cheeks that haunt our Hallmark cards as they once did our church cupolas. The Church had also promoted Baroque as a way of instructing and inspiring those whose faith had grown cold or indifferent, the dramatic paintings of **Peter Paul Rubens** (1577–1640) being a good case in point. The result is an art form, as the *Encyclopædia Britannica* puts it, that is "both sensuous and spiritual."[28] Baroque continues to be the favorite style of religious art in many places, especially Latin America and the Philippines. For Baroque architecture, see p. 43.

## SCULPTURE

*I hated the statues. . . . all the emphasis on the human body. . . . I had done so much injury with this body. How could I want to preserve any of it for eternity?*

—Graham Greene[29]

Sarah's self-loathing reflections in *The End of the Affair* inversely reveal some of the reasons for putting statues in a church. Holiness according to the Catholic faith is something that is literally embodied: just as the rebellious soul of Adam "poisoned" his body with sin, rendering it mortal and frail, so too does grace in the soul spill over and sanctify the body over and above its original goodness.

It is this positive assessment of the body that undergirds the Catholic openness to statuary. Though sculpture reached a magnificent apex in ancient Greece and Rome, the Roman Catholic regard for three dimensional representations was instrumental in preserving the art for future generations. Greek or Byzantine Christianity may have actually pioneered the use of sacred statuary, but it eventually fostered instead a rich tradition of two-dimensional iconography. This left sculpting to the Latin West, which used the art to make reliefs first on its sarcophagi and then along the walls of its churches (see p. 44). By the High Middle Ages, the Roman Church had moved to free-standing works and different materials, such as bronze and wood.[30] During the Renaissance the Church provided not only patronage for brilliant sculptors such as Ghiberti, Donatello, and Michelangelo but an intellectual and cultural framework in which their endeavors could flourish. Like the promotion of painting, this interest was to facilitate an enduring appreciation for the art of sculpture in general.

**Monumental Art.** The combination of Catholic support for three-dimensional art and its respect for the human body even in death also led to the continued development of funeral statuary. The statues keeping vigil in cemeteries, crypts, and mausoleums are a continuation of the sarcophagi tradition from early Christianity. Like burial itself, which is a symbolic gesture of preserving the body for the end times, these customs represent in stone and marble a belief in the day when one's body, reunited with one's soul, will be transfigured and glorified, just as Christ's was on the first Easter Sunday.[31]

**Gargoyles.** One type of Catholic statuary that does not seem eager to affirm corporeal beauty are the strange figures that adorn the perimeter of a Romanesque or Gothic roof. The most recognizable products of medieval sculpting, gargoyles are the animal- or bird-shaped waterspouts that were used on roof gutters prior to the use of a lead drainpipe to shoot rainwater away from the building.[32] Their name, which comes from the old French word for "throat" and "gurgling," attests to their function as open-mouthed conduits. Though examples of lion gargoyles can be found on the Parthenon dating back to the fifth century B.C., they came into their own during the Middle Ages, where they took on grotesque shapes and even exaggerated genitalia. Their symbolic meaning has been the subject of much modern debate, and even during the Middle Ages their presence raised a few eyebrows. As St. Bernard of Clairvaux writes, "What are these ridiculous monstrosities doing in the cloisters in the presence of the brothers as they read?. . . . Why are they here, these unclean monkeys, these savage lions, these monstrous centaurs?. . . . Good God! If we do not blush at such foolishness, should we not at least regret what we have spent on them?"[33]

6

# MUSIC AND THEATER

✠

*Sing joyfully to God, all the earth; make melody, rejoice and sing.*
—Psalm 97:4

The music of the Roman Catholic Church occupies a unique position, not only for its own contributions to the genre but for its influence on all Western music. Such basics as the tonal scale and musical notation are byproducts of the Church. Uniquely Catholic treasures, such as the musical parts of the Mass and the Divine Office, took on a life of their own outside their sacred function, moving from the church to the concert hall. As these pieces were never intended for liturgical use, they are yet another example of a familiar secular phenomenon with a Catholic origin.

Roman Catholic worship not only forever changed the landscape of Western music, it is also responsible for resurrecting Western drama. It is that story—and the terminology that serves as a lingering testimony to it—which shall occupy the second half of this chapter.

## MUSIC

### Musical Compositions and Genres

**Mass.** It would be difficult to underestimate the importance of the Eucharistic sacrifice of the altar, or Mass, in Catholic life and thought. As the nonviolent re-presencing of Our Lord's death and resurrection and the fountainhead from which all graces flow, the Mass has been surrounded with the utmost awe and reverence and celebrated with the greatest acts of homage possible. One of the most important of these acts is singing. To this end, the Second Vatican Council gives pride of place to **Gregorian chant** as the music most congenial to the spirit of the liturgy in the Roman rite.[1] Named after Pope St. Gregory the Great (540–604), who did much to perfect the art, Gregorian chant is a sinuous and gliding form of monophony sung in one of eight different modes, two of which, the Ionian and Aeolian, have become our **major and minor scales**, respectively. The moving echoes of Gregorian chant have been described as the perfect wedding of music and text, with the melodies arousing the heart just enough for contemplating and savoring the meaning of the words, but without drowning the words in an overpowering score. Though Gregorian chant is celebrated in its own right even outside the walls of the church (witness its surge in commercial popularity ten years ago), it has also influenced, as we shall see below, the creation of new forms of music ranging from the sublime to the burlesque.

And if the music of chant has been influential, so too have its verses. Like the Mass celebrated today, the traditional Mass of the Roman rite can be said to have two components: the **Ordinary**, or unchanging parts, and the **Propers**, which vary from week to week. Though the Propers were often given various polyphonic settings prior to the fourteenth century, most composers have focused on producing music for the Ordinary. And though some of these compositions were written for sacred worship, the majority are meant to be performed by a symphony or chorale in a concert, so that the music and not the altar takes center stage. The list of composers, both Catholic and non-Catholic, who have written such Masses is extensive: many if not most of the great composers in the Baroque, Classical, and Romantic periods composed a Mass or at least parts for one (for example, Vivaldi's *Gloria*). And the Mass continues to be the locus of new compositions by serious artists in classical music and even jazz, despite the average American Catholic parish's curious aversion today to anything resembling good music. Recent Masses include Stephen Edward's *Ave Maria Mass,* commissioned by Domino's Pizza magnate Thomas Monaghan in honor of the victims of September 11, and Jean Langlais' *Solemn Mass for Easter.* At the behest of *Our Sunday Visitor,* renowned jazz musician Dave Brubeck composed a Mass entitled *To Hope! A Celebration,* which was first performed in Philadelphia's cathedral in 1980. The composing of the music for the "Our Father" (which came to him in a dream) proved so moving for Brubeck that he converted to Catholicism immediately after.[2]

**The Mass for the Dead, or Requiem.** Named after its opening line, *Requiem aeternam dona eis, Domine* ("Eternal rest grant unto them, O Lord"), Requiem Masses have been written by Wolfgang Amadeus Mozart (1756–1791), Hector Berlioz (1803–1869), Giuseppe Verdi (1813–1901), Antonin Dvorák (1841–1904), Gabriel Fauré (1845–1924), and Maurice Duruflé (1902–1986), among many others. According to some musicologists, the criterion for being considered a truly great master is whether one has written a good Requiem.

The traditional Requiem Mass is an awesome experience, with its black vestments, poignant tone, and distinctive ceremonies. Musically, the Requiem's Propers and slightly modified Ordinary (the *Agnus Dei* is somewhat different) are explored to great effect. Of special note is the sequence, the *Dies Irae,* or "Day of Wrath." Purportedly written in the thirteenth century by Thomas of Celano (St. Francis of Assisi's biographer), the *Dies Irae* is a Latin poem in rhymed, trochaic meter describing in vivid and touching detail the soul as it appears before God on Judgment Day. A masterpiece of both literature and theology, the sequence has been praised by scholars of all faiths as "the acknowledged masterpiece of Latin poetry and the most sublime of all uninspired hymns."[3] The new Roman rite of the Catholic Church no longer uses the Requiem Mass for its funeral services, but the genre continues to attract composers of all creeds.

**The Divine Office.** Though the Church has many different kinds of public rituals, prayers, and devotions, it has, strictly speaking, only two forms of liturgy: the liturgy of the Eucharistic sacrifice (the Mass) and the liturgy of the hours (the Divine Office). The Divine Office traditionally consists of eight times, or "hours," during the day in which primarily the clergy but also the laity assemble in church for prayer. (These hours are Matins, Lauds, Prime, Terce, Sext, None, Vespers, and Compline.) Each hour has a slightly different structure, but every one is invariably centered on the chanting of the **Psalms**. Several parts of the various Offices have become objects of considerable musical interest over the years. For Matins, this includes the **Great Responsories** and the hymn, *Te Deum,* which according to legend was spontaneously composed by Sts. Ambrose and Augustine when the former baptized the latter in A.D. 387. The *Te Deum* is sung at the end of Matins on most Sundays and great feasts of the year and has been set to music by dozens of composers. Vespers, the one hour that admitted polyphonic music, also became popular with composers, especially its canticle the *Magnificat,* the words of the Blessed Virgin Mary to her cousin St. Elizabeth (Luke 1:46–55). Finally, the four Marian **antiphons**—the *Alma Redemptoris Mater, Ave Regina caelorum, Regina caeli,* and *Salve Regina*—that are sung at the end of the hours and especially at Compline (depending on the liturgical season) have been used in several different ways, such as motets in the fifteenth and sixteenth centuries. It is from the antiphons of the Divine Office, incidentally, that we get our word **anthem**.[4]

The Office has also inspired interesting permutations. From the sixteenth to the eighteenth century, for example, brief organ pieces called **Versets** were composed to function as alternate verses during the chanting of a psalm or canticle. Composers typically wrote music for the even-numbered verses, while the odd-numbered verses were sung in plainsong by a choir.[5]

**Lamentations.** *Tenebrae,* the combined celebration of Matins and Lauds during the *Triduum* of Holy Week, left a deep impression upon the faithful. It was the observance of *Tenebrae* in the pre-dawn mornings of Holy Thursday, Good Friday, and Holy Saturday that gave us the word *hearse* (see p. 110) as well as material for enduring and powerful music. On these nights, several passages from the Book of Lamentations by the prophet Jeremiah were used during Matins as nocturnes (nightly readings). Jeremiah's wrenching dirge over the destruction of Jerusalem was traditionally chanted, but beginning in the fifteenth century it became the inspiration for non-liturgical polyphonic settings by several famous composers. These Lamentations are recognized today as among the finest examples of Renaissance and Elizabethan music.

**Ave Maria.** The most recognizably Catholic prayer, the *Ave Maria,* or "Hail Mary," consists of the Angel Gabriel's salutation to Mary (Luke 1:28), St. Elizabeth's greeting to her God-bearing cousin (Luke 1:42), and a petition from the Church beginning with, "Holy Mary, Mother of God." After it reached its final form in 1568, composers, especially during the Romantic era, began supplying music for the *Ave* (almost always in its Latin form). Though many settings have been written by musical luminaries ranging from Mozart to Charles Gounod (1818–1893), the most popular remains that of Franz Schubert (1797–1828).

**Seven Last Words.** The Three Hours' Devotion, or "Seven Last Words of Christ," is a Good Friday service begun by Father Alphonso Messia, S.J., in 1732. From its place of origin in Lima, Peru, it quickly spread to all other countries in Central and South America and from there to Italy, England, and America, where both Catholics and Protestants enthusiastically embraced the devotion. The service, which alternates between homilies on the seven last statements of the crucified Christ and various hymns and prayers, has also inspired the composition of memorable music.

**Passion Music.** In the traditional Roman calendar, all four Gospel narratives of the Lord's Passion were read at some point during Holy Week: the Passion according to St. Matthew on Palm Sunday, the Passion according to St. Mark on the following Tuesday, the Passion according to St. Luke on Spy

Wednesday, and the Passion according to St. John on Good Friday. During a High Mass, these narratives would be chanted by three clerics: a tenor taking the role of the narrator, a high tenor taking the role of the mob and various individuals, and a bass voice taking the role of Christ. The music for these parts is an outstanding example of the power and beauty of Gregorian chant; understandably, it has left a deep impression on the Western imagination. Although the Protestant Reformation in large part did away with the liturgical setting of Holy Week, the association of great music with the Passion thus lingered. Protestant composers soon began writing Passion oratorios to replace the music of solemn liturgy, the most famous of which are J. S. Bach's *Saint John Passion* and *Saint Matthew Passion.*[6]

**Polyphony.** Polyphony, the simultaneous and harmonious singing of different melodic parts, reached its apex of development in the Catholic choirs of the thirteenth century and continued to thrive long after thanks to sixteenth-century masters like Giovanni Pierluigi de Palestrina (1526–1594), Thomas Tallis (1505–1585), and William Byrd (1543–1623). Polyphony began in the late ninth century as *organum,* a new style of singing in which a second part was added to a line of liturgical plainchant.[7] Eventually the parts grew more complicated and autonomous, thus giving us what is perhaps the most beautiful musical use of the voice in the history of humankind. Polyphony, in turn, was also influential in shaping non-liturgical forms of music, such as motets, oratorios, and madrigals.

**Oratorio.** The musical genre made popular today by Handel's *Messiah* (which, incidentally, was written as an oratorio rather than an opera to circumvent the Lenten ban on theatrical performances) received an early and important boost from a Catholic saint. St. Philip of Neri (1515–1595), founder of the Oratorian congregation, encouraged the heartfelt performance of music. St. Philip was particularly fond of *lauda,* a popular form of singing in late-sixteenth century Italy that combined sacred text, interludes of dialogue, and polyphonic texture.[8] St. Phillip used *lauda* to form a new genre, one that, along with his personal influence and mentorship, was to have a profound impact on perhaps the greatest composer of polyphony, Giovanni Pierluigi de Palestrina (1526–1594). After its development, St. Philip's happy medium between sacred and secular music was promoted by the Oratorians wherever they went as a part of their efforts to attract youth to the faith.[9] The genre became known as an "oratorio" because of its perfection in the Oratory of St. Philip in Rome, where, as one awestruck English tourist reported in 1670, "there is every Sunday and Holyday in winter at night, the best Musick in the world."[10]

**Anne Polkas.** In the Roman Catholic calendar, the Feast of St. Anne, the grandmother of Our Lord, is held on July 26. Anne's feast was observed in many different ways. Inspired by an old legend that Anne had been widowed and married three times, young maidens turned to her for help in finding a husband, imploring her, "I beg you, holy mother Anne/ Send me a good and loving man." And because of an old saying that "all Annes are beautiful," St. Anne's Day became the occasion for celebrating all beautiful girls and women with the formal reception of debutantes and elaborate serenades and balls. It was for such balls that both Johann Strausses (1804–1849 and 1825–1899) composed *Anne Polkas.*

**Nursery Rhymes.** Catholicism, of course, embraces not only adult concertgoers and blushing debutantes, but children as well. This is evident to some degree in nursery rhymes, given the fact that these are either sung or chanted in a sing-song fashion. Several Catholic prayers said prior to the establishment of the Church of England in the sixteenth century, for example, survived as nursery rhymes, much to the dismay of Protestant authorities. The rhyme, "**Matthew, Mark, Luke, and John,**" which the editors of the *Oxford Dictionary of Nursery Rhymes* label a "night-spell," was so popular with English children that even after over three hundred years of the Reformation there were rural parts in which this was "almost the only prayer known to children."[11] Other nursery rhymes may contain obscure references to Catholic figures or events. It has been speculated that Cardinal Wolsey, Henry VIII's erstwhile Lord Chancellor, may be **Little Boy Blue**, while **Jack and Jill** falling down the hill may have been inspired by a Greenwich Hill childhood game played on Pentecost Monday. It is commonly held that the beloved rhyme "**Mary, Mary, quite contrary**" refers to something concerning Catholicism. The problem, however, is that no one is certain whether it is pro-Catholic or anti-Catholic. On the one hand, the verses could be "a word-picture of Our Lady's convent," with the "silver bells" representing the *Sanctus* bells that the acolyte rings during Mass, the "cockle shells" symbolizing the badges of medieval pilgrims, and the "pretty maids all in a row" being nuns lined up to recite the Divine Office. On the other hand, the rhyme could be a lament at the reinstatement of the Roman Catholic Church during the brief reign of Queen Mary (1553–1558) or a reference to Mary Stuart, Queen of Scots, whose "gay, French, and Popish inclinations" were very much contrary to "the dour John Knox," founder of the Presbyterian church in Scotland.[12]

Finally, many nursery rhymes from other languages have a Catholic significance. Perhaps the most popular foreign nursery rhyme among anglophones is the French jingle, **Frère Jacques**. It is likely that Frère Jacques is a generic nickname for the Dominican friars, who were called "Jacobins" in France because they built their first convent near the church of St. Jacques, or Sanctus Jacobus, in Paris. (The Jacobins of the French Revolution, a much different group to say the least, were so named after the old Jacobin convent in which they used to assemble.) The song comically describes a monastic scene, that of a sleeping brother whose failure to ring the bells makes his community late for the Office of Matins ("sonnez les matines" means "ring the Matin bells"). The friar's failing is understandable, given the fact that Matins began at 3:00 A.M.

**Carnival Music.** With its annual cycle of feasting and fasting, Catholicism is also a natural vehicle for some rather extravagant celebrating. One popular genre of music, in fact, takes its name from the pre-Lenten period of merrymaking and dancing called Carnival (see p. 12). Carnival music is generally associated with the music of Trinidad and Barbados, though it also describes the music from other parts of the Caribbean and from Brazil. A colorful combination of Spanish, Portuguese, Native American, African, and even Chinese strains, the exact mixture of which varies from country to country, Carnival music has a common origin in saying farewell to fun before the forty-day fast of Lent. Carnival music, in turn, has played an important role in the development of **Latin Jazz**, with the carnival dancing marches of Cuba, for instance, evolving into the **Conga** and **Conjunto**, and the carnival "schools" of Rio de Janeiro influencing the **Samba**.

**Jazz.** Following the efforts of the Church to make the institution of slavery more humane, King Louis XVI issued the 1724 *Code Noir,* a set of laws regulating the treatment of slaves and free persons of color in the French colony of Louisiana. The law was oppressive in many ways, but it also had the salubrious effect of preserving the slaves' African cultures by granting them a fair amount of freedom on Sundays and holy days. As a result, many slaves and free blacks could gather every week at the old Congo Square in New Orleans, where they would dance and sing to the beat of an African drum, an instrument banned in most other parts of the Protestant-dominated American South. (Unlike Catholic slave owners in New Orleans, the Caribbean, and South America, Anglo-American Protestants made a concerted effort to eliminate all vestiges of tribal custom from their slaves, which many believe is why the African American music that would eventually emerge from those regions—namely, the blues—had less of the rhythmic and melodic richness characteristic of music on the African continent.[13]) New Orleans' Catholic liturgical cycle, from its Mardi Gras festivities to its dramatic funerals, also provided an arena for the exercise and development of music, as did the cosmopolitan character of a bustling port city.[14] It was because the sounds of Africa were thus preserved and explored that a new synthesis called jazz could emerge at the beginning of the twentieth century.

**Tobacco Vobiscum?** As mentioned earlier, the subtle and transcendent beauty of Gregorian chant has had an enormous impact on Western music and culture (see p. 54). One of the more surprising examples of this influence is in the auctioning of tobacco. During the nineteenth century, it was the job of the tobacco auctioneer to attract buyers to his employer's warehouse by standing outside the door and using comedy and anything else that could draw favorable attention. One such auctioneer, a formerly unemployed veteran of the Civil War named Chiswell "Chillie" Dabney Langhorne (reputed to be the cousin of Mark Twain), made a name for himself with his own "esoteric and entertaining chant, laced with numbers and stimulating sounds that had not been heard before."[15] Chillie had devised this alluring sound after attending Mass in Richmond with a Catholic friend and hearing Gregorian chant for the first time. Chillie figured that if he could combine the ethereal quality of sacred chant with a staccato rhythm and his own comic antics, he would have a winning formula for selling tobacco, and apparently he was right. Though Chillie's congenital restlessness did not keep him in the auctioning business for long, his style made a deep impact on the trade, where it continues to this day.

## Musical Terms and Techniques

*A cappella. A cappella,* the style of singing without musical instruments, literally means in Italian, "in the chapel," since *a cappella* music is written for sacred spaces too small for orchestras or a pipe organ. The word *chapel* has followed more than one historical twist. A *cappa* in Latin was a large military cloak worn by Roman soldiers. St. Martin of Tours (316–397) was wearing one of these cloaks as a young soldier when he met a half-naked man begging for alms in the name of Christ. Though he was only a catechumen, St. Martin immediately divided his *cappa* and gave the man half. The following night Christ appeared to St. Martin in a dream wearing the part of the cloak given to the beggar and said, "Martin the catechumen hath clothed me with this garment."[16]

After his death the remaining half of St. Martin's cape was revered by the Frankish kings as a relic of his holiness, and so a special oratory was built for its safekeeping. This prayerful cloak-room, as it were, became known as the "chapel" (*cappella*), while the guardians of the cloak were called *cappellani,* or "chaplains." In an odd way, then, the word *chapel* went from referring to a piece of clothing to a sacred building before it would one day designate the unadulterated human voice. Meanwhile, St. Martin's cloak went on to influence the world of haberdashery: the French word for hat, *chapeau,* is so called because it originally referred to a chapel head-covering.

**Dirge.** Our word denoting a burial lamentation or a song of mourning comes from the Office of the Dead for the hour of Matins, the opening antiphon for the first nocturne of which is Psalm 5:8, **Dirige, Domine, Deus meus, in conspectu tuo viam meam,** "Direct, O Lord, my God, my way in thy sight." Though the Matins "dirge" was solemnly chanted in church, it eventually came to take on a much broader meaning; hence in *The Rape of Lucrece* Shakespeare speaks of the Roman matron Lucretia as a pale swan singing "the sad dirge of her certain ending" (1.1612). The term at one point even signified anything connected to the funeral feast, as in the case of "dirge-ale," the beer consumed at a wake or funeral.[17]

**Notation.** The written representation of musical sound and motion began in the monasteries and convents of the Western Church as a way of preserving its rich treasury of Gregorian chant. In order to have music appropriate to the different feasts and solemnities of the liturgical year, the Church's musical treasury grew in size until it became difficult for choirs to remember a complicated piece that they sang only once a year. To remedy this situation, monks in the late seventh century began to use symbols called "neumes" above the text to signify the number of notes in a melody. During the tenth century they added the pitch of the notes as well with the use of a line staff. From this basic schema developed our current system of musical notation.[18]

**Solmization and St. John the Baptist.** Catholic sacred music served as the inspiration not only for musical notation but also for the process of "solmization," the method that simplifies reading music by sight with the use of the do-re-mi scale. The hymn in the Divine Office for the Feast of St. John the Baptist on June 24 is *Ut queant laxis.* Tradition ascribes the hymn to Paul the Deacon, who purportedly wrote it before having to sing the difficult *Exultet* on Holy Saturday night. (Paul was suffering from a hoarse throat and, remembering how Zechariah, the Father of St. John, was cured from a case of muteness, thought it best to direct his prayers to the Baptist). What makes *Ut queant laxis* famous, however, is that it is the source of our musical scale, *do, re, mi.* An Italian monk named Guido of Arezzo (d. 1050) noticed that the melody of the hymn ascended precisely one note of the diatonic scale of C at each verse. Taking the first stanza, he decided to name the notes after the first syllable of each verse:

> *UT* quant laxis *RE*sonare fibris
> *MI*ra gestorum
> *FA*muli tuorum, *SOL*ve polluti *LA*bii reatum, Sanc*Te* *I*oannes.

With the exception of *Ut,* which was later changed in Italy, England, and America to *Do* (ostensibly in honor of *Dominus,* the Lord), these syllables became the first six notes of our scale: *do, re, mi, fa, sol, la.* And this stanza also ended up providing the name of the seventh note, *ti,* which was later taken from the last syllable of the penultimate word and the first syllable of the last word of the stanza: "T" from *Sancte* and "I" from *Ioannes.*[19]

# THEATER

## Theatrical Genres

**Modern Theater.** The modern stage owes its existence to the medieval liturgy of the Church, specifically to its celebration of Easter Sunday. In addition to the dialogic character of the Roman rite, the celebration of Easter, with its Gospel reading's unforgettable plot and characters, was recognized as particularly dramatic. In the tenth century, a primitive **liturgical drama** began to emerge from this holy day, as "tropes" from the Introit of the Mass began to be enacted by the clergy. The first play (if it can be called that) consisted of only four lines comprising the conversation between the holy women and the angels at the tomb and was held after the Office of Matins in the sanctuary of the church. Soon after other parts of the Easter liturgy, such as the beautiful sequence to the Mass, *Victimae Paschali Laude,* began to inspire similar liturgical productions.[20]

With the popular success of the Paschal dramas, the genre soon took on a life of its own, first by expanding to all the other events of Christ's life (especially his Passion), and then by separating from the liturgy altogether. This second stage of development consists of **miracle plays**, so called because of their additional focus on the miracles of Our Lady and the saints. Unlike liturgical drama, miracle plays were often in the vernacular and were held outside the precincts of the church, though they continued to be exclusively religious in theme. They were enormously popular in the twelfth and thirteenth centuries and had a powerful effect on their audience. After seeing the *Play of the Wise and Foolish Virgins,* one spectator was so disturbed by "the failure of the Blessed Virgin to save the foolish virgins" that he suffered a "stroke of apoplexy" and died two years later.[21]

Miracle plays eventually developed into the elaborate and considerably longer **mystery plays** of the fifteenth century, which take their name not from the Christian mysteries of salvation but from the Latin word for an act, *ministerium.* The most famous example of this genre are the **Passion plays**. Financed and enacted by an entire town and prepared by a spiritual lay guild, these plays representing the suffering and death of Our Lord were taken with great seriousness, even to the point of being considered a form of worship. And they were quite sensational: the actor who played Judas often had animal intestines hidden in his clothing, so that when he hanged himself, he could imitate St. Peter's account of the traitor's suicide in Acts 1:18. (After his death, "Judas" would then slide off the stage on a rope into hell.) Pictures representing the soul were hung on the two crucified thieves flanking Jesus; when they died, an angel took the "soul" of the good thief to heaven while the devil took that of the unrepentant thief to hell. The plays were also grueling on the actors. The actors who played Christ often had to memorize more than four thousand lines and one almost literally died on the cross.[22]

By the sixteenth century the old mystery productions had grown decadent with irreverence while there emerged a new kind of play—the most notorious examples being those of the philosopher Niccolo Machiavelli—that even libertines could rightly call immoral.[23] Yet even at this point the Church did not give up entirely on the now fledgling modern theater. The **Society of Jesus**, or *Jesuits,* took an eager interest in drama as part of their reintegration of literature and the humanities into Catholic educational curricula. The purpose of the Jesuits' plays was primarily didactic but it was also meant to hone the linguistic and rhetorical skills of their students, who played all of the roles and staged all the performances in Latin. (Translations of the plays were available for those members of the audience who could not understand Latin.) There was even a practical motive: as one shrewd Jesuit noted, "the sight of poor students performing well on the stage might be expected to move wealthy spectators" to contribute to the school.[24] Regardless of their novel aims, however, the Jesuits kept alive the medieval taste for the spectacular. One play in 1640 represented the infamous demise of Jezebel by placing a model of the evil queen made out of "blood, bones, and pieces of meat" on stage and having it "torn to pieces by dogs."[25]

Though the theater that was born of the Paschal liturgy centuries ago has changed substantially since, the tradition of Catholic drama continues. This is especially true when one considers world-acclaimed productions like the **Passion Play of Oberammergau**, Germany. In 1634 the people of that town vowed to produce a Passion play every ten years if they were spared the Black Death, which had taken fifteen thousand lives in nearby Munich. God heard their prayers, and the town has kept its word ever since, currently producing a play at the beginning of each decade. Today the Oberammergau play is enormous, with seventeen hundred parts to fill, all by natives of the town or residents who have lived there for at least ten years. Like their medieval forebears, people consider it an honor to leave their jobs temporarily and take part in the play. For the sake of authenticity men even start growing a beard one year before the play opens.[26]

The most famous Passion play in the United States is the **Black Hills Passion Play**, the origins of which are even older than Oberammergau's. The play began in 1242 in the Cappenburg Monastery in Germany but moved to America in 1932 when it was driven out by the Nazis. After touring for seven years, the play made its permanent home in Black Hills, South Dakota, where it has more or less stayed ever since. The Black Hills Passion Play features a cast of hundreds and has been commended for the quality of its production, with the world's largest outdoor stage, language redolent of the King James translation of the Bible, and lots of biblical detail, including camels and other live animals.[27]

**Opera.** In addition to their role in shaping modern drama, the Jesuits may also take a good deal of credit for the development of opera. One of the earliest operas ever performed was at the Jesuit Collegium Germanicum in Rome in 1606,[28] and after opera reached its present-day format around 1684, it flourished in the Catholic areas of Europe (such as France, Italy, Bavaria, and Austria) thanks in large part to the influence of the Jesuits there. Here again the Jesuit flair for combining the old and the new was evident. In 1881 the noted musicologist Sabine Baring-Gould could write, "It is in the Opera and the Oratorio that the most flourishing descendants of the old Mystery Plays are to be met with."[29]

## Theatrical Terms

**Pageant and Pageantry.** Our word for pomp and spectacle, procession and parade, comes from the terminology of medieval drama. A *pagina* in Latin refers to the page of a book, but in Anglo-Latin use it came to designate a scene or act in a play. After a while the *padgin,* or pageant, came to be associated with other facets of medieval theater as well, such as the stage on which miracle plays were performed or the stage machinery that made these open-air performances so spectacular.[30] Given medieval drama's love of the sensational, it is not difficult to see how the word has come to take on its current meaning.

**Season.** As we have seen above, modern theater emerged from the liturgical life of the Church in the Middle Ages in order to expound upon the mysteries commemorated throughout the liturgical year. So marked, in fact, was the influence of liturgical drama on the resuscitation of the theater that our current talk of a theatrical "season" can be traced to the different plays that were staged for each liturgical season of the year.[31]

**Termagant.** Our word for a violent and overbearing woman comes from a character in the medieval morality plays that was erroneously assumed to be a male deity worshiped by the Muslim Saracens and that was represented as a raging and overbearing lunatic. Most likely it was because the Termagant was also portrayed in the long and flowing robes of the East that he was over time taken to be a woman, thus narrowing the definition of the term from any violent and turbulent human being to a shrewish female.

**Herod.** As a counterweight to the chauvinist underpinnings of *termagant* we also have a verb for bad male acting, "to out-Herod." In medieval plays like *The Office of the Star,* King Herod was portrayed as "a raging maniac, throwing a wooden spear around, beating clergy and laity alike, creating havoc in both sanctuary and church by his antics."[32] Hence the expression "to out-Herod Herod," which was first used in *Hamlet* to describe ludicrous overacting (III.ii.16), now refers to being "more outrageous than the most outrageous."[33] Hamlet's advice against bad acting has in turn been applied to the actors who now play him, as our use of the word **ham** to describe an overactor is derived not from the pig but from an abbreviation of the Prince of Denmark's name. In a supreme twist of irony, Hamlet has become Herod.

**Old Nick.** Another byproduct of the Catholic theater is a humorous name for Satan. "Old Nick" comes from a character called "Old Iniquity" who appeared in several early modern morality plays.[34] The nickname (no pun intended) also gives us "nickel" and "pumpernickel" (p. 94).

**Twelfth Night.** The twelve days of Christmas, from December 26 through January 6, were not only a time of great merry making but of all sorts of masquerading and role reversals. On Childermas, the Feast of the Holy Innocents (December 28), it was customary to have the youngest member of the family or religious community serve as its head for the day or at least to receive some kind of special attention. Similarly, Catholics in the Middle Ages delighted in events like the "Boy Bishop's Feast" and the "Feast of Fools"—in which a random person was made a "bishop" for a week and made sport of—and the "Feast of the Ass," which honored the lowly donkey that carried Mary to Bethlehem.[35] Ribald though they were, these celebrations reflected the Christian world's joy and astonishment at the ultimate inversion of roles, almighty God humbling himself to become a poor and helpless infant.

The Twelve Days of preposterous feasting culminated on "Twelfth Night," the evening before the Feast of the Epiphany (January 6), an occurrence which has made the night synonymous with masquerading and wild role reversals. (To this day some Catholics have a King's Cake for the occasion which contains a coin or bean; the person whose piece contains the item becomes king or queen for the day.) Thus, Shakespeare's comedy, *Twelfth Night, Or What You Will,* was so named not because the setting is on January 5 (it is not), but because of its gender-bending mumming and topsy-turvy plot.

**Zany.** Our word denoting something ridiculous or clownish comes from the *Commedia dell' arte,* the improvised comedies of the sixteenth century whose roots go back to the rustic Italian farces of the Middle Ages. *Commedia dell' arte* made ample use of local stock characters, one of them named *Zani,* a regional variation of Giovanni, or John. In the Venetian dialect a *zani* was a servant from the mountain country of Bergamo who had taken a job as a porter in a seaside town, and in the plays he was portrayed as a high-spirited clown who imitated his master in a "ludicrously awkward way."[36]

# 7

# SPORTS AND GAMES

✠

*Our Lord the Duke has in his high discretion*
*Considered the destruction and suppression*
*Of gentle blood. . . . Wishing none to die,*
*His Grace now purposes to modify*
*His ordinance.*
　　　　—Chaucer, "The Knight's Tale," *The Canterbury Tales*[1]

It is generally not the function of religion to create new forms of entertainment or competition. Nevertheless, the Judeo-Christian proclamation of the sanctity of human life led to far-reaching changes in the way that Westerners played games, changes that have shaped our modern athletic world. After the Roman Empire embraced Christianity, a successful war was waged against the old athletic festivals and gladiator games, all of which were inherently tied to death cults, animal sacrifice, and even human sacrifice.[2] But the Church never opposed athletic competition per se, and so the field was cleared for new and more wholesome forms of sports to emerge.

In other countries, Catholic life has played a more discernible role in shaping the specific athletic tastes of a culture. In Switzerland, one of the most popular sports is shooting competitions, or *schützenfeste,* which began as training exercises for marksmen who protected the procession of the Blessed Sacrament on the Feast of Corpus Christi from violent Protestants.

What follows are some traces of Catholicism on the sports and games played in the United States.

## ATHLETICS AND RECREATION

**Olympics Motto.** The ancient Olympics were held seventeen hundred years before the birth of Christ and the modern Olympics were created to be an international, secular arena of athletic excellence. Nevertheless, the motto of the Olympic games, *Citius, Altius, Fortius* ("Faster, Higher, Stronger"), was coined by a Dominican friar. Father Henri Didon was the prior of Albert-le-Grand College in Arceuil, France. A well-known character with a penchant for sports (he himself had won many a prize in his youth), Didon encouraged athletic competition at his school as a way of building character. It was at a sports meeting in 1891 that he ended a speech to his pupils with the stirring admonition: *Citius, fortius, altius.*[3] The motto was eventually adopted by the Father of the modern Olympics, Pierre de Coubertin, with one exception. While Didon had placed the word *fortius,* or "stronger," in the middle of the phrase to stress the moral significance of athletics, Coubertin ominously changed the word order to stress the "freedom of excess," which he praised over and against "the unnatural utopia of moderation."[4] Incidentally, the prizes that Father Didon had won as a young man were in "Olympic games" held every two years in the Dominican seminary of Grenoble, France, a half-century before the advent of the modern Olympics.

**Tennis.** Though what is formally known today as lawn tennis is a relatively recent game, only a century or so old, its roots can be traced back to the monasteries of medieval France. Early records make mention of a handball game called *jeu de paume,* or "game of the palm," that was played beginning in the twelfth century in monastic communities. Apparently the game caught on outside the cloister as well; by 1292 there were at least thirteen manufacturers of tennis balls in the city of Paris. Eventually large gloves replaced the players' bare hands, which in turn were replaced by rackets in the late fifteenth century. It was the racket variation of the game that spread to the rest of Europe, thanks in large part to the infectious enthusiasm of French royalty.[5]

**Golf.** Contrary to popular belief golf did not originate in Scotland, though it has become inextricably linked with that country over the years. Many familiar features of the game come from the Scottish, and several of those in turn come from the famous Mary Stuart, Queen of Scots (1542–1587). Mary's Catholicism and *joie de vivre* put her at loggerheads with John Knox, the founder of the (Presbyterian) Church of Scotland (see p. 58), while her faith and bloodline eventually cost her her head under Queen

Elizabeth I, the head of the (Anglican) Church of England. These troubles, however, did not keep Mary from being an ardent devotee of the game. She is said to have been responsible for the first great golf course, St. Andrews, though the likelihood of this is debatable.[6] And it is also speculated that she was instrumental in the use of caddies, a custom that she may have introduced to Scotland after her return from France in 1561 (a "caddy" is a variation of *cadet*, the French word for the youngest boy of the family). Mary's love of the game was even used against her: as evidence of her callousness, her enemies charged her with playing golf a few days after her husband's murder.[7] Does this make her the first golf widow?

**Bowling.** Unlike golf, bowling has a thoroughly Christian derivation. Indeed, according to one reputable source, it may have begun not as a sport but as a religious ceremony held in the cloister of a church. As far back as the third or fourth century, peasants may have placed their clubs (which, like the old Irish shillelagh, they carried with them for protection) at the end of a lane. The club was called a *kegel* in German and was said to represent the heathen (*Heide*). Needless to say, toppling the clubs was an action fraught with symbolic significance. Over time the clubs developed into pins, but the association lingered: to this day, a bowler is sometimes referred to as a *kegler*.

**Fishing.** Fishing as both an industry and a pastime long predates Christianity, but the art of angling was certainly encouraged by Catholic enthusiasts. Dame Juliana Berners' (fl. 1450) *Treatyse of Fysshynge wyth an Angle* provides instructions on fly-fishing as well as advice on life that still rings true today. At least a dozen of the flies she describes are still in use.[8] (Dame Juliana also wrote equally popular treatises on **hawking**, **hunting**, and **fowling**.) Centuries later another Catholic cleric and the inventor of the radio, Father Jozef Murgaš (1864–1929), would add much to the sport by inventing the **spinning reel** (see p. 109).[9]

**Dumbbells.** The weights we use for body-building and the like come from a tool designed to help teach men the art of ringing the large and difficult bells in a church steeple. Because it would have been impossible to practice this art on the real bells (for it would have woken up the whole town), some parishes and cathedrals came equipped with "dumb bells"—bells that behaved like real ones but without the noise. The healthy physique that came from practicing on these dumbbells proved so popular that even men who were not bell-ringers began to use them. Eventually the term was applied to exercise weights.[10]

**Chess.** In its long history this ancient Chinese game has been banned at one time or another by Muslims, Anglicans, Jews, Eastern Orthodox, and Roman Catholics. Despite initial misgivings about the game (which hinged on the question of whether or not chess was an *alea* banned by canon law), chess came to be ardently embraced by some Catholic clergy and laity. St. Theresa of Avila had an extensive knowledge of chess, and medieval moralists were quick to exploit its possibilities for religious instruction.[11] The Catholic appreciation of the game is only appropriate, given that one of the pieces, the bishop, is undeniably ecclesiastical. In fact, the piece, which in English-speaking countries replaced the "aufin" in the fifteenth century, may very well be a testimony to how the rules of the game were modified in Europe to reflect the social structure of medieval Christendom, with the moves of the bishop mirroring the "moves" a medieval bishop could theoretically make vis-à-vis the nobility and the peasantry.

**Playing Cards.** Playing cards were met with similar suspicion by the Church in the early modern period, especially because of their use in gambling. Yet, like chess, the modern deck of cards abounds with traces of a medieval Catholic world. It is believed, for example, that the four suits symbolize the four estates of mankind in medieval society: hearts (originally cups) represent the clergy, spades (originally swords) the nobility, diamonds (originally *denari,* or money) the merchant class, and clubs (originally batons) the peasantry. The identity of the cardboard court is equally suggestive. The King of Diamonds represents Julius Caesar, the King of Clubs Alexander the Great, the King of Hearts Charlemagne, and the King of Spades David from the Old Testament. The Queen of Diamonds is Rachel from the Book of Genesis, the Queen of Clubs is the fictional "Argine" (an anagram for *Regina,* or Queen), the Queen of Hearts is Judith, and the Queen of Spades is the Greek goddess Pallas. Curiously, of all these figures, it is those on the suit associated with the Church that are also quintessentially Catholic. Charlemagne, the King of Hearts, is the only monarch in the deck who was anointed a Catholic emperor, while Judith, the Queen of Hearts, is the heroine of the Book of Judith, recognized by Catholics as part of the Old Testament canon.[12]

**Steeplechase.** A popular form of horse racing in the United Kingdom takes its name from the prominent church landmarks that once marked its starting and finish lines. Today a steeplechase refers to a 3,000–meter race over permanent hurdles and water ditches: it is an event in the modern Olympics, and there is even a track and field obstacle race named after it as well. Originally, however, a steeplechase was a cross-country race from one church steeple to another in which everything in between had to be cleared by horse and rider. The first steeplechase is said to have taken place in 1752 between the steeples of St. Leger Church in Doneraile, Ireland, and of the church in the town of Buttevant.[13] Though it is unclear as to whether the creators of the race were Catholic, their use of the steeple, which was the most visible part of a traditional settlement for miles around, attests to the prominence of the Catholic faith in village life.

**Piñatas.** What we currently associate as meaningless birthday-party fun from Mexico began as good old-fashioned Italian sin-bashing during the holy season of Lent. The idea of a piñata may have come from China via Marco Polo, but Italians in the fourteenth century applied the *pignatta,* or "fragile pot," to their observance of the first Sunday of Lent. The Spanish soon picked up the custom and took it with them to the New World. The "Dance of the Piñata," again on the first Sunday of Lent, was rich in theological meaning. The traditional gaily colored, seven-coned piñata was said to represent the Seven Deadly Sins, all of which appear attractive and beguiling. Since sin is difficult to overcome, the piñata danced on a rope in order to elude being hit, and since sin is difficult to recognize for what it is, the piñata hitter would be blindfolded. Evil, however, can be defeated by good, and so the hitter had several aids at his disposal. The first was Virtue, symbolized by his stick or bat. The hitter also had the three theological virtues of Faith, Hope, and Charity. Faith helped him trust the directions shouted out by the crowd, Hope kept him persevering and directed his actions heavenward, while Charity materialized once he broke the piñata and the treats, representing divine gifts and blessings, cascaded out (see p. 159). The piñata also migrated to the other end of Lent, when effigies of Judas Iscariot would be beaten on Good Friday, and it eventually found its way to the Mexican *posada* festivities that take place from December 16 until Christmas. By this point the piñata had essentially lost its religious significance and was a colorful reward at the end of more explicitly pious devotions.[14]

**Sports Team Names.** Though naming a sports team today after an ethnic or religious group is fraught with controversy, there was a time when such monikers were common. Interestingly, a few lingering Catholic mascots seem to be the only religious nomenclature left, ever since the Boston Puritans changed their name to the Red Sox in 1907 and the Philadelphia Quakers became the Phillies in 1890. The **Anaheim Angels** are named after a city of long Catholic nomenclature (see p. 126), while the **San Diego Padres** are named after the colonial-era Franciscan priests who played a vital role in the development of Spanish and later Mexican California. In football, the **New Orleans Saints** were named after the popular spiritual, "When the Saints Go Marching In." In fact, the franchise was officially christened on November 1, 1966—All Saints' Day.[15]

## ATHLETIC AND RECREATION TERMINOLOGY

**A Hail Mary Pass.** In football a Hail Mary refers to a long pass made near the very end of the game that is usually directed at several receivers in or around the end zone. The precise history of this relatively recent addition to our language is unclear, though some speculate that it was coined by Dallas Cowboys quarterback Roger Staubach, himself a Catholic, in reference to his desperate, "game-winning touchdown pass in the 1975 NFC Championship game."[16] From there the phrase made its way into other sports and eventually into daily discourse: General H. Norman Schwarzkopf, for example, "compared a flanking maneuver to the football play in a 1991 press briefing."[17] What is clear is that the ultimate inspiration of the phrase is the prayer, "Hail Mary, full of grace," often recited by Catholics in times of urgent need.

**Lacrosse.** Sioux Indians in present-day Canada and along the northern border of the United States loved to play a fast-paced and often bloody game involving a hard ball and a long stick topped with a small net. When French explorers witnessed the game, they were particularly struck by the shape of the stick, which reminded them of the crook of a bishop's staff, or crozier. Hence they named the sport *la crosse,* the French word for *crozier.*[18]

**Dominoes, fact and fiction.** There is a legend that the game of dominoes was invented by French monks and that the game's name comes from the opening verse of the first psalm of Sunday Vespers, *Dixit Dominus Domino meo,* which the winner would recite as a way of declaring his victory. The truth of the matter is that dominoes dating back to A.D. 1120 have been found in China and that the European name derives from a sartorial source. A "domino" was a hood, black on the outside and white on the inside, worn by canons (a kind of cleric). Interestingly enough, one theory about why the hood was called a domino is that it comes from the final versicle of Vespers, *Benedicamus Domino.*[19] Ironically, then, the name may be from Vespers after all.

# Part III

# *The Tree of Knowledge*

# 8

# FLOWERS AND PLANTS

✠

*To see a World in a grain of sand*
*And a Heaven in a wild flower,*
*Hold Infinity in the palm of your hand*
*And Eternity in an hour.*
                    —William Blake, "Auguries of Innocence"

Just as Catholic thought echoes the opening line from Psalm 18, "the heavens shew forth the glory of God," so too do Catholics see in the natural world around them small testaments of their faith. When "reading" the characteristics of holly, for example, one sixteenth-century poet compared the leaf's white blossom to Christ's purity, its red berry to his Passion, its prickles to the sharpness of the winter morn in which Christ was born, and its bitter bark to the gall which Christ drank on the cross. This connecting of the natural to the supernatural is not so much an artificial imposition of Catholic "values" on the botanical as it is the recognition that everything, by its very nature, potentially points to something beyond itself. Like William Blake, the Catholic mind recognizes that the smallest wild flower reveals an entire Heaven of meaning to the pious and attentive eye.

And the smallest wildflower may serve as an apt reminder of God's friends as well. According to the research association Mary's Gardens, there are over eight hundred plants and trees that have been named after the Trinity or the saints.[1] Following is an overview of that impressive list. After this tour through the greenhouse of things inspired by God and the Church Triumphant, we will look at the flora named after the Church Militant.

## GOD THE FATHER, SON, AND HOLY SPIRIT

**Trinity Plant.** *Tradescantia Virginiana* is a plant that produces small, colorful flowers with three petals, thus earning it the nickname "Trinity plant." Trefoils of various kinds have long been associated with one of the most fundamental Christian mysteries. Stories abound about St. Patrick teaching his Irish audiences about the three Persons in one God by comparing them to the three leaves of a single **shamrock**, while the Wake Robin (*Trillium grandiflorum*) is also referred to as a **Trinity lily**. Lessons on the eternal processions of the Divine Persons have even been adduced from plant life. **Aloe vera**'s tendency to have a third spear sprout between two others has been likened to the Catholic doctrine of the *filioque,* which holds that together the Father and the Son "spirate" the Holy Spirit in love.[2]

**Nativity Flowers.** Many flowers have been named in honor of Christ's birth. The **Cradle orchid** (*Anguloa clowesii*) is believed by some to evoke the memory of Jesus' crib in Nazareth, while lungwort, or **Bethlehem sage** (*Pulmonaria*), recalls the town of his birth. Perhaps the best known flowers to evoke the first Christmas are the several varieties of the **Star of Bethlehem** (*Ornithogalum umbellatum*), a native of the Holy Land most likely brought to Europe by the Crusaders. According to one legend, after the star faithfully guided the Magi to the manger, it exploded in the sky, scattering little pieces that burst into white blossoms.[3] (For more flowers pertaining to the birth of Jesus, see pp. 78 and 84).

**Passion Flowers.** As common as the flowers recalling the Nativity are those named after Our Lord's Passion. The centaury or **Christ's ladder** (*Erythræa Centaurium*), for example, appears to be named after the ladder used during the crucifixion. The **Christ-thorn** (*Paliurus spina-christi* and *Zizyphus spina-christi*), **Crown of Thorns** (*Euphorbia splendens*), and glory bower or **Holy Crown of Jesus** (*Clerodendrum japon*) obviously hearken to the spiky crown on Christ's head, while **bloodleaf** (*Iresine herbstii*) and **blood-drop emlets** (*Mimulus luteus*) recall the blood he shed on Good Friday. Several other plants, by contrast, reflect the beauty of Christ's everyday appearance, such as *Christ's-eye* (*Inula oculus-christi*) and **Christ's-hair** (*Scolopendrium vulgare*).[4]

**The Passion Flower.** Perhaps the most famous blossom representing the suffering Christ and certainly the most theologically rich is the Passion flower (*Passiflora*). Discovered in the sixteenth century in Paraguay by "the gentle poet-priest Martin del Barco,"[5] the flower was so named because missionaries saw in its exquisite and beautiful features an allegory of Our Lord's

Passion. The flower's five sepals and five petals purportedly call to mind the ten apostles (minus Judas and St. Peter) who deserted but did not betray Christ. The corona (a double row of colored filaments) represents the Crown of Thorns, while the vine tendrils symbolize the flagella used in the scourging. The five stamens represent the Five Wounds, and the three spreading styles the nails that transfixed Christ's hands and feet. The column of the flower, on the other hand, betokens the pillar of the scourging, the fragrance signifies the spices the women brought to the tomb, the round fruit recalls the world that Christ's death redeemed, and the red spots on some species hearken to the drops of blood he shed.[6]

**Crucial Flowers.** Given the power of the Passion on human imagination, it is not surprising that several plants have been named after Christ's suffering and death. The **Santa Cruz lily** (*Victoria cruziana*) is one of the world's largest water lilies, growing up to six feet in diameter. Its fragrant white flowers, which have more than fifty petals, open up in the late afternoon. Within two days, the petals redden before withering up and being replaced by a large berrylike fruit. Other crosslike plants include the **crosswort** (*Crucianella*), **Maltese cross** (*Lychnis chalced.*), and **iron cross** (*Begonia masoniana*).

Since death did not ultimately claim Christ, the final word should go to the **Resurrection plant** (*Selaginella lepidophylla*). This desert native of the Americas derives its name from the way that it tightens into a ball and turns brown when there is no water, and unfurls and turns green when the water returns.[7]

**Dove Orchid.** God the Son is not the only divine person to inspire floral nomenclature. Several plants have also been named after the Holy Spirit. The dove orchid (*Peristeria elata*), or **Holy Ghost flower**, is an exquisite orchid from the Americas and the national flower of Panama. The column in its center bears a peculiar resemblance to a dove.

**Holy Ghost Pear.** An old cognomen for an avocado is a Holy Ghost pear. What possible relation could there be between the Holy Spirit and the unusual green fruit from which guacamole is made? *Avocado* was used as a convenient Spanish substitute for the Aztec word *ahuacatl,* since the two sound somewhat similar. *Avocado* in Spanish means "advocate," one of the titles of the Holy Spirit (this, for instance, is the meaning of the word *Paraclete*). Given the avocado's oily richness, perhaps it is not inappropriate that it shares a name with the divine person who is also called our "Spiritual Unction."[8]

## MARY'S FLOWERS

Flowers have long been associated with the Mother of God, aptly praised in one hymn as the "loveliest rose of the vale." Not too long ago **Mary gardens** filled with plants "ascribed by love and legend" to the Blessed Virgin[9] adorned the yards of Catholic homes, while Catholic brides and young "May queens" continue to dedicate their bouquets to her. Almost every flower known in the Middle Ages had a Marian legend attached to it, and more than a few, as we shall see, still take their name from her.

**Madonna Lily.** According to legend, the Madonna lily (*Lilium candidum*) first sprang from the tears of Eve after her expulsion from Paradise, but it was turned white when Mary touched the lily that was being held in the angel Gabriel's hand. (Notice that artwork depicting the Annunciation frequently shows Gabriel holding a lily.) The Venerable Bede (673–735), a learned Benedictine monk, tells us why the Madonna lily is a fitting symbol of the Virgin:

> the white petals [signify] her bodily purity,
> the golden anthers the glowing light of her soul.[10]

Indeed, the "lily among thorns" mentioned in the Song of Songs (2:2) was thought by some to be the Madonna lily.

**Our Lady's Bedstraw.** Yellow bedstraw (*Galium verum*) is a small plant with slender ascending stems crowned with clusters of small flowers. It has also been called Our Lady's bedstraw. According to a colorful legend, after Mary and Joseph were turned away at the inn, Joseph went to the stable and made a bed for Mary that consisted of dried straw, thyme, and sweet woodruff. When Jesus was born, these same grasses, most noticeably the yellow flowers of the bedstraw, burst into blossom.[11]

**Sainfoin.** A similar story surrounds sainfoin (*Onobrychis viciifolia*), or "holy hay." According to a French tradition, sainfoin was also used to help make a resting place for the Blessed Virgin, and when Jesus was born and placed on a bed of hay, the sainfoin around his head bloomed.[12]

**Marigolds.** "What flower is that which bears the Virgin's name/ The richest metal joined with the same?"[13] The answer to that riddle by John Gay is the marigold, or Mary's Gold. Marigolds (*calendula*) took on a Marian association because they were in bloom during virtually all the feast days of the Blessed Virgin. The flowers were especially popular on Lady Day, the Feast of the Annunciation on March 25, when they would be twined into garlands and used to decorate the church. But the flower is called Mary's Gold for a different reason. There is an old legend that says during the flight into Egypt a gang of robbers took Mary's purse; when they opened it, marigolds fell out. Perhaps as a result of this story there developed the custom of placing marigolds instead of coins around the statue of Mary.[14]

**Rosemary.** According to legend, Mary washed the tiny garments of Jesus during their flight to Egypt and spread them over the branches of a rosemary bush (*Rosmarinus officinalis*) to dry them. In reward for this service to his Son, God conferred upon the rosemary, or Mary's rose, a fragrant aroma.[15]

**Virgin's Bower.** Rosemary was not the only plant to aid the Holy Family in their escape from Herod's henchmen. In Sicily there was a story that a **juniper** bush courageously hid Jesus, Mary, and Joseph from the soldiers, an act that God rewarded by bestowing on the plant the power of putting evil spirits to flight. Similarly, in Germany it was said that the species of clematis called virgin's bower (*Clematis vitalba*) provided shelter for the besieged family. The twenty-foot high hedges functioned as a bower, or dwelling, for the Holy Family at night and a shield from the sun during the day.[16]

**Our Lady's Thistle.** The scientific name for milk thistle, a prickly weed with small purple flowers, is *Carduus marianus,* or Mary's thistle. Early botanists referred to the plant as *Lac Beatae Mariae* (Blessed Mary's milk), while today it is more popularly known as lady's thistle. It is said that the white veins of the plant were made by a few drops of Mary's milk that fell on its leaves as she was nursing her son.[17]

**Lady's Slipper.** Lady's slipper is a name that has been applied to several plants, such as the **bird's-foot trefoil**, which in France was said to have grown on whatever soil Our Lady and her young son trod. But it is the yellow orchid *Cypripedium calceolus* that is best known as lady slipper. According to legend, Jesus placed his mother's foot into the opening of this flower when he was a little child.[18] How long this allusion to the Mother of God will last, however, is another question. Since the toe of the slipper can also look like a prominent chin, several flower shops have begun to call this the Jay Leno orchid.

**Lady's Smock.** The cuckoo flower (*Cardamine pratensis*) is also known as lady smock. The smock in question is the seamless robe that the Virgin Mary wove for her Son and that was worn by him on Good Friday (this was the same garment for which the Roman soldiers cast lots as described in John 19:24). According to an ancient tradition, Our Lady was raised in the Temple as a little girl and became an expert weaver.[19]

**Our Lady's Thimble.** Bluebell, or *Campanula rotundifolia,* is also related to the seamless garment of the Gospels. The tiny bell-shaped flowers of the plant are called lady's thimble in honor of the plausible assumption that it was Mary who sewed all of Christ's clothes.[20]

**Lily of the Valley.** The name for the fragrant *Convallaria majalis* comes from one of the verses in the Song of Songs traditionally viewed as an allegorical allusion to the Blessed Virgin: "I am a lily of the valley" (2:1). Lily of the valley is also known as **Mary's tears**, for from a distance its tiny droop-ing flowers look like teardrops. An old legend recounts how the flowers first blossomed from the soil on which Mary's tears had fallen as she stood weep-ing at the foot of the Cross.[21] No doubt this genealogy could also be applied to the similarly named **Queen's tears** (*Billbergia nutans*).

**Rosary Vine or Plant.** Finally, even the devotions to the Blessed Virgin are duly represented in the plant world. *Ceropegia woodii* and *Crassula ru-pestris* are both plants that have been named rosary vines after their resem-blance in one way or another to rosary beads. Such floral associations are only fitting: *rosary* comes from the Latin word for a bouquet of roses (*rosar-ius*). In fact, there is an old legend that the first rosary was made by the Blessed Mother herself, who took rosebuds from the lips of a young monk as he recited *Hail Mary*'s and wove them into a garland for her head. We do know that a **bead** originally referred to a prayer, and that our current use of the word for a small, perforated ball comes from the prayers of the rosary rather than vice versa. The rosary, incidentally, is a cherished form of prayer consisting of one Apostles' Creed, six *Our Father*'s, six *Glory Be*'s, 153 *Hail Mary*'s, and one *Hail, Holy Queen*. It is recited on a special string of beads while meditating on the joyful, sorrowful, or glorious "mysteries," events taken from the lives of Our Lord and Our Lady. In 2002, Pope John Paul II added a fourth set of mysteries called the *luminous,* which focus on Christ's earthly ministry.

## THE CHURCH TRIUMPHANT:
## THE COMMUNION OF SAINTS

**Plants from on High.** More than a few members of the vegetable kingdom have been named after the Heavenly Hosts. These include but are not limited to: **angelica** (*Angelica archangelica*), **angel wing begonia** (*Begonia,* var.), **angel's tears** (*Soleirolia soleirolii* or *Narcissus,* var.), **angelonia** (*Angelonia,* var.), **angel's wings cactus** (*Opuntia microdasys*), **angel wings** (*Caladium bicolor,* or Heart of Jesus), **angel's trumpet** (*Brugmansia* or *Datura*).[22] Of course, we cannot forget Lucifer, the most notorious fallen angel, after whom **devil's tongue** (*Amorphophallus rívieri*), **devil's backbone** (*Pedilanthus tithymaloides*), **devil's tomato** (*Solanum eleagnifolium*), and **devil's ivy pothos** (*Epipremnum aureum*) are named.

**Jacob's Ladder.** The *Polemonium caeruleum* is a garden plant with blue or white flowers. The pinnate growth of its leaves resembles a ladder, and so it was named after the dream in which Jacob saw "a ladder standing upon the earth, and the top thereof touching heaven: the angels also of God ascending and descending by it" (Genesis 28:12). Given the traditional popularity of

Jacob's ladder as an exemplum of spiritual progress, it is not surprising to see it invoked for a number of different items. "Jacob's ladder," for example, is also a **rope ladder** with wooden steps used to ascend the rigging on a sailing ship[23] as well as a charming **folk toy** made of moving wood blocks connected by ribbons.

**Joseph's Coat.** Jacob's favorite son can also claim an eponymous plant. The variegated leaves of the summer poinsettia or Joseph's coat (*Amaranthus tricolor*) recall the multi-colored coat that Jacob gave to the son of his beloved wife Rachel (Genesis 37:3).[24] It is to be hoped that the presence of Joseph's coat does not cause the same discord among the other flowers of the garden as it did among Joseph's envious siblings.

**Moses in the Bulrush.** *Rhoeo discolor* or *spathacea* is a native of Mexico and the West Indies. The plant's long, waxy leaves are evocative of the bulrushes that line the River Nile and that figure in the dramatic narrative of Moses' infancy in Exodus 2:1–10. It has taken on a number of Mosaic sobriquets—such as Moses-in-the-boat, Moses-in-the-cradle, Moses-in-the-basket, and Moses-in-the-bulrush—because the way in which it cradles its small white flowers suggests Moses in the makeshift ark when he was discovered by the Pharaoh's daughter (Exodus 2:3–6).

**Aaron's Beard.** Several plants have been named after the flowing facial hair of Moses' older brother and ancient Israel's first high priest, including great St. John's wort (*Hypericum calycinum*), the strawberry geranium (*Saxifraga sarmentosa*), the ivy-leaved toadflax (*Linaria cymbalaria*), the shrub *Spiraea salicifolia,* and the cactus *Opuntia leucotricha.*[25] Each plant in its own peculiar way bears a resemblance to the psalmist's colorful description of fraternal unity as the precious oil that runs "down upon the beard, the beard of Aaron" (Psalm132:2).

**Aaron's Rod.** Aaron's staff also occupies an important place in the Scriptures. The symbol of his priestly power, it was turned into a serpent by Moses in the presence of the Pharoah (Exodus 7:10) and became one of the three items placed in the Ark of the Covenant—the stone tablets of the Ten Commandments and some of the manna that fell from heaven being the other two (Numbers 17:10). It is the time that the staff sprouted blossoming buds and leaves (Numbers 17:8), however, that inspired the lending of its name to several tall-stemmed flowers such as the great mullein or hag-taper (*Verbascum thapsus*) and the golden rod (*Solidago virgaurea*).[26]

**Job's Tears.** This species of grass, which can grow several feet high, produces tear-shaped grains that are used to make rosary beads. The sorrow and tribulations of Job are proverbial even within the Bible itself, and so it is fitting that his name be attached to a plant associated with tears. It is interesting to note, however, that Job is described in Scripture as rending his garments and shaving his head in grief (Job 1:20), as scraping his ulcerous skin with a potsherd in agony (2:8), and even as sitting on a dunghill in misery, but, unlike his three friends, he is never actually described as weeping.[27]

**Peter's Plants.** Several individual apostles have also been memorialized in botanical nomenclature. Chief among these is, fittingly enough, the chief apostle. **St. Peter's keys** or **St. Peter's wort** (*Primula veris*), **St. Peter's plant** (*Cuphea llavea*), **St. Peter's wreath** (*Spiraea hypericifolia*), the single-grained wheat **St. Peter's corn** (*Triticum monococcum*), and **Peter's cress**, or samphire (*Crithmum maritimum*) are all named in honor of Simon Bar Jonah.[28]

**St. John's Wort.** One apostolic plant famed for its healing properties is *Hypericum perforatum,* or johnswort. According to one legend, St. John the Evangelist, who was the only apostle who stood at the foot of the cross, gathered the herb after he noticed it drenched in Christ's blood. Others believe the plant may be named after St. John the Baptist, as some legends link the wort to his beheading: the red spots on the plant are said to be drops of his blood. One corroborating piece of evidence in support of the Baptist theory is that the plant is considered most potent around the time of June 24, the Feast of St. John the Baptist.[29]

**St. Barnaby's Thistle.** *Centaurea solstitialis* is a kind of knapweed named in honor of St. Barnabas, "a good man and full of the Holy Ghost and of faith" (Acts 11:24), who first introduced St. Paul to the rest of the apostles and who first persuaded Paul to preach the Gospel to the gentiles (Acts 9:27 and 11:25). Consequently, the Church honors Barnabas with the title of Apostle even though he was not one of the original twelve. The thistle is named after St. Barnabas because it flowers around June 11, the saint's feast day.[30]

**Costmary.** *Chrysanthemum balsamita* is reputedly named after St. Mary Magdalene, whose feast is July 20. The name is most likely an allusion to the precious ointment that St. Mary Magdalene used to anoint the head of her Savior (Matthew 26:7). Maudlin, another nickname for costmary, likewise alludes to the great penitent (see p. 153).[31]

**Veronica.** An entire genus of perennial ground cover is named after the saint who tradition tells us wiped the bloody face of Our Lord with a napkin as he was carrying the cross. Also known as speedwell, these plants are said to resemblance the impression of Our Lord's countenance that was left on St. Veronica's napkin.[32]

**St. Barbara's Cress.** *Barbarea vulgaris* or herb-Barbara is named after the patron saint of artillerymen and miners because it is grown and eaten around the time of her feast day on December 4. St. Barbara, a virgin who was killed by her father for converting to Catholicism, has long been associated with flora. There is an old custom, for example, of putting cherry branches in water on her feast day; if the branches bloom before Christmas, it is a sign that the new year will bring good luck.[33]

**St. Augustine Grass.** A favorite grass for lawns in the southern states and throughout Mexico and South America, St. Augustine is most likely named after the city of St. Augustine, Florida, which has been cultivating the grass for its lawns since the 1890s. A native North African who spent most of his life in present-day Algeria, St. Augustine (354–430) once complained of how chilly he found the winters in Italy. Thus, though the grass has only a homonymous connection with the famous sinner-turned-saint, it does seem to share with St. Augustine a love of clement weather.

**Filberts.** Filberts are a kind of hazelnut from the birch tree family (*Corylus avellana*). Though popular since the days of the Romans, filberts take their name from a medieval saint. Philibert (608–685) was a Benedictine abbot and bishop whose feast day, August 20, happens to fall around the time when the sweet nuts are harvested.[34]

**Marguerite.** The daisy *Bellis perennis* is named after St. Margaret of Cortona (1247–1297). Margaret wasted her youth as the mistress of a man who promised to marry her but never did, even though she bore him an illegitimate son. One day Margaret noticed a dog acting as if it wanted her to follow him; she did so, and the dog led her to a woodpile, under which she found the body of her murdered lover. Margaret immediately repented of her past, abandoned her gay dress and pretty jewelry, and joined the Third Order of the Friar Minors (the Franciscans). She became renowned for her holiness, her generosity to the poor, her mystical visions of Christ, and her ability to see into the hearts and consciences of others. The reason her name has been used to denote this particularly daisy is aptly expressed in an old poem:

> There is a double flouret, white and red,
> That our lasses call herb-Margaret,
> In honour of Cortona's penitent,
> Whose contrite soul with red remorse was rent;
> While on her penitence kind heaven did throw
> The white of purity, surpassing snow;
> So white and red in this fair flower entwine,
> Which maids are wont to scatter at her shrine.[35]

Incidentally, having a flower named after St. Margaret is particularly appropriate given the miracle that has followed her death. Even to this day her body remains incorrupt (showing no sign of decay) and is known to emit a fragrance like sweet perfume.[36]

**St. Ignatius' Bean.** More recent saints have also had their influence on botanical nomenclature. Jesuit missionaries named the seed of a Filipino tree after the founder of their order, St. Ignatius of Loyola, christening it the *Ignatia,* or Ignatius bean.[37]

# THE CHURCH MILITANT

The traditional liturgical calendar, with its rich array of fasts and feasts, customs and observances, did more than inspire the imagination; it imbued the monotony of time with the sparkle of Christian mysteries. Here are some of the floral fruits of that celestial infusion.

**Christmas Flowers.** Given the popularity of Christmas, it is not surprising that at least a dozen flowers have been named after it. Most plants, such as the **Christmas cactus** (*Schlumbergera, varii*) and **Christmas daisy** (*Aster grandiflorus*), take their name from the time of the year when they bloom, though a few, such as the **Christmas fern** (*Polystichum acrostichoides*) and **Christmas bush** (*Ceratopetalum gummiferum*), are so named because they were used as Christmas decorations.[38]

**Christmas Rose.** *Helleborus niger* is variously known as the Christmas flower, Christmas herb, Holy Night rose, rose de Noël or, as is most common, the Christmas rose. The rose most likely takes its name from the fact that it blooms at Christmastime, but there is also a rich codex of legend attached to it. Several medieval mystery plays, for example, tell the story of Madelon, a young shepherd girl who tagged behind the other shepherds to whom the angel had appeared as they made their way to the manger. Madelon watched as the shepherds played lullabies on their rustic pipes and as the three kings gave gifts of gold, frankincense, and myrrh. Because she had nothing to offer, however, she was filled with sorrow and began to weep. Suddenly the angel Gabriel appeared to her and asked her why she was crying. "Because," she replied, "I have nothing to offer the infant Jesus. If only I had some flowers to give him I should be happy, but it is winter, and the frost is on the ground." Gabriel then took Madelon's hand and led her away to a secluded spot. The cold seemed to vanish as they were enveloped in a bright, warm light. Gabriel touched the frozen earth with his staff, and suddenly there appeared white blossoms tinged with pink. Madelon gratefully gathered the roses in her arms and took them to the manger, where she decorated Jesus' crib.[39]

**Christmas Holly.** The name for American or Christmas holly (*Ilex opaca*) hearkens back to a number of beautiful stories about this popular holiday plant. Holly was made a Christmas garland not as a holdover from pagan yuletide customs (as is sometimes thought) but, as we mentioned in the introduction to this chapter, because of its symbolic properties. According to one tradition, holly's prickly edges and red berries point backward to the thorny bush glowing red with fire that Moses saw on Mt. Sinai as well as forward to the bloody crown of thorns that the newborn King would one day wear. The use of holly as an emblem of the burning bush is particularly appropriate. On the testimony of the traditional Advent liturgy, it is not just God but God the Son who appeared to Moses in the bush, the same God who would become a helpless babe in a manger. Similarly, the bush itself was seen as a type of the Blessed Virgin Mary, whose virginity was preserved despite childbirth just as the bush was preserved despite the fire engulfing it.[40]

**Candlemas Bells.** The feast that falls on February 2 has been known by many names: the Purification of the Blessed Virgin Mary, the Presentation of Our Lord in the Temple, and the Encounter of Our Lord with Simeon the Prophet. But one of the more popular names for the feast was the Mass of Candles, or "Candlemas," because of the elaborate candlelight processions and the blessing of candles that took place on that day. The feast also had its own flower, the snowdrop or Candlemas bells (*Galanthus nivalis*). The pure white flower was seen as a symbol of Mary's purity and was a reminder that although Mary dutifully went to the temple to obey the Mosaic laws of postpartum purification, she who was conceived without original sin was in no need of it.[41]

**Simnel Squash.** This species of squash (also known as simlin or cymling) takes its name from a once-popular mid-Lenten treat. Laetare Sunday, notable for its rose vestments, occurs in the middle of Lent and provides a small break from the austerity of the season. On this Sunday in the traditional Roman rite, the faithful would hear the Epistle reading in which St. Paul declares "Jerusalem above" to be our mother (Galatians 4:26). Laetare Sunday thus came to be known in England as "Mothering Sunday," and it became a time for honoring one's "mother church" (one's childhood parish) as well as one's mother (see p. 15). Children would on this occasion give their mothers simnel cakes, rich currant cakes crowned with eleven marzipan eggs (the number of the apostles minus Judas). Since the scalloped edge of the gourd *Cucurbita verrucosa* bears a vague resemblance to this unusual cake top, it came to be known as a simnel squash.[42]

**Palm Willow.** The palm willow, or *Salix caprea*, takes its name not from any biological affinity with palm trees but from the fact that it was used as a substitute for palms on Palm Sunday in England. The same obtains for the **yew tree** in Ireland, which is sometimes referred to there as a palm tree. Such liturgical substitutions, incidentally, are common. In the Ukraine and other parts of Eastern Europe, Palm Sunday is called **Pussy Willow Sunday** for that very reason.[43]

**Easter Lily.** It is hard to believe that *Lilium longiflorum,* or Easter lily, has been in the United States for only a little over a century. First exported into this country from Japan in 1882, the elegant white lily quickly became a staple of altar and sanctuary for the annual Feast of the Resurrection. Though the Easter lily is relatively new to Western worship, however, lilies have been associated with Mary and Jesus ever since the Sermon on the Mount's injunction to "consider the lilies of the field" (Matthew 6:28). Sometimes referred to as the "white-robed apostles of hope," lilies have been linked in folklore to the Garden of Gethsemane after Our Lord sweat drops of blood onto the soil.[44]

**Paschal Flowers.** The Easter lily is not the only flower named after the Feast of the Resurrection. Other examples include the **Pasque flower** (*Anemone pulsatilla*), **Easter lily cactus** (*Echinopsis multiplex*), the **Easter cactus** (*Schlumbergera gaertneri*), and **Easter bells** (*Stellaria holostea*).

**Rogation Flower.** *Polygala vulgaris* is a European species of milkwort that is associated with the Rogation Days of the traditional Church calendar. The Rogation Days fell on April 25 and on the Monday, Tuesday, and Wednesday before the Feast of the Ascension. This was a solemn time to *rogare,* or petition God for bountiful crops, protection from natural disaster, and spiritual security. Plaintive litanies and impressive processions through town and country would be conducted, affording the priest the opportunity to bless his parishioners' fields and land. Rogationtide was also theologically rich in meaning, simultaneously reminding us of the goodness of the fruits of the earth and of our human vulnerability to the forces of nature. (The Rogation Days before Ascension were instituted in A.D. 470 by Bishop Mamertus of Vienne, France, whose diocese was being rocked by a terrifying series of storms, floods, and earthquakes.) One of the traditions that grew around the Rogation Days was of making garlands and nosegays out of milkwort for use in the procession. It is from this custom that the *Polygala vulgaris* took its common name.[45]

**Michaelmas Daisy.** Michaelmas is the traditional nickname for what was formerly the Feast of St. Michael and the Angels on September 29. (In the current Roman calendar, the feast is in honor of all the angels.) Michaelmas was a great day of celebration, and in England it was also one of the quarter days, one of the four times in the year when rents were due. Consequently, there are a number of old expressions that arose from the holiday, such as **Michaelmas summer** for Indian summer, **Michaelmas moon** for the harvest moon, and the **Michaelmas blackbird** for the ring ouzel (*Turdus torquatus*). And, of course, flowers that bloomed around the time of St. Michael's feast also took on the name. A **Michaelmas crocus** is an obsolete term for a meadow saffron (*Colchicum autumnale*), but a name still in currency is the one used for the North American *Aster novi-belgii,* the **Michael-mas daisy**.

## RELIGIOUS AND CLERICAL ORDERS

**Jesuit Bark.** *Quinaquina* was the name the Incans gave to a plant that contains quinine, the alkaloid that is used as a remedy for malaria. Formally known as cinchona, the plant was discovered by a Jesuit missionary in Peru, and hence it is more commonly known as Jesuit bark.[46]

**Monkish Habits...** A number of plants have been given names based on their resemblance to monks. After its pappus is blown off, the dandelion **Monk's head** (*Taraxacum*) looks like the tonsured head of a monk, while the helmet-shaped sepal of **Monkshood** (*Aconitum*) and the hot pepper **Monk's hat** (*Capsicum annum*) resemble monastic headwear.[47]

**... and Monastic Medicine.** Monastic gardens were once great centers of herbal healing, which is why plants used medicinally—such as *Rumex patientia,* or **monk's rhubarb**—now bear their names. One peculiar example is *Vitex agnus-castus,* which was revered in pre-Christian times as an antidote to violent sexual passion. The plant came to be called **monk's pepper tree**, for it was seen as something that could help monks keep their vows of chastity. The ancient belief in the plant's properties, incidentally, may have some merit after all. Vitex has estrogenlike properties, which are used today to relieve premenstrual syndrome (PMS) and menstrual cramps.[48]

**Episcopal Flora.** Further up on the hierarchical scale are plants named after the successors of the apostles. These include the genus *Mitella,* called **bishop's cap** or **miterwort**, **bishop's hat** (*Epimedium alpinum*), **bishop's leaves** (*Scrophularia aquatica*), and **bishop's wort** (*Stachys betonica* or *Nigella damascene*).[49]

**Cardinal Flower.** Because the color of the North American scarlet lobelia, which is prized for its beautiful blossoms, resembles that of a cardinal's robe and hat, it is also known as the cardinal flower (for more on the color cardinal red, see pp. 107–108).[50]

**Pope's Head.** And if a cardinal is to have his own plant, then certainly the pope should as well. The spiny head of the cactus *Melocactus communis,* which grows in South America and the West Indies, bears a curious resemblance to the papal tiara formerly worn by the Supreme Pontiff.[51]

# INSECTS, ANIMALS, AND OTHER NATURAL PHENOMENA

✠

*How great are thy works, O Lord! Thou hast made all things in wisdom: the earth is filled with thy riches.*

—Psalm 103:24

*The world is charged with the grandeur of God.*
—Gerard Manley Hopkins, S.J., "God's Grandeur"

The works of nature are God's silent words, and since not even the din of contemporary life can drown them out entirely, they continue to speak to us. Little wonder, then, that Catholics of old responded to the charged grandeur of these words with pious nomenclature of their own, naming the creatures around them in honor of their common Creator. Of course, God also writes straight with crooked lines, and many names are the product of bizarre historical twists. Regardless of the process, what follows are several members of the animal and insect kingdoms that directly or indirectly take their names from Catholic life.

## ANIMALS AND INSECTS

**Ladybug.** One of the nursery's most celebrated insects and one of a gardener's best friends is named after the Blessed Virgin Mary. This could be because ladybugs are plentiful in May, one of the two months of the year dedicated to Our Lady, though the more likely reason is that its seven black spots were seen as symbolic of the Seven Sorrows of the Blessed Virgin.[1] The pest-eating beetle, incidentally, has had more than one pious moniker in its day, including lady-bird, lady-cow, duck, Marygold, God's Little Cow, and Bishop that Burneth.[2]

**Cardinal.** Because of the deep crimson of its plumes, the beautiful state bird of Illinois, Indiana, Kentucky, North Carolina, Ohio, Virginia, and West Virginia is named after the distinctive red habit of the College of Cardinals (for more on this color, see pp. 107–108).[3]

**Chartreux Cat.** The breed of cat that is jokingly referred to as a "potato on sticks" is named after the Carthusian monks in France who also make Chartreuse liqueur (see p. 33). Though stories abound about the quiet felines with oddly canine behavior being raised by the monks for companionship, it is also possible that they were named after a Spanish wool that their coat resembles. Regardless, their association with the French monastery remains: an experimental breed that is being developed in Great Britain from long-haired Chartreux, for example, is being called **Benedictine**.[4]

**St. Bernard.** The dog whose reputation is forever adorned by heroic legend is named after St. Bernard of Menthon or Montjoux (923–1008), a holy archdeacon who was determined to bring Christianity to the mountain peoples living in the Alps. As part of his evangelization effort and in order to help French and German pilgrims on their arduous trek to Rome, Bernard founded two monasteries and hospices along a pass that crossed the Pennine Alps, one of which was at the pass's highest point, eight thousand feet above sea level. This treacherous part of the mountains is covered with seven to eight feet of snow the year round with drifts reaching as high as forty feet, and it is susceptible to avalanches in the spring. Though Bernard's hospices were renowned for their generosity to all travelers, they are best known for the valor of their monks and their well-trained dogs, who would scour the area after a storm, rescuing those in trouble and burying those who had perished.[5] Today not only the dogs but the pass and the two hospices bear St. Bernard's name.

The St. Bernard is an ancient breed, though its use for search and rescue probably began in the seventeenth century. And while our storybook pictures of St. Bernards with barrels of brandy around their neck is myth, it is true that these strong and noble dogs have been credited with saving the lives of approximately twenty-five hundred people in the three hundred years that their breed has been documented. When the dogs, who can smell a person buried in several feet of snow, find a person, they lick him and lie next to him to keep him warm while another dog returns to the hospice for help. Originally, however, it is speculated that St. Bernards were bred as guard dogs, and that one resourceful cook at the monastery used them to power a rotating spit in the kitchen.[6]

**Pigeons.** Trumping the dog category with its solitary St. Bernard is the pigeon. Several breeds of this common bird have Catholic or clerical names, most likely because of their physical resemblance to this or that religious habit. These include the **Archangel**, **German Nun**, **Nun**, **Old Dutch Capu-chine** (which actually looks more like a Dominican friar than a Capuchin), **Priest**, **Saxon Monk**, and **Saxon Priest**.[7]

**Priest-fish.** The blue or black rockfish (*Sebastichthys mystinus*) can be found along the Pacific coast from Alaska to Baja California at depths of up to three hundred fathoms (1,800 feet) below the surface of the sea. Though it is known by several names, one of the more interesting is priest-fish, presumably because of its black scales and sometimes white-striped forehead.[8]

**Guadalupe Bass.** The species of black bass known as *Micropterus tre-culii* takes its name from its home in the Guadalupe River of southwest Texas, but that waterway was in turn named by its European discoverer in honor of Our Lady of Guadalupe in 1689. Alonso De Leon was a Spanish ex-plorer whose expedition marched under the patronage of Our Lady; in fact, the royal standard that the troops carried had her image painted on it.[9]

**Requiem Shark.** As we saw earlier (see p. 55), the Requiem Mass was for centuries the principal way to grieve over the loss of one's beloved dead. The word *requiem,* or rest, in fact, came to mean not only any kind of funeral dirge but any kind of repose or rest from labor. And it also came to signify a family of sharks known in scientific circles as the *Carcharhinidae,* which in-clude dozens of species ranging from harmless bottom feeders to the fero-cious tiger and bull sharks. Apparently it was French and Portuguese mariners who coined this term on the observation that these sharks tended to appear when the ocean was calm.[10] But given the fact that a few species of *Carcharhinidae* sharks can be deadly for swimmers, there may also be a more morbid reason why the name is appropriate.

**Monkfish and Angel-Sharks.** Requiems are not the only sharks with Catholic nomenclature. The *Squatina* genus of sharks, better known as **monkfish**, are so-called because their head looks like a monk wearing his cowl.[11] And one of the more famous species of monkfish also has a nomi-nally religious identity. The **angel-shark**, which lives on the ocean's bottom, is named after the spirits that dwell in the heaven's heights because its pec-toral fins resemble an angel's wings.[12]

**John Dory.** *Zeus faber* is a tasty species of fish with a distinctive, yel-low-ringed black mark about the size of a United States quarter on each of its two flat sides. According to an old legend, this is the fish that St. Peter caught when Christ told him: "go thou to the sea, and cast in a hook; and that fish which shall first come up, take: and when thou hast opened its mouth, thou shalt find a stater [silver coin]" (Matthew 17:26). To commemorate the honor bestowed on it, the legend continues, the fish henceforth bears on its sides the mark of a coin (other versions of the story say the black marks are St. Peter's fingerprints). Inspired by this legend, the Spanish call the fish *San Pedro* and the French *Saint-Pierre,* but in English it is known as **John Dory**. This may seem to have little in common with the name that Christ gave his chief apostle, but it is possible that the word is a variation of one of St. Peter's titles, the *Janitor,* or Doorkeeper, of Heaven. In Italian, for example, the fish is called a *janitore.*[13] Appropriately, the John Dory remains a favorite traditional dish on the Feast of St. Peter, June 29.

**The Petrel.** The John Dory is not the only creature to take its name from the first bishop of Rome. "Petrel," a diminutive of Peter, is given to the sea bird *Procellaria pelagica.* English seamen gave the bird this honor centuries ago because its habit of touching the water with its feet while still in flight reminded them of St. Peter walking on the lake of Genesareth (Matthew 14:29). (The Norwegian *Soren Peders* and *Peders fugl* and the German *Peters vogel* involve a similar ascription.) Given that St. Peter went only a few feet before his faith flagged and he began to sink, one wonders how successful a sea walker the petrel really is. In any event, over one hundred species of birds are now called petrels, including the family *Procellariidae* and the order *Tubinares.*[14]

**Monk Seal.** No one is certain why this rather rare genus of seal is named after monks, though some speculate that the Friar Tuck appearance of their bald heads, the cowl-like fold of skin on the nape of their necks, or their rather solitary habits account for this title. (If it is due to the latter, they would have been better called hermit seals, for most monks live in community.) In any event, all three species of monk seals—the Caribbean, Mediterranean, and Hawaiian—have unfortunately become endangered, not unlike several monastic orders over the past thirty years.[15]

**Monk Parakeet.** One monastic creature that is showing no signs of abatement is the monk parakeet (*Myiopsitta monachus*). This green and gray parrot is originally from South America but has invaded several other continents and is now common in several parts of the world. (Monks, for example, have been flourishing in the New York area ever since a crate of them broke open at the Idlewild Airport in the 1950s.) These ingenious birds may be named after monks because they are the only species of parrot that intricately builds a nest made entirely out of sticks. A single nest, which can reach the size of a small automobile, can contain dozens of birds in several different apartments.[16] The parakeet does not seem to mind having a religious affiliation of one kind or another. When it is not being called a monk, it is referred to as a **Quaker parrot**.

**Bishops.** Not to be outdone by monks, bishops can claim an eponymous connection to the bird kingdom with the genus called *Euplectes*.[17] Bishop-birds are very common in Africa; in fact, they are considered a pest by local agricultural communities. Though no one is certain why they are named after the apostles' successors, it is interesting that some of them, such as the **red bishop** (*Euplectes orix*), look like an African prelate on Pentecost Sunday. Moreover, the scientific name for the **orange bishop** is *Orix franciscanus,* the "Franciscan" bishop.

**St. James's Shell.** During the Middle Ages the most famous pilgrimage site in Western Europe was the shrine at Compostella, Spain, in honor of the country's patron saint, St. James the Greater, one of the three "princes" of the apostles. Pilgrims to the shrine wore a scallop shell that over time took on the saint's name, the *Pecten jacobeus* or St. James shell.[18]

## Miscellaneous Natural Phenomena

**St. Vitus' Dance.** This evocative phrase appears to have originated from a medieval belief that dancing in front of a statue of St. Vitus on his feast day (June 15) would guarantee a year of good health. Today it is used to describe two different phenomena. First, St. Vitus' dance is the name given to a dancing madness characterized by contortions and convulsions that swept Germany and other parts of Europe in the fifteenth century. It is generally believed that this was a form of **mass hysteria**, possibly an anxious pantomime of the epilepsy-like symptoms of the Black Plague, rather than a biological ailment. Second, St. Vitus' Dance is a synonym for Sydenham chorea (short, in fact, for *chorea Sancti Viti*). According to the *Encyclopædia Britannica,* chorea is "a **neurological disorder** characterized by irregular and involuntary movements of muscle groups in various parts of the body that follow streptococcal infection."[19] Interestingly, chorea generally affects boys and girls between the ages of five and fifteen, the same general age group as St. Vitus at the time of his martyrdom.

**St. Anthony's Fire.** Ergotism, a gangrenous and sometimes fatal disease caused by tainted rye and other cereals, takes its more popular name from Christianity's most famous hermit. In the eleventh century, ergotism swept through various regions of Europe, especially France, and caused tens of thousands of deaths. According to tradition, those who sought the intercession of St. Anthony of Egypt (251–356) were miraculously spared from this pestilence, and so the malady previously known to medievals as the "sacred fire" henceforth bore his name. In 1093, for example, a father and his son who were among the miraculously cured founded the Hospital Brothers of St. Anthony, or "Antonines," in order to care for those afflicted by the disease (the order was eventually suppressed during the French Revolution).[20] It has been conjectured that St. Anthony's intercession was invoked because one of the effects of the disease is convulsion and hallucination, symptoms similar to those of demonic possession. And as St. Athanasius' *Life of St. Anthony* relates, Anthony struggled with many devils during his solitude in the desert.

**St. Elmo's Fire.** A very different kind of fire is that which takes its name from the patron saint of sailors. St. Elmo's fire denotes "the luminous appearance of a naturally occurring corona discharge about a ship's mast or the like, usually in bad weather."[21] St. Elmo, or Erasmus, was an Italian bishop martyred around A.D. 303. Though little about him is known, there is a legend that one day St. Elmo was preaching when lightning suddenly struck the ground next to him. Unfazed, the saint continued his sermon, much to the astonishment of his audience. Elmo's fearlessness became an inspiration for sailors, who soon began to invoke his name when a thunderstorm threatened their ship. They took the harmless static discharge around their vessels as an indication that God had heard their prayers.

**Laurence.** Heat as well as light seems to attract sanctoral nomenclature. The name for the miragelike waves that shimmer up off a road on a hot day is a laurence. The most likely reason for the designation is that the Feast of St. Laurence falls on August 10, during the dog days of August when such heat shimmers are most likely. It is interesting to note, however, that St. Laurence's martyrdom is famously linked to heat in a more direct way. Laurence was a Roman deacon and assistant to Pope Sixtus II in A.D. 258. After boldly giving the Church's riches to the poor instead of to the prefect, Laurence was slowly roasted alive on a gridiron. His bravery and holiness were so extraordinary that Christians less than a century later attributed the conversion of pagan Rome to his intercession and to the powerful testimony of his death.[22] It is therefore somehow fitting to say that there were laurences emanating off the body of Laurence the holy martyr.

**Nickel.** Nickel is a malleable and ductile metal used in corrosion-resistant and magnetic alloys, in plating, and in rechargeable batteries. Its name, however, refers to a creature much more ethereal and much less helpful. *Kupfernickel* in German literally means "devil's copper," "nick" being a humorous name for Satan (see p. 65). Nickel earned this dubious appellation because it is generally found in the earth with arsenic. When German miners in the fifteenth century accidentally discovered it instead of copper, they were poisoned by contact with nickel's lethal neighbor.[23] Incidentally, another German nickname that has found its way into English is the coarse rye bread from Westphalia called **pumpernickel**. According to some, the word means "devil's fart," the logic being that the bread is so difficult to digest it would force even Beelzebub to break wind.[24]

**Angelite.** Angelite is another name for lilac-blue anhydrite, a calcium sulfate mineral rock that is multi-layered and somewhat translucent. The mineral most likely takes its name from its "angelic" color, but coincidentally the word *angelite* originally designated a small group of fifth-century heretics from Alexandria, Egypt, who held strange views on the Blessed Trinity.[25] The two words are thus homonymous, though given the popularity of angelite crystal in New Age healing and celestial telepathy, its coincidental association with an Alexandrine heresy is eerily appropriate. Despite Alexandria's well-earned reputation for producing philosophers and saints, it is not without reason that Evelyn Waugh referred to the once-great metropolis as that "ancient asparagus bed of theological absurdity."[26]

**Valentinite.** Another mineral with a passing connection to heresy is the lustrous material known as valentinite. Antimony oxide received its more popular name in honor not of St. Valentine but a fifteenth-century Benedictine monk named Basil Valentine who practiced alchemy and subscribed to the Gnostic heresy known as hermeticism. Given his shady interests, Basil hid his writings in a hollow column in the abbey of which he was prior, but they were discovered many years later.[27] Though Basil was a practitioner of an occult science, some of his writings were later of use to chemists—he is the first, for instance, to mention the mineral **bismuth**—which may explain why valentinite was named after him in 1845.

**Wulfenite.** The mineral wulfenite (a yellow lead molybdate, $PbMoO_4$,) takes its name from a more orthodox pillar of the church, the Austrian Jesuit Franz Xaver Freiherr von Wulfen (1728–1805). An extraordinary botanist who specialized in lichens (see p. 100) as well as an expert Alpine mountaineer, Father Wulfen was also more than competent in mineralogical studies.[28] His discovery in 1785 of the mineral that would one day bear his name is testimony to that fact.

# SCIENCE

✠

*Are you surprised that the same civilization which believed in the Trinity discovered steam?*

—G. K. Chesterton[1]

*All things were made by him: and without him was made nothing that was made.*

—John 1:3

Periodic sensationalist accounts of the Galileo affair and half-baked conspiracy theories continue to distort popular perceptions of the Church's love affair with higher learning. Such distortions also obscure the deeper truth that Christian insights into a created and contingent world may have actually *opened up* new avenues of exploration, while Catholicism's teachings on the capacity of human reason even after the Fall to know the intelligibility of God's created order proved to be instrumental in grounding the very possibility of scientific activity.[2] This is an enormous topic, and since it would take an entire tome to enumerate all of the contributions of Catholic scientists to their fields as well as the institutional support given to them by the Church, the following chapter is limited to the principal ways in which Catholic men and women have shaped the sciences.

**Aeronautics.** Though the Wright brothers dominate our imagination when it comes to human flight, it was **John J. Montgomery**, a Catholic professor of physics at Santa Clara College (now University) who is credited with being "the first successful practitioner and teacher of the art of controlled free flight." Montgomery was known to conduct thrilling public exhibitions of his research throughout the San Francisco area, but his inaugural exhibition took place on the campus of Santa Clara. On April 29, 1905, Montgomery had a manned monoplane glider lifted 4,000 feet in the air by a hot-air balloon and then cut loose. During the glider's eight-mile journey, the pilot, Daniel Maloney, made all kinds of daring maneuvers, including steep dives and figure-eights. The plane eventually landed at a previously designated spot three-quarters of a mile away, "so lightly that the pilot was not even jarred."[3]

**Agricultural Science.** The head of the chemistry department of the first agricultural college in the United States was a devout Catholic who helped establish the first Catholic church in Amherst, Massachusetts. Before coming to the Massachusetts Agricultural College, Professor **Charles Anthony Goessmann** (1827–1910) had earned a reputation in his native Germany as an outstanding chemist, having discovered the chemical composition of the oils derived from various kinds of nuts. Once in America, Goessmann was looked upon as a leading authority "in the use of chemistry for the improvement of farming." But the man to whom the United States owes the most "for putting agriculture on a scientific basis" is a convert to Catholicism named **Eugene Waldemar Hilgard** (1833–1916). Hilgard had contributed much to our knowledge of coastal geology along the Gulf of Mexico and the doctrine of the "Mississippi Embayment" before turning his attention to agricultural chemistry. After serving as a professor of science at the University of Michigan, he joined the new agricultural department at the University of California, where his studies of California soil changed the perception of the state from a barren desert to a geographical territory with enormous agricultural potential. The success of California agriculture and horticulture is due in large part to his pioneering work. Despite his many achievements, however, Hilgard stated near the end of his life that nothing "had given him more satisfaction than his membership in the Church."[4]

**Astronomy.** The ancient science of astronomy received a revolutionary boost from the Polish cleric and possible priest, **Nicolaus Copernicus** (1473–1543). Copernicus was a veritable polymath: he held a doctorate in canon law; he practiced medicine for six years, tending to the poor for free; and, because of a Latin treatise he wrote on finance, he held a position as deputy counselor of the financial regulations of Prussia. But Copernicus is best remembered as the astronomer whose heliocentric hypothesis upended the thousand-year-old Ptolemaic understanding of the universe. Even before the publication of his treatise on the subject, Copernicus had such a stellar reputation as an astronomer that the Lateran Council asked for his opinion on the reform of the ecclesiastical calendar. Copernicus modestly replied that the solar year was not yet understood well enough for him to make an educated conclusion, but the question inspired him to pursue the matter on his own. His findings formed the basis of the Gregorian calendar seventy years later (see p. 9).

Several high-ranking churchmen were dazzled by Copernicus' thoughts on the revolution of the earth around the sun; Cardinal Schonberg and Pope Clement VII were among his strongest admirers. Yet Copernicus was hesitant to publish his views, given the near-universal outcry it would provoke, not just from certain quarters of the Church but from the general population, the university, and the new followers of Luther and Melancthon, who were particularly critical of heliocentrism on biblical grounds. Copernicus eventually published *On the Revolutions of the Celestial Bodies* near the end of his life; the first edition was placed in his hands only hours before he died.[5]

Copernicus was only one of many clerics to make advances in the field of astronomy. The **Vatican Observatory**, one of the oldest astronomical research institutions in the world, is headquartered at the pope's summer residence in Castel Gandolfo outside of Rome, and it also has a research branch at the University of Arizona in Tucson. Its astronomers have recorded positions of more than five hundred thousand stars.

As they did in many sciences, the Jesuits made outstanding astronomers. Father **Christopher Scheiner** (1575–1650) was the first astronomer to study the sun systematically; Scheiner's halo is named after him.[6] He may have also discovered sunspots before Galileo, but his discovery was so contrary to the opinions of the time "that his superiors begged him not to publish. . . . under his own name for fear of ridicule."[7] Father **Pietro Angelo Secchi** (1818–1878) surveyed over four thousand stars; his fourfold division of spectral types became the basis for the Harvard classification system.[8] Father **Benedict Sestini** (1816–1890), who was said to have two passions, "one for pure mathematics, the other for pure Catholicism," made the first comprehensive study of star colors.[9] Fathers **Francesco Maria Grimaldi** (1613–1663) and **Giambattista Riccioli** (1598–1671) made a notably accurate selenograph—a detailed map of the moon's surface—that now graces the entrance of the National Space Museum in Washington, D.C. In tribute to their incomparable contributions in mathematics, astronomy, and other sciences, individual Jesuits have no fewer than thirty-five craters of the moon named after them.[10]

**Bacteriology.** The celebrated microbiologist and founder of bacteriology is **Louis Pasteur** (1822–1895). After groundbreaking work in fermentation and putrefaction, Pasteur was asked by the French government to save the national silkworm industry from a pestilence that was ravaging it. Pasteur did so by finding the diseases from which the silkworms were suffering and simply segregating the healthy specimens from the sick. Pasteur now found himself interested in germs and their relation to disease. He discovered the bacterial cause of anthrax and childbed fever and developed a vaccine for rabies. (The Russian population, which was frequently attacked by wolves from the steppes, was particularly grateful for the latter, and the tsar honored him with a personal visit.) Pasteur, however, is best known for the method that bears his name. Pasteurization was a boon to the wine, vinegar, and beer industries of France, just as it is to the American milk industry today. Not only does the heating process destroy harmful germs, but it prolongs the storage life of the product.

Much of Pasteur's work was motivated by his Catholic faith. Pasteur marveled at the failure of his scientific colleagues to recognize the existence of God. On his deathbed he asked to have the life of St. Vincent de Paul read to him: like St. Vincent, he had worked to alleviate the suffering of children. He died with his rosary in his hands.[11]

**Botany.** The father of modern botany is considered by many to be **Andreas Caesalpinus**, a professor at the University of Padua and physician to Pope Clement VIII. In his *De Plantis,* published in 1583, Caesalpinus classified the 1,520 plants known at the time into fifteen categories based on the fruit they produced.[12]

Botany appears to be a science in which Catholics thrive. In addition to the plants discovered or named by Catholic explorers (see Chapter Eight), several genera and species have been named after botanist priests such as Father **Franz von Paula Hladnik** (1773–1844) and the Austrian Jesuit **Franz Xaver Freiherr von Wulfen** (1728–1805).[13]

**Cosmology and the Big Bang Theory.** This branch of science needed a retooling after Einstein's theory of relativity and Hubble and Shapley's discovery that the universe was expanding. The scientist to do so was a Belgian Catholic priest named **Georges Lemaître** (1894–1966). As a professor of astrophysics at the University of Louvain, Lemaître proposed in 1927 what has come to be called the Big Bang Theory, which explains "the recession of the galaxies within the framework of Albert Einstein's theory of general relativity."[14] After almost eighty years and a minor revision by George Gamow, Big Bang remains the leading theory of cosmology.

**Crystallography.** The father of modern crystallography is a priest who was imprisoned for his faith during the French Revolution. Father **René-Just Haüy** (1743–1822) was a professor of literature, pioneer developer of pyroelectricity, and amateur botanist who one day fell into mineralogy literally by accident. While examining a crystal collection, he unintentionally dropped a mineral called a calc-spar, shattering it into pieces. Haüy looked at the fragments closely and became fascinated not by their chemical or geological composition but by their shapes. This initiated a lifelong study in which Haüy discovered that crystals of the same composition had the same nucleus, regardless of their external shape and that the forms of crystals are perfectly definite and based on fixed laws.[15]

**Entomology.** According to some the "real founder" of the modern study of insects is a priest by the name of Pierre-André Latreille (1762–1833). After being left destitute by his parents Latreille was adopted by Abbé Haüy, a pioneer in the field of crystallography (see above). Latreille discovered and classified many genera of insects despite irregular persecution by the new regimes that arose in the wake of the French Revolution.[16]

**Experimental Physics.** According to one historian of science, the Society of Jesus may be considered "the single most important contributor to experimental physics in the seventeenth century."[17] Father **Giambattista Riccioli**, for example, was the first person to determine the rate of acceleration of a freefalling body and the first to invent a pendulum so accurate that with it he was able to calculate the constant of gravity. It was also a Jesuit, **Francesco Maria Grimaldi**, who discovered the diffraction of light (the fact that light does not proceed in a rectilinear fashion) and who assigned the word "diffraction" to the phenomenon. Among other things, Grimaldi's discovery led to hypotheses on the wavelike character of light and to Isaac Newton's interest in optics.

Among the obscure scientists deserving far greater acclaim perhaps none is more worthy than Father **Roger Boscovich** (1711–1787). In addition to significant contributions in astronomy and architectural statics, Father Boskovich is credited by some as the true father of atomic physics, his well-developed work on the matter having appeared a century before the emergence of modern atomic theory.[18]

In the field of **electricity**, it is in honor of three Catholic laymen—**André Ampère**, **Alessandro Volta**, and **Charles Coulomb**—that we have amps, volts, and coulombs as the designations for different kinds of electrical units (an amp is a measurement of an electrical current's strength, a volt is a measurement of electrical pressure, and a coulomb is a measurement of electrical quantity.) Several priests have also made substantial contributions to the study of electricity. Abbé **Jean-Antoine Nollet** (1700–1770) was the "first to recognize the importance of sharp points on the conductors in the discharge of electricity," a discovery that later proved instrumental in the invention of the lightning rod. The lightning rod itself was then invented in 1754 by a Norbertine priest named **Procopius Divisch** (1698–1765), who erected it before news of Benjamin Franklin's theories reached France. (Divisch was also one of the first to use electricity for the treatment of disease.)

It was the Philadelphian's device, however, that the Italian priest and scientist of atmospheric electricity **Giuseppe Toaldo** (1719–1797) preferred; his promotion of Franklin's invention did much to turn European opinion in favor of it. Though Franklin is also sometimes reputed to have invented the electric chime, the real credit goes to a Scottish Benedictine monk named **Andrew Gordon** (1712–1751), whose chimes Franklin adopted for his experiments with lightning rods.[19] Perhaps our familiar images of Ben Franklin and his kite should be supplemented with a row of black-cassocked men in the background.

**Genetics.** Building upon the Catholic legacy of botany is the father of modern genetics, an Augustinian monk named **Gregor Mendel**. When Father Mendel became abbot of the Abbey of St. Thomas, in Brunn, Austria, he was forced to abandon his research, in part because his energies were then to be consumed fighting an unjust tax being levied on all religious houses in the country. Prior to that, however, Mendel had made an enormous breakthrough, the proof that hereditary traits are transmitted by agents we know today as genes. Dissatisfied with Darwinist theory, Mendel conducted a number of experiments involving peas in the large gardens of his monastery over a period of eight years. He discovered that the traits were passed on according to a particular pattern, what we would call today dominant and recessive genes. The discovery of this "Natural Law," as Mendel put it, has placed Mendel in the eyes of some on par with other great pioneers of science such as Sir Isaac Newton.

Though Mendel published his findings in 1866, it was not until 1899, fifteen years after his death, that three scientists almost simultaneously rediscovered his work and began to promote it. During his life Mendel was frustrated at the lack of attention his views were receiving, but he never lost confidence in their accuracy. As he used to tell his friends, "My time has not yet come."[20]

**Linguistics.** Much is owed to the German Jesuit polymath, Athanasius Kircher (1601–1680), the father of **Egyptology**, whose pioneering work in ancient Egyptian and Coptic (he was the first to see a connection between the two) made possible the celebrated deciphering of the Rosetta Stone years later.[21] In addition to fostering the science of **chemistry** by definitively debunking alchemy, Kircher is also credited with the invention of the forerunner of the **slide projector** (see p. 108).

**Pathology.** The reputed father of the modern study of disease was a devout Catholic whose advice was sought by five different pontiffs. **Giovanni Battista Morgagni** (1682–1771) was a gifted Italian physician and professor of anatomy at the University of Bologna. His work on tuberculosis changed the way the disease was viewed, and his opposition to bleeding patients was years ahead of its time. Several parts of the body, such as the hyatid of Morgagni and the columns of Morgagni, are named after him, as are the ailments Morgagni syndrome and Morgagni hernia. Morgagni was deeply loved and respected; on two occasions, when armies were set to invade Bologna, their generals gave strict instructions that no harm should come to him. In his personal life Morgagni was so successful at hiding his generosity to the poor that his charitable activities became known only after his death. Morgagni had fifteen children: all of his eight daughters became nuns, and one of his sons became a Jesuit.[22]

**Seismology.** Contributions to the study of earthquakes by members of the Society of Jesus have been so numerous and profound that it has been nicknamed the "Jesuit science." The Jesuit Seismological Service, established in 1909, took advantage of the Jesuit universities and colleges scattered throughout the United States; with a seismograph at each institution, the Jesuits were able to collect valuable data that would be passed on to the International Seismological Center in Strasbourg. The Service was reinvigorated in 1925 by the noted Jesuit seismologist **J. B. Macelwane**, who wrote the first textbook in America on the field in 1936 and who served as president of the Seismological Society of America and later the American Geophysical Union. To this day the American Geophysical Union awards a James B. Macelwane Medal to exceptional geophysicists under thirty-six years of age.[23]

A subtler testimony to the Jesuit influence on seismology may perhaps be found in one of the more curious blessings found in the old Roman Ritual, a 1924 blessing for a seismograph. Among other things the priest is instructed to pray that the proper operation of the blessed seismograph may be "for the greater glory of God"—the motto of the Jesuits.[24] And perhaps it is no coincidence that the horizontal pendulum used in making seismographs at the time had been invented over half a century earlier by a Catholic priest named Father **Lawrence Hengler** (1805–1858), for the pastoral zeal of priests in protecting their flock from calamity was a key motivator of their work.[25]

**Statics.** One of the earliest Catholic contributions to statics mechanics is **Blaise Pascal** (1623–1662), the great mathematician and author of the powerful defense of Catholic Christianity, the *Pensées*. Pascal invented a calculator (see p. 108) as well as the first public transportation system, the proceeds of which he is reputed to have donated to the poor. In statics mechanics Pascal is remembered for discovering the **fundamental relation of hydrostatics** and the fundamental principle of hydrostatics, known today as **Pascal's Law**.[26]

**Stratigraphy.** The study of geological strata in the earth owes its existence in large part to Blessed Nicolaus Steno (1638–1686), a former

Lutheran turned Catholic priest and bishop who was beatified by Pope John Paul II. Father Steno's groundbreaking treatise *De solido* decisively opened up the possibility that the land itself had a history and that this history could be read from the earth's sedimentary layers and the fossils contained therein. Three cornerstones of stratigraphy are still known today as "Steno's principles."[27] Before turning to stratigraphy, Steno was a first-rate anatomist: the **Stenonian** or **parotid duct** was discovered by him and hence named in his honor. But above all Steno was a good and faithful servant of God and his Church. After being consecrated a bishop only two years after his ordination to the priesthood, he gave all he had to the poor and lived an austere and ascetic life. Blessed Nicolaus was eventually made Vicar Apostolic for the northern missions in Germany where he worked nine years until he died at the early age of forty-eight.[28]

**Tide Tables.** Carefully recording the ebb and flow of the tide, so important for marine transportation, appears to have been done first by the monks of St. Albans, who measured the Thames River at London Bridge in the Middle Ages. The monks based their calculations on the "phase of the moon within its cycle of 29.6 days revolution around the earth."[29] Centuries later a French cleric named **Jean de Hautefeuille** (1647–1724) would invent a device for measuring tides called a **thalassameter**.[30]

# INVENTIONS

✠

*Christianity, which is a very mystical religion, has nevertheless been the religion of the most practical section of mankind. It has far more paradoxes than the Eastern philosophies, but it also builds far better roads... Christendom has mysteries—and motor cars.*

—G. K. Chesterton[1]

In a move that is often mystifying to the secular world, believers have been both wary of unfettered technologies and pioneers in its development. Arthur Fry invented the Post-it Note as a bookmark for the hymnal he used when signing in the choir of his Presbyterian church, while an early version of the answering machine was devised for the benefit of Orthodox Jews who could not operate their telephones on the Sabbath.[2] As we have already seen in this book, Catholics have also made their mark on the man-made world. Below is but a tiny sampling of some other accomplishments, including various devices named after Catholic phenomena. We begin with the world of fashion.

## CLOTHES

It is not surprising that Catholicism should have an influence on the sartorial. From the shabby aprons of Adam and Eve's fig leaves to the splendid white robes of the martyrs mentioned in the Book of Revelation, clothes mentioned in the Bible bear an important symbolic meaning. The same is true of Catholic liturgy. Though the **vestments** that the priest wears for Mass are derived from everyday Roman dress, each article also represents something worn by Christ during his Passion. For example, the priest's chasuble (the poncho-like outer vestment) signifies the purple cloak mockingly placed on Jesus's shoulders by the soldiers; the priest's cincture (a rope-like belt) symbolizes the cord that bound Jesus to the pillar as he was scourged; and the priest's stole recalls the cross Jesus was forced to carry. Such symbolism powerfully reminds the faithful that the priest is acting *in persona Christi,* or in the place of Christ, and that the Mass sacramentally makes present the actual crucifixion and resurrection of Our Lord. Similarly replete with significance is the bishop's hat, or **miter**. The two tips of the hat represent the two Testaments the bishop is charged with proclaiming and defending as well as the horns of glory that adorned the head of Moses after he came down from Mt. Sinai (Moses' horns are based on a mistranslation of Exodus 34:29–30, but they are still useful symbolically). Even the **black attire** worn by nuns, priests, and bishops in their daily lives may be said to represent their death to the world.

Though the Catholic impact on secular fashion has been far less pronounced, it is by no means negligible, as the following entries attest.

**Tartans.** St. Margaret of Scotland (1045–1092) was a holy English princess who married King Malcolm III of Scotland (the man who defeated the nefarious Macbeth). Margaret was a ray of sunshine in her adopted home, bringing piety and civility to a dreary and rustic land. She endeavored to lead by example, softening the rough ways of the noblemen with a comely appearance. It is said that her love of bright colors inspired the development of the now famous Scottish tartans.[3]

**Pants.** Our most common word for trousers comes from a saint who probably never wore or even saw a pair in his life—or if he did, he would have probably been like most ancient Greeks and Romans and dismissed them as an effeminate product of Persia. St. Pantaleon was a physician martyred in Nicomedia in A.D. 303 under the reign of Emperor Diocletian. Pantaleon is considered one of the Fourteen Holy Helpers—saints whose intercession in particular ailments was considered especially efficacious—and he is thus invoked for consumptive diseases. Though the cult of the Fourteen Holy Helpers was popular throughout the Middle Ages, Pantaleon was especially popular in Venice, partly because, it is speculated, his name (*Pantaleone*) resembles the Venetian battle cry *Piante Lione* ("Plant the Lion"). The term *Pantalone* thus came to designate a Venetian character in Italian comedy, and since the character generally appeared wearing distinctive Venetian breeches, the breeches came to be known as pantaloons, or pants for short.[4]

**Cardinal Lace.** A modern pattern of lace found in window treatments and the like is named after the College of Cardinals, whose taste in formal apparel from the Renaissance on has been rather delicate.[5]

**Monkwear.** Monastic habits were adopted to signify the monk's death to the world and all its entanglements, but they have paradoxically left a minor mark on the realm of worldly fashion. A **monk shoe** or **monk strap**, for example, is a shoe with a fully-covered instep, fastened by a side buckle, and **monk's cloth** is a heavy fabric now used for furnishing.[6] It should be noted, however, that monks were not alone in their influence. The **domino hood** worn by canons (clerics) later inspired a graceful cloak for women (for more on this see p. 72)

## COLORS

**Black . . .** Black was the standard color of mourning in the West long before the Christian era, but our current use of black as the funerary color par excellence is owed to medieval Catholicism. From what we can tell, early Christian funerals used white as the primary liturgical color to distinguish Christianity's hope in the resurrection from pagan despair over the afterlife. Why, then, did later generations of believers revert to an ostensibly pagan custom? The most likely reason is that after the death of the old gods, it was now safe to appropriate the use of black without appropriating paganism in the process. Black acts as a kind of catharsis for mourners: it gives silent voice to the sorrow that lingers in their hearts (even if they hope in the Resurrection), and it gently helps them confront the reality of death, mitigating as it does against the human proclivity for denial or psychological suppression. Perhaps this is why even though the Church currently allows white as well as black vestments to be used at funerals, mourners still fill the pews wearing somber hues.

**. . . and Blue.** In traditional Roman Catholic religious art, blue rather than white is the color that betokens purity. As Ben Jonson writes in *Cynthia's Revels,* "bluenesse doth expresse truenesse."[7] Hence a bride, even after introduction of the white gown, wears "something borrowed, something blue" (see p. 119 for more on this). And hence the Blessed Virgin Mary is generally portrayed in paintings with a blue mantle as a sign of her purity. Indeed, it is this convention that accounts for the exclamation *Sacré Bleu*. By invoking the sacred color of the Blessed Mother's mantle, the French are pleading for protection under her protective cloak.

**Cardinal.** The color that has been described as "halfway between scarlet and crimson" takes its name from the College of Cardinals, the several dozen "princes" of the Church who wear distinctive red cassocks, sashes, buttons, hats, cloaks, and even stockings. Pope Paul II (who reigned from 1464 to 1471) dressed in this color, and he instructed his cardinals to do the same. Though Paul II's decision was probably motivated more by vanity than piety (he was a great lover of pomp and splendor), over time the color came to symbolize a willingness to shed blood for the faith. In 1566 the pontiff's attire was changed to white with the election of the Dominican friar Pope St. Pius V, who preferred to wear the habit of his order. The color of the cardinalate, however, remained unchanged.[8]

Incidentally, the word *cardinal* means *principal* in Latin and has been used since the days of Pope St. Gregory the Great (d. 604) as a title for the principal churches of Rome. The pastors of those churches were frequently consulted by the pope, and hence they too came to be known as "cardinals." Thus the word has passed from meaning a crucial hinge to an important church to an important cleric to a color to a bird to a flower (see pp. 87 and 90).

**Chartreuse.** The peculiar yellowish green we call chartreuse is named after the mysterious liqueur invented and made by Carthusian monks (see p. 33).

**Red.** Worldly lovers borrowed this color from the Roman Catholic cult of martyrs, as red is the liturgical color used to celebrate the feast day of someone whose blood has been shed for Christ. The transfer is fitting, for the willingness to die for someone is, as Christ reminds his disciples, the ultimate manifestation of love (see John 15:13).[9] Red is also used on the Feast of Pentecost, which commemorates the Holy Spirit's descent upon the apostles in the form of fiery red tongues. Here, too, there is a strong association with love, for the Holy Spirit is understood to be the *caritas,* or love, that proceeds from the Father and the Son.

## TECHNOLOGY

**Calculator.** Although there are earlier examples of the calculator, the first truly operative mechanical calculating device was invented in 1642 by the great French philosopher, mathematician, and Catholic apologist, Blaise Pascal. Pascal developed a calculator to assist his father, a tax official, with his work. His "pascaline," as he called it, measured about four by twenty inches, had eight dials on its face, and could add and subtract with great accuracy.[10] Because the pascaline can also be considered the world's first computer, the computer language "Pascal" was named in his honor.

**Slide Projector.** The slide projector owes its existence to the "Magic Lantern," a contraption invented by an extraordinary German Jesuit scholar, Athanasius Kircher (1601–1680). In addition to mastering physics, mathematics, hieroglyphics, linguistics, and natural science, Kircher devised a box lit from within by a candle that could project hand-painted images on glass plates. These lanterns became enormously popular in Europe and by 1845 they were mass being produced. Our photographic slide projectors are only the latest development of Kircher's invention.[11]

**Radio and Wireless Communications.** Father Jozef Murgaš (1864–1929) was born in Tajov, Slovakia, and spent most of his life as a parish priest in Wilkes-Barre, Pennsylvania. After noticing that the Morse code was inordinately slow because of its use of dashes, Murgaš went to his laboratory in the back of the rectory and devised a much faster **Rotary-spark-system** that used musical tones. The seventeen patents he took out for his wireless telegraph (the first of its kind) later became the foundation of radio technology. Murgaš himself pioneered the development of radio, erecting the first aerial station in the country and successfully making the first wireless voice transmissions, but he was forced to abandon his work after his financial backers were unable to provide the necessary funding. In the interests of science and the common good, Father Murgaš decided to give his patents and his research notes to the younger scientist Guglielmo Marconi, who is now credited with inventing the radio.[12] Murgaš, however, went on to benefit mankind with an even better invention: the fishing reel (see p. 69).

**Television.** TV developed from a long series of discoveries and innovations, beginning with a breakthrough made in 1862. Abbé Castelli, an Italian-born priest working in France, proved that variations of light "could be transmitted down a telegraph wire as electrical impulses."[13] From here it was only a matter of time before images formed from these impulses would be made.

**Barometer.** Evangelista Torricelli (1608–1647) was a mathematician and physicist best known for his invention of the barometer. Torricelli was working for Galileo when a question arose concerning the question of water pressure. Creating a hermetically sealed tube filled with mercury, Torricelli was able not only to demonstrate the error of his master's hypothesis but also to create a way to measure changes in atmospheric pressure. The mercury barometer went on to become one of science's most important instruments.[14]

Being finely attuned to external pressure seems to be a Catholic talent. The Jesuit astronomer Pietro Angelo Secchi later built upon "Torricelli's tube," as it was sometimes known, by inventing a device that simultaneously records temperature, barometric pressure, wind direction, velocity, and rainfall called a **meteorograph**.[15]

**Mercedes.** The celebrated manufacturer of luxury automobiles unwittingly took its name from the Blessed Virgin Mary. In 1900 Daimler began to manufacture a new engine called Daimler-Mercedes in honor of Emil

Jellinek, a daredevil businessman who raced under the the name of his ten-year-old daughter, Mercédès. Though the Mercedes-Benz website states that Mercedes is "a Spanish girls' [sic] name meaning grace,"[16] the word really refers to a fee or ransom—an appropriate moniker, come to think of it, for a car as costly as a Mercedes! Specifically, the term is used to refer to *Our Lady of Ransom*, the title given to Mary when in 1218 she appeared to St. Peter Nolasco, St. Raymund of Peñafort, and King James of Aragon and asked them to found the Mercedarian Order. The purpose of the order was the ransoming of Christians who had been abducted and enslaved by Muslims along the Mediterranean. The Mercedarians went on to do great good, collecting ransom money in order to buy slaves their freedom and often giving up their own freedom in exchange for that of others.[17]

**Hearse.** Speaking of cars, our word for a coffin-carrying vehicle comes from a candlestick used during Holy Week. In old English, a *hearse* referred to an iron-spiked, A-shaped rake that was used to pulverize and prepare the soil for sowing. A fifteen-stick candelabrum used during the office of Tenebrae on the night of Spy Wednesday, Holy Thursday, and Good Friday (see p. 56) visually resembled this tool and so came to be known as a hearse. The hearse plays an important role in the Tenebrae service, as each of its candles are extinguished during the liturgy until the entire church is enveloped in darkness (hence the name *tenebrae*, or darkness). Only one candle, which is hidden by the side of the altar before the *Miserere* is chanted, remains lit at the end. According to some, the extinction of the fourteen candles calls to mind the fourteen holy men mentioned in the Bible who, from the foundation of the world to the very threshold of Christ's coming, were slain by their own wicked brethren, while the hiding of the fifteenth candle signifies the death and resurrection of Christ Himself. Over time, however, the word *hearse* also came to designate an elaborate frame connected to a funeral bier for candles and other decorations until eventually it was applied to the carriage or car that carried the bier and coffin.

## MISCELLANEOUS

**Priest.** Combining the black humor of the Irish with their peculiar line of reasoning is the Irish word for a fish-killing hammer. A "priest" in Ireland refers not only to a man of the cloth but to a wooden mallet that is used in delivering the coup de grace to a foundering fish. The idea is that the mallet is brought in "to perform the last offices" of finishing off a feisty salmon or pike just as a priest is called in to administer last rites to a dying parishioner.[18] (*Last rites*, which consist of anointing the forehead and hands of a sick or dying person to give them spiritual aid and strength, is the common name given to the sacrament of extreme unction, or anointing of the sick.) The priests made today range in style and function, some being a part of an aluminum, multi-tool gadget, others containing unhooking devices for easy catch-and-release. That the priest can now be used to get something "off the hook" may also be symbolically appropriate given the purpose of last rites in preparing one for the afterlife.

There is more than one piscatorial use of the word *priest*. In fly-fishing, a priest can refer to an artificial fly with white feathers and a black-and-white shoulder and cheek that resemble a Roman collar.[19] Given the Gospel injunction to the apostles to be "fishers of men" (Matthew 4:19), the name is certainly appropriate.

**Catherine Wheel.** St. Catherine of Alexandria was a virgin-martyr of the early Church and one of the fourteen Holy Helpers (see p. 106). According to tradition, St. Catherine was sentenced by Emperor Maximus II to die from slow torture on a spiked wheel especially made for that purpose. As she approached the wheel, however, lightning or the power of an angel miraculously struck it, killing the executioner and breaking the bonds of the young maiden. Furious, the Emperor had her beheaded, and, according to legend, angels carried her body to Mt. Sinai. The **Catherine-wheel firework**, a series of rockets that spin on a rotating disc fixed to a pole, can be seen as a combination of the angel's lightning and the executioner's wheel, and thus it is fittingly named. Incidentally, a Catherine wheel is also the synonym for a **cartwheel** and the name for a **window** in architecture (see p. 44).[20]

**Artificial Fertilization.** Dom Pinchon was a monk of Reome Abbey, near Montbard, France, who wished to provide sustenance for the populace during the numerous days of the liturgical calendar in which the faithful abstained from flesh meat. In 1420 he successfully fertilized trout eggs by taking the eggs from a female fish and the milt from a male and agitating the water into which they had been placed. Next, he placed the newly fertilized eggs in a wooden case with a wicker grill at each end and then put the case in gently running water. Though Pinchon's experiment worked, it was ignored until a German naturalist reinvented the "hatching box" three and a half centuries later.

**Cemetery.** The Greek word *koimetērion* refers to a dormitory or "sleeping-place," not a site at which the dead are interred. Christians were the first to call their graveyards cemeteries as a reminder that death was merely a kind of nap: soon the body would reunite with the soul on Judgment Day and rise from its slumber, glorified and transfigured. The belief in the "resurrection of the body," as the Apostles' Creed puts it, also accounts for the great dignity that is accorded the body in Christian burial, a symbolic gesture to preserve its integrity for the Second Coming rather than annihilating it through such procedures as cremation.[21]

**Roadside Shrines.** Since we are on the subject of bereavement, the impromptu crosses and flowers on many American roadsides that mark the site of fatal accidents also reflect a Catholic sensibility. Roadside shrines are a feature of many cultures, Western and Eastern, Christian and non-Christian. Contemporary American shrines, however, most likely spring from a Catholic influence on the country, specifically, from recent Hispanic immigration (this despite the fact that Catholics from other ethnicities have been erected road shrines in the country for centuries). To date, however, substantive documentation on the phenomenon is lacking.

# EDUCATION AND SUPERSTITION

✠

*How can we say that the Church wishes to bring us back into the*
*Dark Ages? The Church was the only thing that ever brought us*
*out of them.*

—G. K. Chesterton[1]

Despite its foundation on the relatively unlettered apostles (whom one pagan critic dismissed as "theologizing fishermen"), Christianity quickly came to distinguish itself as "a learned religion."[2] The worship of God as Word, or *Logos*, was to have far-reaching effects on the world of learning, giving rise to new alphabets and promoting education on all levels, from basic primers to the creation of colleges and universities.

Of course, despite its vigorous efforts to the contrary, Catholic Christianity also gave indirect rise to several superstitions, mostly through a misappropriation of orthodox doctrine.

## EDUCATION

**Colleges and Universities.** Though there were great schools of learning in classical antiquity, the modern-day college or university is the product of the medieval Catholic Church. Many of the features we associate with college life—a permanent campus, a stable student body, regular examinations and coursework, the conferral of degrees, an academic year, even town-gown frictions—can be traced to the medieval university. After the fall of the Roman Empire and the invasions of barbarian hordes throughout Europe, political and cultural conditions for educating even a significant minority of the population were destroyed. It was left to the Church, especially to religious orders, to preserve learning in the West, primarily through the copying of manuscripts. Eventually monasteries and convents developed their own schools, with prominent dioceses following the precedent not long after. The **monastic school** was thus replaced by the **cathedral school**, but after classical learning (especially Aristotle) was reintroduced into the West, leading churchmen realized that a new kind of institution, the **university**, would be necessary to meet the intellectual challenges of the day.[3]

When this new kind of formal education began to materialize, many of the students were members of the **clergy**, young men who had been tonsured and who had received at least minor orders in the Church. Those who had not, however, still wore clerical dress because lay university students were given the same privileges normally reserved for the clergy. (Students were also expected to remain single during their matriculation.) Regardless of their ecclesiastical status, however, students were notoriously rowdy, crammed in dilapidated quarters, and ill-fed. It was after religious orders, such as the Benedictines, Dominicans, and Franciscans, established houses and colleges in conjunction with the main university that student life began to improve. Many of the semi-monastic features of contemporary college life, such as taking meals in common and living together in dormitories, come from this influence, as did the former requirement of daily chapel, a common feature on the campuses of private universities, Catholic and non-Catholic, as recently as a generation ago.

Several colleges and universities began as portable student unions, which would threaten to leave town if innkeepers did not provide discount rates for their housing: the words *college* and *university* actually come from the guilds of faculty and students, not from any curriculum being followed. But because education was seen as a great good for the Church and hence in its service, several other schools received their charter directly from the pope, so much so that by the thirteenth century it was not uncommon to view the papacy as the only valid source for a charter. The popes, in turn, were generally good to the university, exempting students from taxation and military service and protecting academic institutions from civic encroachments.

It has been argued that Christianity is the only world religion that could have created the university, as it is the only major religion that places *primary* emphasis on a divinely revealed Word that is to be known and loved rather than on a divine Law. This is especially the case with Roman Catholicism, which characteristically exhibits a cautious yet earnest openness to the life of reason. Interestingly, one of the propositions made by the proto-Protestant reformer John Wyclif (1324–1384) that was condemned by the Church was the opinion that "universities with their studies, colleges, graduations, and masterships, were introduced by vain heathenism" and that "they do the Church just as much good as the devil does."[4]

**Caps and Gowns.** Given the university's Catholic origins, it is not surprising that one of the more conspicuous features of higher education should derive from medieval Catholic life. The academic cap and gown, worn during commencement ceremonies by students and faculty alike, can be traced in general to the clerical dress of the Middle Ages and in particular to the conventions of Oxford University. The **square cap** or **mortarboard** descends from the standard clerical headwear of the day: in fact, the mortarboard cap and the biretta, the ecclesiastical hat worn by priests and seminarians as recently as a generation ago, developed from the same medieval prototype. Jokesters have pointed out that such a cap is only appropriate, as its shape resembles the books that scholars read, while its four corners betoken the fact that scholars are (or at least should be) more mentally stable than common folk.[5] Similarly, the **academic gown** is akin to the cassock, its long length—according to an Oxford statute promulgated in 1358—befitting the dignity of the clergy. The **academic hood**, on the other hand, derives in part from the cowls commonly worn in the Middle Ages, especially those of the monastic orders.

Caps and gowns, incidentally, were not originally a part of most American colleges, but they became standard after a widespread student demand for them in 1885. Americans took the Oxford customs as their basic template but added their own variations. An intercollegiate board determined the designs of the various gowns for bachelors, masters, and doctors, as well as what academic disciplines were to be symbolized by what colors on the hood. The United States also introduced the idea of caps and gowns for non-college graduates. In the 1910s, high school principals began promoting the idea for their commencement ceremonies—for the sake of democratic leveling. As one school superintendent complained, too often wealthy students spent exorbitant amounts of money on their graduation outfits, turning a solemn intellectual occasion into a "cheap peacock parade."[6] Having all students rent the same cap and gown for a modest price guarded against an undue display of social inequality.

**Primary and Secondary Schools.** Catholicism has influenced not only advanced learning but all levels of education. In the early Middle Ages distinctively Christian schools began to emerge in the wake of a decadent

Roman Empire. Monastic orders, especially the Benedictines, instructed boys and girls, lay folk and members of their own community, in the seven liberal arts and in the tenets of the faith These educational efforts were greatly enhanced and expanded during the Counter-Reformation with the advent of the Jesuits, Oratorians, Christian Brothers, and Salesians, new orders that were formed at least in part for the express purpose of training the young. All of this intense activity also led to a distinctively Catholic institution of education, the parish or **parochial school**. In the United States, poor Catholic immigrants, clergy, and religious communities (especially orders of nuns) used the parochial-school model to build the largest independent educational system in the history of the world. It is no exaggeration to conclude that "the whole parochial school movement during the nineteenth century forms one of the most remarkable chapters in the history of education."[7]

**Primer.** One would think that a primer, which is defined as "an elementary school-book for teaching children to read," derives its name from its function as a "primary" educational tool. It is likely, however, that the name comes from the **Office of Prime**, one of the eight canonical hours of the day for chanting the psalms and praying (for more on the Divine Office see p. 55). Prior to and shortly after the Reformation in England, the laity used devotional manuals and prayer books called *prymers,* which principally consisted of excerpts from the Divine Office adapted for private use. The name was later applied to those books by which children learned both to read and pray.[8]

**Limited Corporal Punishment.** Because stereotypes of nuns whacking their students' knuckles with rulers prevail, it may be surprising to learn that the first advocate of limiting corporal punishment as a pedagogical tool was St. Augustine of Hippo. Augustine reckoned that although corporal punishment may be a grudging necessity in a sinful world, it should not necessarily be used as an exclusive or even primary means of maintaining discipline.[9] The implication was that disciplinary measures should be subordinated to charity and a genuine love of learning (as opposed to a fear of being punished for *not* learning). This may seem like a minor shift, but it was in fact a crucial reassessment of an assumption that had gone unquestioned for centuries. In Augustine's day there was an adage, "The ears of a child are on his back," which meant that the only way to get children to listen was to cane their tender backs. Seen against this backdrop, one wonders if the European custom of spanking children on their well-cushioned *gluteus maximus* was not a Christian softening of Roman brutality.

**Crisscross.** Given the Church's role in educating young minds, it is not surprising to still find traces of this influence in our language. Our common term for zigzagged lines, crisscross, is actually a more recent spelling of *christcross,* a cross (usually shaped like a X) that was formerly placed at the beginning of the alphabet in what were called hornbooks. (Hornbooks were wooden frames with handles on which alphabets and numbers were attached in order to help children learn to read, figure, and spell.) The christcross was placed there as a mnemonic device to help the student remember the alphabet and to invoke God's aid in learning and growing wise. The christcross is so named because of the phrase it betokened, "Christ's cross me speed," that is, may Christ's cross speed me in my endeavors. The following formula from 1597 is typical:

> Christes crosse be my speede, in all vertue to proceede, A, b, c, d, e, f, g, h, i, k, l, m, n, o, p, q, r, s, & t, double w, v, x with y, ezod, & per se, con per se tittle tittle est. Amen. When you have done begin againe, begin againe.[10]

**The Cyrillic Alphabet.** Christianity takes its evangelical duty to go and teach all nations so seriously that its saints have even invented letters for those languages that had none before. Sts. Cyril and Methodius, the "Apostles to the Slavs," brought Christianity to several Slavic peoples in Eastern Europe, such as Bulgaria, Moravia, and Bohemia. According to an old tradition, the saints were such industrious missionaries that they not only translated the entire Bible into Slavonic, but they devised a special alphabet for the hitherto oral language. The Cyrillic alphabet, as it came to be called, was based on the Greek, but because Slavonic had more sounds, several new letters were added to the alphabet, including some from Hebrew. Slightly different versions of Cyrillic continue to be used today for Russian, Ukrainian, Bulgarian, and Serbian, and, because of the former Soviet Union, even for non-Slavic languages such as Turkmenian, Azerbaijanian, and Kurdish. And Cyrillic is still the official alphabet of the Slavic Eastern Orthodox and Eastern Catholic churches. Having a lettering system with an ecclesiastical origin is entirely appropriate; after all, the very word *alphabet,* which comes from the first two letters in Greek, *alpha* and *beta,* was introduced to the Latin West by Tertullian, an author from the second and third century who was a Catholic at the time.[11]

**Sign Language.** Letters on a page, however, are not the only kind of alphabet. It was a French priest and abbot, Charles-Michel d'Epée (1712–1789), "who made a most profound contribution in developing the natural sign language of the deaf into a systematic and conventional language to be used as a medium of instruction."[12] D'Epée, who opened the first free deaf school in 1760, is said to have been inspired by two deaf sisters who had developed their own system of hand signs. D'Epée's work was carried on by his monastic successor, Abbé Roch-Ambroise Cucurron Sicard, whose manual system, or silent method, was to have a strong impact on the teaching of the deaf in America.[13]

## SUPERSTITION

While there are a number of explicitly Catholic superstitions around today, such as burying a statue of St. Joseph upside down in your yard in order to sell a house, it is surprising to learn that many of the most common superstitions in our society today—four-leaf clovers, open umbrellas inside the house, and rabbit's feet, to name a few—are ones that long predate Christianity. What follows are the superstitions that have more than a passing connection to Catholicism.

**Crossing One's Fingers.** Making the sign of the cross while saying, "In the name of the Father, and of the Son, and of the Holy Spirit," is a simple but meaningful acknowledgment of two great Christian mysteries: the Crucifixion and the Blessed Trinity. The gesture was already widespred by the second century, and thus it could very well have been instituted by the apostles themselves. As Tertullian, who was born around A.D. 160, writes: "In all our travels and movements, in all our coming in and going out, in [the] putting [on] of our shoes, at the bath, at the table, in lighting our candles, in lying down, in sitting down, whatever employment occupieth us, we mark our foreheads with the sign of the cross."[14]

Because Christians recognize the power of Christ's cross in definitively defeating death, the sign of the cross has also long been used as a blessing. Consequently, the sign of the cross has been made in response to virtually every ailment pertaining to body and soul, from alleviating cramps and sicknesses to preventing frostbite. One mildly superstititious variation of this was to cross one's fingers for good luck in the face of danger or adversity.[15] Crossing one's fingers while lying, on the other hand, implies that the blessing of the cross will cancel out the "evil" of the lie.

**Knock on Wood.** The cross is remembered not only by virtue of its shape or form, as with the sign of the cross, but by virtue of its material. The instrument of Christ's death was often the object of reflection by the Church Fathers, Christianity's illustrious early thinkers and bishops, who saw the wooden cross as the new tree of eternal life that rescues us from the slavery to which Adam and Eve's sin with the tree of the knowledge of good and evil bound us. The superstition of knocking on wood is thus a way of invoking the power of the cross in the face of danger or misfortune. In some areas it is even said that one is supposed to knock on wood three times, one for each Person of the Trinity.[16]

**Friday.** Though the cross is a symbol of Christ's triumph over death and evil and is hence cherished and revered, the day on which Christ died has always been shrouded in sorrow and penance. It is most likely this fact, coupled with the penitential character of Friday (witnessed by such customs as abstaining from meat on this day), that accounts for its reputation as the unluckiest day of the week. Beginning anything on a Friday—be it a new job, a voyage, or a journey—was considered bad luck, as was moving, courting, getting married, being born, or even hearing news on that day.[17] **Friday the thirteenth**, in turn, was considered especially unlucky because it joins the day of Christ's passion with the number of Christ and his twelve apostles, one of whom was the traitor, Judas Iscariot.

**Thirteen.** The number sometimes referred to as a baker's dozen had an inauspicious reputation long before the night of the Last Supper. Thus, Christianity may not even be responsible for thirteen's infamy. In the Middle Ages, for example, thirteen was considered lucky *because* it was the number of Christ and the twelve apostles. Hence in the days when it was common to bless coins as well as a ring during the wedding ceremony, events not exactly alien to superstition, thirteen coins were often used and are in fact still used in Latino cultures today.[18] Some time in the early modern period, however, thirteen came to take on the opposite connotation, and it is that stigma with which we are now most familiar.

**Something Blue.** The superstition of the bride wearing something blue on her wedding hearkens back to the days when the color blue, not white, signified purity (see p. 107 for more on this). Since weddings tend to evoke a traditional instinct many never knew they had, a modicum of blue was retained in the bridal costume even after the white gown became popular in the nineteenth century. Incidentally, Catholic sensibility is also responsible for another familiar nuptial feature. After the exchange of vows and rings, it was customary for the priest to wrap his stole around the clasped hands of the couple as he formally declared them married. It is believed that from this ritual arose the popular slang term for getting married: **"tying the knot."**

**Horseshoe.** Apparently the horseshoe has been a good luck charm in several different cultures, but since the Middle Ages it has been associated in the West with St. Dunstan (d. 988), Archbishop of Canterbury. According to legend, Dunstan was a blacksmith before entering the religious life and was visited one day in his workshop by the devil. When the devil asked him to shoe his cloven feet, the quick-thinking Dunstan told him that he would have to first bind him to the wall. The saint then made this process so painful that the devil begged him for mercy, which Dunstan granted on condition that the old fiend never enter a house where a horseshoe was placed above the door. Though it is unlikely that St. Dunstan was ever a blacksmith (his more reliable biographers tell us that he was of noble birth), it is true that he was not afraid to battle evil or confront the well-heeled. St. Dunstan's reproach of the miscreant King Edgar, for example, was so powerful that the king broke down crying and begged him to assign a suitable penance. When the holy bishop prescribed a seven-year sentence of almsgiving, fasting twice a week, and not wearing a crown, the king gladly accepted. In any event, it was St. Dunstan's legendary link to horseshoeing that not only gave rise to the superstition about a horseshoe above the door but also to the horseshoe-shaped door knocker.[19]

# Part IV

# *The Body Politic*

# 13

# AMERICAN PLACES

✠

Catholicism has made a conspicuous mark on city and street names throughout those parts of the world in which it has been practiced. Pope Pius II (1458–1464), for example, convinced his hometown in Tuscany to change its name in his honor, and hence "Corsignano" became "Pienza." The United States also has a significant number of Catholic site names, though usually for more pious reasons (no pun intended). Over one hundred cities and counties as well as one state in America take their name from the Catholic faith. Catholic nomenclature was apparently so popular that it even spawned a few impostors. It is to highlighting a fraction of such sites that this chapter is dedicated.

## STATES

**Florida.** One would think that Florida, which is Latin for "flowery," was named after its lush tropical foliage, but the Sunshine State was actually named after Palm Sunday and Easter. Because it was the custom in several places to bless not only palms but flowers on Palm Sunday, the feast was sometimes called "Flower" or "Blossom" Sunday. In Spain it was called *Pascua Florida,* a term that over time was applied not just to the Sunday before Easter but to the whole season of Easter week. Thus when Ponce de Leon first spotted the coast of Florida on March 27, 1513 (Easter Sunday), he had a name for the new land ready at hand.[1]

**And New York (sort of).** Contrary to popular belief, the state of New York is named not after York or Yorkshire, England, but James II (1633–1701), the brother of King Charles II (1600–1649) who would go on to profess Catholicism and lose his crown as a result (see below).[2] So while the Empire State was not named after a figure who was Catholic at the time, its name nonetheless designates England's last Catholic monarch.

## COUNTIES AND PARISHES

There are sixty-six counties and parishes in the United States that, thanks mostly to the French and Spanish, bear the names of Catholic dogmas, the Blessed Virgin Mary, and the saints. (And, of course, the very term that the state of Louisiana uses for its civil districts, **parish**, comes from the ecclesiastical parishes of the Roman Catholic Church, the districts having originally been drawn according to preexistent parochial territories.) While we cannot list them all, we can at least mention some of the more unexpected, such as **Liberty County, Texas**, named after the Most Holy Trinity of Liberty (*Sanctissima Trinidad de la Libertad*); **Ventura County, California**, named after St. Bonaventure (1221–1274); **Dolores County, Colorado**, named after Our Lady of Sorrows; and **Kings County, California**, named after the Magi who visited the infant Jesus in Bethlehem.

One county that deserves special mention in this regard is **Las Animas County, Colorado**, for it is perhaps the only district in the world named in reference to the doctrine of Purgatory. According to Catholic teaching, Purgatory is the place or condition where spiritually imperfect yet nevertheless saved souls are purged of their debts and defects before they are admitted into the bliss of Heaven. The doctrine, which is attested to in the writings and practices of the early Church, thus encourages the faithful on earth to pray for the "poor souls," as they are often called, in order to lessen their pain and hasten the attainment of their eternal reward. One may even venture to say that any Christian who prays for the dead implicitly confirms a belief in Purgatory, since prayer for those who go immediately to Heaven is unnecessary and prayer for those who go to Hell futile. Prayer was certainly the motivation behind the name of Las Animas County, which was coined in order to commemorate the souls of a group of Spanish soldiers found slain in an Indian raid by the banks of the Las Animas River.[3] Since they died suddenly and thus without the benefit of having been absolved of their sins in the sacrament of confession, later settlers prayed that their souls would not have to suffer too much in Purgatory.

There are also several counties named after illustrious Catholic figures. The most famous, of course, is **Christopher Columbus**, the nominal inspiration for ten counties. But there are others as well. Twelve counties and two parishes are named after **Charles Carroll** (1737–1832), the last surviving signer of the Declaration of Independence who also happened to be the only Catholic signatory.[4] Michigan and Wisconsin each have a county named in honor of Father **Jacques Marquette, S.J.** (1637–1675), a Jesuit explorer and missionary who, after accepting an invitation from the Illinois Indians to catechize them, became the first European to navigate and map the Mississippi River.[5] Ravalli County, Montana, is named after Father **Antonio Ravalli, S.J.** (1811–1884), a remarkable Jesuit missionary who was fluent in several Native American languages and skilled in medicine, architecture, and sculpting.[6]

Perhaps the most unusual category of "Catholic" counties are those named after English Catholic monarchs—unusual given the fact that England had long been a Protestant nation by the time it founded the American colonies. Several counties, such as **Albany** in New York, take their name from a king whose Catholicism would jolt the monarchy and destroy his reign. King James II (1633–1701) converted to Catholicism after marrying Mary of Modena (1658–1718), a decision that led to civil war and his eventual exile.[7] Mary, after whom New York state's **Dutchess County** is named, would have become a Salesian nun had not others convinced her that she could do a greater service to the Church by marrying James, who was already showing Catholic leanings. Mary was England's last Catholic queen, but before her there was Catherine of Braganza (1638–1705), after whom **Queens County** in New York is named. Catherine was a popular monarch who was loving even to her husband's illegitimate children, but because her life grew uncomfortable under the reign of the very Protestant William of Orange (1650–1702), she retired to Portugal in 1689.

## CITIES AND TOWNS

The following are several of the many municipalities whose names have a Catholic pedigree of some sort.

**Boston, Massachusetts.** One wonders whether the Puritans, who were not known for their love of Catholicism, were aware that they were naming their shining city on a hill after a Benedictine saint. St. Botolph founded Ikanhoe monastery in A.D. 654 and was renowned as a wise and holy abbot. After his death, Botolph became a popular medieval saint in his native land: seventy churches and five towns and villages in England (one of which, in Lincolnshire, is the original home of the Pilgrims) still bear his name. These municipal centers were named Botolphstown (with the *t* pronounced like a *d*), a name that over time was contracted to "Botolphston," then "Botoston," and eventually "Boston." There is a Botolph Street in downtown Boston that serves as a small reminder of this ancient connection.[8]

**Corpus Christi, Texas.** Franciscans who came to the shores of a bay in the Gulf of Mexico named it in honor of the Feast of the Body of Christ, or Corpus Christi. Later, the town that came to be built on the bay took on the same name.[9]

**De Pere, Wisconsin.** The site of Father Marquette's death (see p. 125) was originally known as *Rapides des Pères*, "rapids of the priests," because of the mission there.[10]

**Los Angeles, California.** Surprisingly, the once Spanish and Mexican "city of the Angels" is named not after God's celestial messengers but after the Blessed Virgin Mary, a Franciscan feast, and an Italian chapel. When the Franciscan priest Father Juan Crespi came upon a large river in southern California on August 2, 1769, he named it *El Rio de Nuestra Señora La Reina de los Angeles de Porciuncula*, "Our Lady, Queen of the Angels of Portiuncula." Crespi chose this name because the previous day, he and the expedition of which he was a part had celebrated this feast. (The Portiuncula is the name of the chapel located in the basilica of Our Lady of the Angels near Assisi, Italy, that is essentially the birthplace of the Franciscan order. The Benedictines had given St. Francis this *portiuncula*, or "little portion" [of the basilica], when he began his own order.) Later on, Filipe de Neve, the governor of California, founded a small settlement near the river on September 4, 1781, calling it *El Pueblo de Nuestra Señora La Reina de los Angeles de Porciuncula*. The daunting title was shortened by common usage so that by the time California became a United States territory in 1850, the *pueblo* was known as the City of Los Angeles.[11]

**Sacramento, California.** The state capitol of California is named after the river that runs through it, a river that had been named *Sacramento* by the Franciscan missionaries in honor of the Blessed Sacrament. Naming a body of water or place after the Blessed Sacrament is by no means unusual in North America. On the other side of the country, St. Isaac Jogues, the Jesuit martyr who would be slowly tortured to death by the Iroquois, discovered **Lake George** in upstate New York on May 30, 1636, the vigil of Corpus Christi. Because of the feast, Jogues named it *Lac du Saint Sacrament*, a name that remained until 1756 when it was changed in honor of the British monarch King George II.[12]

**San Antonio, Texas.** When Spanish explorers to Texas discovered a river on June 13, 1691, the Feast of St. Anthony of Padua (1195–1231), a Franciscan member of the expedition named the waterway in honor of the Franciscan saint. A marvelous preacher whose sermons moved tens of thousands to repentance and the popular saint to whom people pray when they lose something, St. Anthony is the only male saint besides St. Joseph and the prophet Simeon who is customarily portrayed in Catholic art holding the infant Jesus. Anthony holds this distinction because of a miraculous incident in which the Holy Infant came to Anthony, lept into his arms, and showered him with kisses until the saint responded in kind.[13] When in 1718 a city was founded near the San Antonio River, it too took on St. Anthony's illustrious name and patronage.[14]

**San Diego, California.** Contrary to what some Catholics might think, the city of San Diego is not named after St. Juan Diego (1474–1548), the recently canonized Aztec Indian who was visited by Our Lady of Guadalupe, but St. Didacus of Alcalá, Spain (d. 1463), a Franciscan saint whose name in Spanish is *San Diego*. St. Didacus was a lay brother who was made superior of a Franciscan community in the Canary Islands, a rare honor for someone with that vocation. Renowned for his humility and the miracles he worked, Didacus was canonized about a hundred years after his death.[15] The Franciscans kept his feast on November 12, and so when on that day in 1602 the Spanish explorer Don Sebastian de Viscaíno stepped onto the shore of a beautiful bay in California and had Mass celebrated, it was natural to name the bay in honor of the saint. (Coincidentally, Viscaíno's flagship was also named *San Diego*.) Later on, the "Apostle of California," the Franciscan friar Blessed Junípero Serra, arrived in the area and in 1769 founded what would become the first of California's nine celebrated missions. The mission, San Diego del Alcalá, became the center of the eponymous city that would grow up around it.[16]

**San Francisco, California.** San Francisco is named after St. Francis of Assisi (1181–1226), the popular saint whose religious order extensively evangelized the American Southwest. How it got that name, however, is mildly surprising. Though a Franciscan priest named the northern California bay in honor of St. Francis of Assisi on November 7, 1595, the settlement itself was called *Yerba Buena,* or "Good Herb," on account of the abundant mint that grew in the area. It was an American naval officer, Commodore John Sloat who, after capturing the city in 1846 during the Mexican-American War, renamed it for its mission, *San Francisco de Asís de Dolores,* that is, St. Francis of Assisi of the Sorrows. The "Sorrows" in that title refer to the nearby laguna and arroyo, which were named after the Seven Sorrows of the Blessed Virgin Mary: they give the mission its more familiar name, Mission Dolores.[17]

**Santa Fe, New Mexico.** New Mexico's capitol and the second oldest city in the United States was founded by the Spanish around 1610. The Governor, Don Pedro de Peralta, named the new settlement *La Villa Real de la Santa Fe de San Francisco de Asís,* that is, the Royal City of the Holy Faith of St. Francis of Assisi. The city was called royal because it was the seat of the Spanish government in the upper Rio Grande and presumably it was named after St. Francis' faith because of the central role the Franciscans played in evangelizing the native population. Over time, the city's name was shortened to Santa Fe.[18]

**St. Augustine, Florida.** The oldest permanent European settlement on the North American continent and the oldest continuously inhabited city in the United States, the city of St. Augustine began as a fort built by the Spanish to expel a colony of French Huguenots who had settled nearby and whose fort and fleet were threatening Spain's interests. The commander of the Spanish forces, Don Pedro Menendez de Aviles, discovered a safe harbor on August 28, 1565, the Feast of St. Augustine of Hippo (354–430).[19] Menendez subsequently named the camp he set up on the harbor's shores after Augustine, the North African bishop who, after a riotous youth, was converted to Christianity and went on to become one of the Latin Church's greatest and most influential intellectual treasures.

**Saint Marys, West Virginia.** One of the more unusual place-name stories surrounds the town of St. Marys, which was founded by Alexander Creel in 1849. According to the received account, "Creel was traveling by steamboat down the Ohio when he beheld a vision of the Virgin Mary who told him that a city founded at the joining of the Ohio River and Middle Island Creek would be happy and prosperous. Creel bought the land, marked off the streets for his city, and named it in honor of the Virgin Mary."[20]

**St. Louis, Missouri.** In February 1764, Auguste Choteau, a deputy of Pierre Laclede Ligueste, established a fur trading station on what would become the future city of St. Louis. When Ligueste arrived, he laid out plans for a town that soon became informally known as Laclede's Village. Given its strategic location and potential, however, Ligueste had grander plans for the village, declaring, "This settlement will become one of the finest cities in America." Perhaps that is why he gave it the more illustrious name of St. Louis, in honor of the Crusader king, Louis IX of France (d. 1270). Louis was a monarch renowned for his piety and justice who chose a life of celibacy, even though this meant forsaking the possibility of an heir.[21]

**St. Paul, Minnesota.** There are numerous towns named after "the least of the apostles," but the naming of Minnesota's state capitol is noteworthy for two reasons. First, it mercifully replaced the town's earlier name, Pig's Eye Landing. Second, St. Paul was originally the name of a Catholic chapel built by Father Lucien Galtier, who chose the saint partly in distinction to a nearby parish called St. Peter's. Galtier's other (and rather wry) reason, however, was that St. Paul is the apostle to the Gentiles, who were "well represented in the new place in the persons of the Indians."[22]

**Washington, D.C.** The present-day District of Columbia was created from territories that belonged to two Catholic barons of Baltimore, Notley Young and Daniel Carroll of Duddington, a relative of the first American bishop, John Carroll.[23] Washington received immediate cooperation from the owners when he approached them, a cooperation that inspired other leaders of the landed gentry to do the same. The choice of a site near the Potomac was no doubt motivated by pragmatic considerations, but there is something symbolically appropriate about building the seat of government on land that was part of Catholic Maryland, the first haven of religious freedom in the New World.

## STREET NAMES

There are thousands of streets, boulevards, avenues, lanes, and roads in the United States with Catholic names, far too many to be summarized here. And, of course, were we to expand our search to the rest of the world, we would find many more, such as **Pope John XXIII Street** in Istanbul, Turkey, named after the pope in honor of his services to that country as Apostolic Delegate from 1934 to 1944, and **Pope Paul VI Street** and **Pope John Paul II Street** in Bethlehem, in honor of their visits to the ancient city.[24] For the sake of brevity we will mention only one unusual American street name and the peculiar history that it evokes.

**Pio Nono Avenue.** The city of Macon, Georgia, has a thoroughfare named after Pope Blessed Pius IX (Pio Nono in Italian), the controversial pontiff who spent most of his papacy (1846–1878) reviled for his opposition to modernity in general and Italian nationalism in particular. The avenue took its name from a now-defunct diocesan college in Macon, but there is more than an accidental affinity between the beleaguered pope and the Old South. Thanks to the diplomacy of an Irish Catholic priest who convinced the pontiff that the South merely wished to defend itself from Northern aggression, Pope Pius IX wrote a letter to Jefferson Davis addressing him as president, an appellation many at the time (incorrectly?) viewed as a de facto recognition by the Holy See of the Confederacy.[25] When Davis was placed in solitary confinement for two years after the Civil War, Pius, himself the first "prisoner of the Vatican" after the fall of the Papal States, hand-wove a crown of thorns and sent it to him. (Pius probably even hurt himself making the crown, as each of the thorns is approximately two inches long.) The crown is currently on display in the New Orleans Confederate Civil War Museum.

The odd rapport between Pius and the South stands in sharp contrast to the North's earlier reception of the pope's gestures of friendship. When Pius IX donated a marble stone from ancient Rome's Temple of Concord for the construction of the **Washington Monument** in 1854, the anti-Catholic "Know Nothing" Party halted all construction and stole it. Though no arrests were made over the vandalism of the "Pope Stone," as it came to be called, the incident did lead to a call for greater religious toleration. However, it also delayed the completion of the monument for decades. A replacement stone was not installed in the monument until 1983.[26]

## PSEUDO-CATHOLIC

Apparently Catholic naming is contagious. Below are several names that appear to be Catholic but are not.

**Saint Tammany Parish, Louisiana.** A popular chief of the Delaware Indians, Tammany or Tamenend was not a Catholic saint, but he was well-regarded by the colonists, some of whom jokingly referred to him as their patron saint. In the eighteenth century, populist citizens of New York City even named a political action group after him, though ironically, "Tammany Hall," as it was known, eventually came to be associated with political corruption and boss control rather than reform.

**Holy Wives?** Several cities and towns are named not after Catholic saints but after the wives of their founders. **St. Anna, Missouri**, is named after the wife of Bob Williams; **St. Martha, Missouri**, is named after the wife of W. R. Wild; and **St. Francis, Kansas**, is named after Frances Emerson, the wife of one of the founders.[27]

**Holy Founders?** In other places, the founders themselves or other local prominent persons came to be "canonized" by their town. **St. Paul, Texas**, is named after W. H. Paul; **St. James, Missouri**, after Thomas James; **St. Thomas, Pennsylvania**, after Thomas Campbell; **Saint Edward, Nebraska**, for the Catholic priest Edward Serrels; **St. Joe, Texas**, after Joe Howell; and **Saint Michael, Nebraska**, for Mike Kyne. Sometimes the names were given ironically, as in **Holy Jim Canyon, California**, named after a local beekeeper known as "Cussin' Jim."[28]

# 14

# INTERNATIONAL, NATIONAL, AND STATE SYMBOLS

✠

I n the days when Christendom reigned in Western Europe, it was not un-common to find Catholic Christian motifs in political symbols. Though virtually all of the former lands that comprised Christendom are now secular nation-states, vestiges of this former custom still remain. This is even true, surprisingly enough, of political dominions that were never Catholic, such as the United States federal government and a number of individual states. The following chapter introduces us to some of the "hidden" Catholic signs that can be found on the international, national, and state levels.

## FLAGS FROM AROUND THE WORLD

**The Dannebrog.** The Danish flag, or *Dannebrog,* consists of a white cross on a red field and is the oldest continuously used national flag in the world. According to legend, the *Dannebrog* fell from the sky when King Waldemar II defeated the Estonians in battle on June 15, 1219. The white cross represents the Catholic faith of the Danish kingdom at the time. Similar crosses may be found on the flags of **Norway**, **Iceland, Sweden**, and **Finland**.

    **Dominican Republic.** When the Trinitarians (members of the Dominican Republic's independence movement) were fighting for their independence from Haiti in 1839, they took the national colors of Haiti and added a large white cross to symbolize their Catholic faith. The flag was adopted as the national flag in 1844. Some Dominican flags also feature a coat of arms in the center, which includes a Bible opened to the Prologue of the Gospel of John. The tiny Caribbean island nation of **Dominica** (no relation) has an even more explicitly Christian flag for its predominantly Roman Catholic population: it not only has a cross to symbolize faith in Christ, but the cross has three stripes to represent the Trinity.[1]

**The French Royal Arms.** Before the French Revolution (1789–1792) one of the more recognizable French flags was that of three yellow fleurs-de-lis on a blue field, the arms of the French royal family. (A variation of this may be seen today in the flag of Quebec.) In 1365 Charles V reduced the number of fleurs-de-lis on the royal arms to three in honor of the Trinity.[2] Given the fleur-de-lis' three pedals, it is a fitting symbol.

**The French Tricolor.** After the fall of the old regime, the French National Convention officially adopted the tricolor flag of three red, white, and blue vertical bars in 1794. It is said that the flag is the product of the French Revolution: red and blue were the livery colors of Paris, the heart of the Revolution, while white symbolizes French royalty. The peaceful coexistence of all three on the same flag symbolizes the truce reached between the king and the revolutionaries (apparently, decapitating one of the parties ensures a certain measure of peace). Later on, however, the tricolor also came to be interpreted in light of France's pre-Revolutionary history. Red is considered the color of St. Denis, the patron saint of Paris; white is the color of the Blessed Virgin Mary, the patroness of France, and also of St. Joan of Arc, whose victory over the English in the fifteenth century helped shape the French kingdom; and blue is the color of St. Martin of Tours, the famous soldier and eventual bishop who gave half of his cloak to a beggar in the snow (for more on St. Martin, see p. 60).[3]

**Great Britain's Union Jack.** The flag that flew over the Empire on which the sun never set contains symbols of three of Christendom's most famous saints: the soldier-dragonslayer St. George, who is generally portrayed in art with a scarlet cross on a white flag; the Apostle St. Andrew, whose symbol is a white diagonal cross, or saltire, in a blue field, in honor of the X-shaped cross on which he was slowly martyred; and St. Patrick, whose cross is a red saltire with a white background. The reason for these three crosses appearing in the design of Great Britain's flag is that they represent the 1801 union of three countries: England, whose patron saint is St. George; Scotland, whose patron saint is St. Andrew; and Ireland, whose patron is St. Patrick. (Though Wales is also a part of the United Kingdom, it is not represented on the Union Jack.) Despite St. Patrick's obvious connection with Catholicism in Ireland, however, his cross should probably not be considered

Catholic, as it seems to have been invented in 1783 by the British and is generally preferred by Ulster Unionists and Masons in Northern Ireland.

**The Irish Flag.** The flag of the Republic of Ireland gives equal billing to both Catholics and Protestants. The flag, which features three vertical bars of green, white, and orange, was first used in the mid-nineteenth century by the Young Ireland movement, a group that called for the independence of the entire island. The flag dramatizes that vision: the green symbolizes the Catholics (predominantly in the south) as well as the Gaelic tradition of Ireland, the orange symbolizes the pro-British Protestants in the north (nicknamed the Orangemen after William of Orange), and the white symbolizes peace between the two groups. Despite this commendable meaning, however, the flag still tends to be associated with Sinn Fein, the political wing of the I.R.A.[4]

**The Lebanese Flag.** Lebanon's flag reflects its ancient Maronite Catholic heritage. In the eighteenth century the Maronites used a white flag with a cedar tree in the center, citing as their inspiration, Psalm 92:12: "The just shall flourish like the palm tree: he shall grow up like the cedar of Lebanon." Later, under French influence, two horizontal red bars were added, giving the flag its current appearance.[5]

**The Mexican *Bandero Nacional.*** Since 1957, Mexico's tricolor flag of green, white, and red has been interpreted in a secular way, with green representing hope, white unity, and red parenthood and the blood of patriots.[6] Originally, however, the colors represented what were meant to be the three founding pillars of the Mexican nation: Independence (green), Religion (white), and Union (red). During Mexico's War of Independence from Spain (1815–1821), Catholic authorities in Mexico agreed to support the Mexican cause provided that the secular powers promise what became known as the "Three Guaranties" (*Tres Garantias*): 1) promotion of the Roman Catholic apostolic religion, 2) independence under a moderate monarchical government, and 3) the equality of native and European peoples. Thus, the white of the Mexican flag is the symbol of the Catholic faith.[7]

**The Flag of Montserrat.** Montserrat is a tiny island nation in the Caribbean named by Columbus after the Spanish Abbey of Montserrat, where St. Ignatius of Loyola had had the vision that inspired him to found the Jesuit Order. After the island was eventually settled by English and Irish Catholics from nearby St. Kitt's, it gained a reputation as a safe haven for Catholics under British rule, attracting persecuted Catholics from as far away as Virginia. The influence of Irish Catholics on the island may be seen in Montserrat's flag, which features Ireland, or Erin (personified as a lady), holding an Irish harp and a large passion cross.[8]

**The Swiss Flag.** Switzerland's flag consists of a white "Greek" cross (that is, a cross with equidistant arms) on a red field. Though today the flag is associated with the defining characteristics of modern Switzerland (such as neutrality and democracy), it was patterned after that of the Holy Roman Empire (from which most Swiss cantons acquired their sovereignty) and thus has a Catholic connotation.[9]

**The Vatican City Flag.** It should come as no surprise that the world's smallest nation flies a flag with unmistakable symbols of the papacy. The papal coat of arms, place on a gold and white flag, features the triple-crowned tiara formerly worn by a pope to signify his three degrees of authority: Bishop of the diocese of Rome, Patriarch of the Western Church, and Supreme Pontiff of the universal Church. Below the tiara are two crossed keys (one gold and the other silver), symbols of the power that Christ gave to his first Vicar, St. Peter: "That thou art Peter; and upon this rock I will build my church, and the gates of hell shall not prevail against it. And I will give to thee the keys of the kingdom of heaven. And whatsoever thou shalt bind upon earth, it shall be bound also in heaven: and whatsoever thou shalt loose upon earth, it shall be loosed also in heaven" (Matthew 16:18, 19). When these keys are represented on the Vatican City flag, the silver key appears on the right; but when they appear on the flag of the Holy See (which is the central governing authority of the Catholic Church, not the tiny nation *per se*), the keys are reversed and the silver key appears on the left.[10]

## SYMBOLS OF THE UNITED STATES

**The Trinity and the One-Dollar Bill.** Though it was best known for its use by Masonic lodges, the reverse of the Great Seal of the United States was originally a Catholic symbol of the Holy Trinity. This symbol, an unfinished pyramid topped by a single eye surrounded by rays, is on the back of every one-dollar bill. According to the State Department, the pyramid "represents strength and duration" and the eye "Providence," presumably that of God's providence, for the adjoining motto, *Annuit Coeptis,* means, "He has favored our undertakings." Prior to its inclusion in the Great Seal, however, the single triangle represented one God, its three sides represented the three persons of the Trinity, the eye signified God's omniscience and providence, and the rays betokened divinity. The design was once quite popular in Europe and may still found there on roadside shrines and in churches.[11] And it may also be found on the great seal of the state of Colorado.

## STATE FLAGS, SEALS, AND MOTTOS

**Alabama.** The Heart of Dixie has as its flag a scarlet St. Andrew's cross on a white field in imitation of the Confederacy's Army of Northern Virginia battle flag, since most Alabamans fought under this flag during the Civil War. St. Andrew's cross was featured in most Confederate flags, possibly because of the Scottish ancestry of many Southerners. Whatever the reason, it is an indirect if unintentional tribute to St. Andrew. Similarly, because Alabama's coat of arms features Great Britain's Union Jack and pre-Revolution France's fleur-de-lis flag (among others),[12] it incorporates the symbols of not only St. Andrew, but St. George, St. Patrick, and the Blessed Virgin Mary (see p. 132).

**Arizona and New Mexico.** To commemorate the Catholic country that first colonized them, the Grand Canyon State and the Cactus State contain the national colors of Spain: red and yellow.[13] The Spanish flag may also be found on the coat of arms of Alabama.

**Florida.** Like Alabama, Florida had a large number of its citizens fight in the Army of Northern Virginia during the Civil War. Hence the Orange State also has St. Andrew's cross in its design.[14]

**Georgia and Mississippi.** Most of the Confederacy's flags featured St. Andrew's cross in one way or another. This is certainly true of the most famous symbol of the Confederacy, the Confederate battle flag, which is featured in the flags of the Peach State and the Magnolia State.

**Hawaii.** The only American state flag with the Union Jack on it, the Aloha State's flag was created by King Kamehameha I in 1816, when Hawaii was an independent kingdom with close ties to Great Britain. By including the Union Jack, however, the Hawaiian flag also indirectly pays homage to Saints George, Andrew, and Patrick (see p. 132).

**Idaho.** Idaho's state motto, *Esto perpetua,* "May it be forever," is said to have been coined by a Catholic priest and the first person to write a history of the Council of Trent. Father Pietro Sarpi (1552–1623) was a learned theologian, mathematician, and historian. In addition to being the Procurator General of the Venetian province of the Servite Order and an acquaintance of such luminaries of the day as St. Charles Borromeo, St. Robert Bellarmine, Galileo, and Hugo Grotius, Sarpi was also a loyal citizen of the Republic of Venice who sided with Venice against the pope in a number of jurisdictional disputes. Sarpi apparently applied the phrase *Esto perpetua* to Venice in 1623. The National Grange of the Patrons of Husbandry adopted it as their motto in 1867, as did the state of Idaho in 1890.[15]

**Iowa.** The flag of the Hawkeye State includes the French tricolor of red, white, and blue to commemorate that United States' acquisition from France of the territory that would one day become the state of Iowa in the Louisiana Purchase. In including the French colors, Iowa is also paying indirect tribute to St. Martin, the Blessed Virgin Mary, and St. Denis (see p. 132).

**Louisiana.** The flag and seal of the Bayou State feature a pelican piercing its own breast in order to feed its young. This striking symbol of self-sacrifice was most likely chosen because of the numerous pelicans in this historically Catholic state (the brown pelican is in fact the state bird), though it is interesting to note that the pelican lacerating itself is one of the oldest Catholic symbols of the Eucharist. According to an ancient myth, a father pelican returned to the nest after a three-day absence to find his brood killed by a serpent. To bring them back to life, he tore open his breast and let his blood drip onto them. Early Christians like St. Jerome saw in this tale an allegory of the Eucharist and the Cross. Just as the pelican feeds its offspring with itself, so too does Christ; just as the pelican saves its offspring with its own blood, so too does Christ. There is even a hymn, sometimes used, appropriately enough, during the Benediction of the Blessed Sacrament that begins with the words, *Pie Pelicane, Jesu, Domine*—"Merciful Pelican, O Lord Jesus."[16]

**Maryland.** While several states have mottos taken from the Bible, Maryland is the only one with a motto that can be directly traced to a Catholic edition of the Scriptures. *Scuto Bonae Voluntatis Tuae Coronasti Nos,* which means "Thou hast crowned us as with a shield of thy good will," is taken from the Latin Vulgate translation of Psalm 5:13.[17] No doubt the verse reflects the faith of Maryland's founder, Sir George Calvert (Lord Baltimore), a Roman Catholic nobleman who was renowned for his religious tolerance, relatively fair treatment of Native Americans, and commitment to protecting his co-religionists from the persecution they were suffering in England and the rest of the colonies. The beautiful state flag of Maryland also bears testimony to Sir George's beneficent influence, as it consists of the coats of arms of the Calvert and Crossland families (Crossland was the family name of the mother of the first Lord Baltimore).[18]

**Rhode Island.** The flag and the seal of the Ocean State feature a gold anchor and the word, *Hope.* The anchor has been associated with Rhode Island since its founding under the Cromwellian Patent of 1643 and has survived a royal charter in 1663 (which officially granted the state religious freedom), the Revolutionary War, and beyond.[19] Though the anchor is a universal symbol for all Western Christians to appreciate, it is also one of the Catholic Church's oldest symbols for the theological virtue of hope. The Epistle to the Hebrews mentions Christian hope "as an anchor of the soul, sure and firm"(6:19), while the catacombs of Rome abound with images of the anchor from as early as the first century. The anchor was most likely popular not only because it expressed Christianity's hope in the salvation of its dead but also because its cruciform shape could be cherished as a symbol of the Cross without arousing the suspicion of the Church's persecutors.[20]

# 15

# LAW

✠

*Yes, I'd give the Devil benefit of law, for my own safety's sake.*
—Sir Thomas More in *A Man for all Seasons*

As St. Thomas Aquinas points out, law is a constitutive element of the virtue of justice that makes "men good by habituating them to good works."[1] Since the Church is passionately concerned with justice and since its principal goal is to make its members saints, it is not surprising that it would have prudent recourse to law. This is aptly reflected in the first principle of canon law (the Church's body of legislation), the principle that both trumps and grounds all others: "The supreme law is the salvation of souls."

The Church's justice-driven development of law has also had a benevolent effect on the legal systems of the West and, by extension, the world. Saints like Thomas More recognized civic law's great value even when forced by conscience to disobey it. But more fundamentally, it was the development of **canon law** in the Middle Ages that retrieved, transformed, and then re-presented the long-forgotten Justinian code of the ancient Roman Empire to emerging European polities in dire need of good juridical models. It was, in fact, the emergence of ecclesiastical courts after Pope Gregory VII that prompted civil courts to imitate and eventually supercede them.[2]

In this chapter we review some of the effects of this transfigured emergence of the rule of law, from the paramount to the piddling. Needless to say, our review would be much longer if we included the norms and customs of every Western nation. In France, for example, the senior advocate is called a *bastonier* or *batônnier* (literally, a banner holder) because it was his privilege to carry the banner of St. Catherine of Alexandria, patron saint of attorneys, in her feast day procession.[3] Fortunately though, there are plenty of examples closer to home.

**Consent, Contracts, and Marriage.** There is more than one salubrious side effect to the Catholic teaching on marriage. According to Professor Harold Berman, the Catholic stipulation that marriage requires the free consent of a man and a woman provided "the foundations not only of the modern law of marriage" but of a number of basic tenets to modern contract law, such as the concept of free will, mistake, duress, and fraud.[4] This in turn had the further effect of eliminating the practice of infant marriage in Europe and in every other culture that would be shaped by the Christian religion.[5]

**Christianity and the Common Law.** The legal systems of continental Europe may be the distant scions of ancient Roman law, but the Anglo-American legal tradition, or common law, is grounded in an explicitly Christian framework. As John C. H. Wu writes, "[W]hile the Roman law was a deathbed convert to Christianity, the common law was a cradle Christian." Anglo-American common law presupposed that the same God who governs the "laws of nature" (such as gravity and generation) also governs the "natural law," those universally binding moral precepts that are knowable to all men and women because they are written on the tablets of their heart (Romans 2:15). The Christian pedigree of common law was clearly recognized by jurisprudence theorists like Sir William Blackstone, whose *Commentaries on the Law of England* was to exert an enormous influence on British and early American law. Indeed, in 1829 Joseph Story could write, "There never has been a period in which the Common Law did not recognize Christianity as lying at its foundations." The shift to a pure secularism that eventually did occur in the United States seems to be the result of Justice Oliver Wendell Holmes, who ridiculed the law's relation to the divine and instituted a positivist approach based on judiciary opinion.[6] The planks for Holmes's rejection, however, had been laid a century earlier by Thomas Jefferson, who vigorously denied that Christianity is or "ever was a part of the common law."[7]

**The Rule of Law.** One of the most important maxims undergirding modern law is "the rule of law not men," that is, the sovereignty of an impartial law over and against the exercise of arbitrary power. Although this principle may be found in several ancient civilizations, its reintroduction to the West is most likely the result of the medieval Church in its dialectical tension with secular authority. According to Professor Charles Donahue, Jr., the concept of the rule of law may have emerged as early as the Magna Carta. Donahue speculates that several unique factors contributed to this development, including 1) the "dual" aspect of medieval society, with its conflicts between altar and throne; 2) a plurality of legal jurisdictions, including ecclesiastical courts and royal courts; and 3) the Catholic belief in the transcendence of God and in overarching immutable principles that transcended particular legal codes.[8]

**Equity.** Another byproduct of the legal system to emerge from the crucible of medieval Catholic tradition is the concept of equity, the fair settlement of grievances and injustices often beyond the purview of statutory law. It was the ecclesiastical courts and religious orders of the Church that introduced the idea of equity to the English realm and hence to Anglo-American law. By combining aspects of Greco-Roman law, Celtic-Saxon custom, and Judeo-Christian principles in their efforts to be fair when adjudicating canon law cases, the Church and its courts became the locus for equitable justice in medieval England. This, however, was seen as a threat to the civil courts, and so in 1349 the king transferred this power to his Chancery. The once exclusively religious dimension of justice was then definitively secularized by Henry VIII, who eliminated all ecclesiastical courts in 1534 when he subjected the Church in England to the authority of the state. Equity courts such as the Chancery existed separate from law courts in the United States and Great Britain until the nineteenth century, when the two were conflated into one system.[9]

**Intent and Liability.** As canon lawyers in the twelfth century began to reflect on the nature of innocence and guilt, they were slowly able to replace the Germanic preference for ordeals by fire and water as a means of deciding guilt with trials that were governed by more rational principles. One of the fruits of this was the development of the concepts of intent and liability in judiciary evaluations, concepts that are still with us today. Canonists mulled over elaborate scenarios in order to flesh out the importance of both of these factors. Here is one example: a man throws a stone at his friend with the intention of frightening him. The friend jumps in order to dodge the stone and badly injures himself. The friend then seeks medical assistance but receives poor treatment from a physician and dies. To what extent is the man liable for his friend's death?[10]

**International Law.** It was Catholic conscience confronting the evils of New World colonialism that led vicariously to the development of the modern system of international law. In 1511 a Dominican priest on the island of Hispaniola (modern-day Haiti and the Dominican Republic) launched a fiery volley against Spanish exploitation of the natives, which prompted King Ferdinand of Spain to convene a council of theologians and to draft legislation for the humane treatment of his new subjects. Though most of the new laws were poorly enforced in the faraway colonies, they did "set the stage for the more systematic and lasting work of some of the great theological jurists of the sixteenth century." Chief among these is Father Francisco de Vitoria (1486–1546), the Thomist scholar whose explication of just war theory essentially rejects a European "right" to conquer the inhabitants of the New World in the name of civilization or Christianity. The alleged abuse or neglect of life and property by Native Americans, Vitoria taught, was not in itself sufficient grounds for waging war on them or subjugating them. Native Americans were fully human and as such were entitled to rule themselves, no matter what a European power, even the papacy, said. Such teachings, which were inspired by the Catholic natural law tradition and the Catholic understanding of the unity of the human race, contributed much to the idea of an international law.[11]

**Going Out in Your Right Mind.** A common feature of legislation involving the death penalty in the United States and other Western countries is that a condemned convict who goes insane after his sentencing cannot be executed until he recovers from his madness. This odd stipulation is based on the Catholic notion of forgiveness and repentance. Even a doomed convict should have the opportunity to repent of his wrongdoing and be reconciled to God through the sacrament of confession before going off to meet the Eternal Judge, but he can do this only if he is sane.[12]

**X Marks the Spot.** When an illiterate person had to sign a legal document, he or she wrote an X for his name. X is a St. Andrew's cross as well as the first letter of *Xristos,* the Greek word for Christ. Fraught with this religious significance, the X came to signify a sworn oath and became a legally recognized mark. After writing it, the signatory often kissed the X as a gesture of sincerity, just as kissing a Bible sometimes accompanies the taking of an oath. It is from this custom that there originated writing *XXX* at the end of a letter as a sign for a **kiss**.[13]

**The Courtroom.** Not just the form but the forum of law may be inspired by Catholic practice. Though a strict historical causality is difficult to trace, there is a remarkable resemblance between traditional church architecture and the design of the American courtroom. Public seating in a courtroom gallery, for example, is akin to the pews in the nave of a church; the space for the lawyers and judge is similar to the sanctuary where traditionally only the clergy and their ministers would be allowed (note that many courtrooms demarcate this space with a rail similar in appearance and function to a communion rail); the judge's bench, elevated and set apart, assumes the same importance as the similarly situated high altar, which only certain members of the clergy are permitted to approach and only at certain times; the jury benches resemble the choir stalls found in many medieval churches;

and the personnel who move in and out of the bench area, such as the bailiffs, resemble the acolytes serving the priest. Even the drama of the court echoes the drama of the liturgy. In a fascinating article entitled "Courting Reverence," Father Paul Scalia, son of Supreme Court Justice Antonin Scalia, argues that both the Mass and the court deal with forgiveness and punishment, innocence and guilt, life and death, and that the appropriate response to both as a sense of awe and respect.[14] After all, in the Creed recited at Mass we acknowledge Christ as the Judge of the living and the dead. Taking Father Scalia's argument a step further, one wonders if something cannot be made of the connection between the court and the opening line of the old Latin Mass: *Judica me, Deus, et discerne causam meam de gente non sancta: ab homine iniquo et doloso, erue me*—"Judge me, O God, and distinguish my cause from the nation that is not holy: deliver me from the unjust and deceitful man" (Psalm 42:1).

**Judicial Garb.** One thing is certain; it is no coincidence that our judges wear black robes. The judical **gown** hearkens back to the cassock and the days when only the clergy studied and practiced law or when students wore clerical dress during their matriculation (see p. 115). In England and other parts of the world, the indebtedness to medieval church custom is even more conspicuous. The **wig** worn by judges and barristers in Great Britain and the Commonwealth is a substitute of the tight-fitting skull-cap worn by medieval clerics, and the prohibition against wearing **gloves** on the bench mirrors the rubric against priests wearing gloves during Mass.[15] Further, when a British judge sentences a guilty person to death, he is required to put on his **black hat** when he does so; this is in imitation of a priest, who was once required to wear his biretta when hearing confession.[16] Even the British **law terms**, the vacation times during which the court is not in session, are a product of the Church, which prohibited the adjudication of legal disputes at certain times so that the feasts of the liturgical year would be duly observed. The winter vacation is a relic of Advent and Christmastide, the spring vacation of Lent, the summer vacation of Pentecost, and the fall vacation of Michaelmas (for more on Michaelmas, see p. 86).[17]

**Clerking.** The legal debt to the Catholic clergy is more than skin deep. When a law student graduates, he or she often "clerks" for a judge, assisting in the judge's research, drafting of opinions, and so on. The legal custom of calling a young assistant for a judge a "law clerk" and an administrative officer of the court a "court clerk"[18] testifies to the days when virtually all practitioners of the law were members of the clergy, men who been tonsured (made a monk) or who had taken at least one of the **four minor orders** of the Church: acolyte, lector, doorkeeper, and exorcist. (The major orders, by contrast, are deacon, priest, and bishop.) Because clerics were literate (a rare skill in those days), they were called upon to do a number of office-related tasks, especially in matters pertaining to the law. Over time the association of the minor clergy with administrative and other bureaucratic duties grew so strong that the jobs themselves became known as "clerical" and the people who performed them as "clerks."[19]

# Part V

# *Our Mother Tongue*

# WORDS, WORDS, WORDS—
# CATHOLIC, ANTI-CATHOLIC,
# AND POST-CATHOLIC

✠

Much of *Why Do Catholics Eat Fish on Friday?* is linguistic in nature, reflecting as it does on the origin of words. This is eminently appropriate, since the first Latin author to use the term for the study of word origins, **etymology**, was St. Isidore of Seville.[1] As we have seen, the impact of Catholicism on language is considerable, yet it is only part of the story. In addition to words authored by Catholics there are a number of implicitly or explicitly anti-Catholic terms as well as a growing list of "post-Catholic" vocabulary, that is, Catholic terms forced to take on non-Catholic meanings. The following chapter is thus dedicated to the Catholic, anti-Catholic, and post-Catholic nomenclature of the English-speaking world.

## CATHOLIC

*New names must be put on new things.*

—Cicero[2]

The new realities revealed by Christ and preserved by apostolic tradition required a new terminology adequate to the task of designating them. Words such as *incarnation, atonement, transubstantiation,* and *grace* thus entered the Western lexicon and have remained there ever since. But the Catholic exercise in verbal discipline and meaning also led to a number of equally original but less conspicuous contributions. The following list focuses on only a few of the everyday words that were coined by Catholic saints and scholars.

**Integrity.** Our word for moral probity originated from a man whose life was a reflection of it. St. Thomas More had been a scrupulous Chancellor of England known for his honesty, but when King Henry VIII divorced Catherine of Aragon and subsequently severed himself and the nation from the Catholic Church, More could not in good conscience support these actions and quickly resigned. More had no intention of publicly dissenting, but even his refusal to endorse was a silence too defeaning for the king, who had him beheaded after years of imprisonment in the Tower of London. Before his death, More had written a book in which he used the word *integrity* to signify wholeness or completeness, thus endowing it with one of its more common definitions today. Appropriately enough, an early biographer of More was one of the first to apply the term in a moral sense when describing More's behavior as conserving "the integritie of a good conscience."[3]

**Utopia.** St. Thomas More has also given us the popular word for an ideal political or social community. *Utopia* is the title of a work by More in which the main character, Raphael Hythloday, enthusiastically reports on what he deems to be a model island nation in the New World. In everyday discourse *utopia* can also refer to an impossible plan or idea, but More would not have been offended. He coined the word from the Greek so that it could mean either "good place" or "no place" in order to underscore the impossibility of a perfect society.[4] Unfortunately, since most of his readers did not know Greek, many thought that More was serious and that an island called Utopia really did exist on the other side of the Atlantic.[5] And even more unfortunately, later utopian thinkers like Marx and Hegel rejected More's sober realism and treated the idea of a perfect society not only as a possibility but as a historically inevitable certainty, one that justifies any injustice and bloodshed that would hasten its arrival.

**Agony.** One of the chief ways in which Christian authors transformed the languages they spoke was by internalizing or spiritualizing the meanings of words that had previously referred to purely external or physical phenomena. *Agony* is a good case in point. The Greek word *agōn* was defined as any contest or combat in the public games.[6] For Christians, however, the real combat or struggle was not against flesh and blood, but against the invisible "spirits of wickedness in the high places" (Ephesians 6:12). *Agony* thus came to signify not only the public games (see II Maccabees 4:18) but the struggle that takes place within the soul given one's own propensity to sin. The primary example of this new kind of contest is Our Lord's suffering in the Garden of Gethsemane, where St. Luke describes him as being in agony (22:43). Interestingly, though this archetypal agony of mind obviously took place internally, it too led to bloodshed. St. Luke, who according to tradition was a physician, records that during the Agony in the Garden, Jesus' "sweat became as drops of blood, trickling down upon the ground" (22:44). Doctors now recognize this phenomenon as *hematidrosa,* in which the blood capillaries of the face rupture under extreme stress. Luke's observation thus indicates the tremendous extent of Christ's agony.[7]

**Ruminate.** Another example of spiritualizing the physical is one of our words for meditating or mulling over something. *Ruminare* in Latin means "chewing the cud," which is why cattle and other animals with more than one stomach are classified today as "ruminants." Early Christians saw in the ruminant's processing of its food an apt metaphor for dwelling on the sacred text.[8] In one of his explications of a Psalm, St. Augustine invites his listeners to chew, or ruminate, on what they have heard.[9] But in his *Confessions* he goes one step further, describing memory as the "mind's stomach," which recalls things from its vast recesses and mulls over them like a cow retrieving its cud and chewing on it.[10]

**Soliloquy.** Given that St. Augustine was one of the chief agents in transposing physical imagery onto a spiritual plane—or rather, in recognizing the profound metaphysical link between the two—it is appropriate that he coined the literary term for what today is often referred to as a monologue. The *Soliloquies* is a dialogue written by Augustine between himself and a mysterious interlocutor whom he calls Reason. Reason interrogates Augustine about his life, his desires, and his opinions, while Augustine in turn pressures Reason for answers to his questions about the soul and God. The simple conceit of the work belies its revolutionary quality; by internalizing a conversation between himself and reason, Augustine had single-handedly transformed a centuries-old tradition of philosophical dialogues, which previously had taken place only between two or more characters.[11]

**Snack Food.** According to Notre Dame professor Brian Khrostenko, Augustine's psychological astuteness also had unintended consequences on the naming of party food. When analyzing the inordinate desire for physical pleasure, Augustine notes the phenomenon of heightening discomfort in order to induce a greater experience of gratification. Drunkards, for example, often eat *salsiuscula,* or "little salty things" to increase their thirst so that the subsequent slaking will be all the more enjoyable.[12] Since Augustine invented the word *salsiuscula,* he may be rightly regarded as the father of the term "snack food."[13]

**Rubrics.** One of our words for a rule or injunction comes from an old English word for red. How did a color become associated with commands? The answer lies in the books of the Catholic liturgical tradition. From the early Middle Ages on it has been the custom in liturgical manuals to print all ceremonial instructions in red and all prayers and readings that are to be recited during the service in black. This enables the celebrant to distinguish easily between the parts he is to pray and the parts he is to follow. Over time this convention found its way into other types of print, such as British legal documents, until it became synonymous with written direction.[14]

**Red-Letter Day.** Our expression for an especially happy or memorable day comes from a similar usage. Church calendars for the liturgical year once put a saint's feast day or holy day in red letters to set it apart from regular ferial days; thus a red-letter day was more festive than those in black. So closely associated, in fact, was this convention with Catholicism that a "Red-Letter" became an English nickname for a Roman Catholic person or thing.[15]

**Devil's Advocate.** Though his official title was *Promotor Fidei,* or Promoter of the Faith, the cleric whose duty it was to compile as many negative things as possible against a candidate for canonization is better known as the Devil's Advocate. The Devil's Advocate was supposed to ensure that all of the procedures for canonizing a saint were meticulously observed, but it was his role in raising all sorts of objections regardless of whether he believed them or not that inspired the phrase, "to play the devil's advocate." Hence John Stuart Mill, no great friend of Catholicism, writes: "The most intolerant of churches, the Roman Catholic Church, even at the canonization of a saint, admits, and listens patiently to, a 'devil's advocate.' The holiest of men, it appears, cannot be admitted to posthumous honors, until all that the devil could say against him is known and weighed."[16] Alas, because of recent changes to the process of canonization, which have rendered the proceedings less dramatic and more academic, the office of Devil's Advocate has been relegated to the category of bygone curiosities.

**When in Rome, Do As the Romans Do.** This popular proverb hails not from the glory days of ancient Rome and it does not refer to wearing togas or watching gladiator games. Rather, it is inspired by the way in which a Christian bishop replied to a query about local fasting practices. According to the story, when St. Augustine and his mother St. Monica asked St. Ambrose of Milan whether they should follow the weekly fasting traditions of Rome (which included a Saturday fast) or of Milan (which did not), Ambrose replied: "When I am here, I do not fast on Saturday; when I am in Rome, I fast on Saturday."[17]

**Quo Vadis?** Another expression from ancient Christian sources is *quo vadis?* or "whither are you going?" According to tradition, St. Peter, who had been shepherding the Church in Rome for a number of years, was fleeing the city during the first wave of persecution when he saw Jesus Christ walking toward him carrying his cross. Astonished at the sight, Peter asked him, "Where are you going, Lord?" Jesus answered him: "To Rome to be crucified again." Peter then realized that it was his duty to be martyred for Christ. He returned to Rome, but because he did not consider himself worthy to die as his master, he insisted that he be crucified upside down.[18] The location of Peter's encounter with Our Lord on the Appian Way became the site of a church that ranked among the most popular destinations in Rome for medieval pilgrims, in part because it contained what was believed to be the footprints Christ made when he met St. Peter. But it was the visit of one man centuries later that would immortalize Peter's question. Henryk Sienkiewicz (1846–1916) received the idea for his Nobel prize-winning novel *Quo Vadis* when a friend took him to the church in the late 1800s.

**Holy Smoke.** It is possible that this once-popular exclamation has its origins in Catholic practice. Two well-known Catholic uses of smoke could have easily inspired the phrase: incense and the election of a new pope. **Incense** is a treasured part of the Church's liturgical heritage that is prefigured not only in the Temple worship of the Old Testament but in the widespread belief held by several different world cultures that incense betokens the divine. (Note that the pagan Magi who adored the infant Jesus offered him frankincense, a gesture that is traditionally interpreted as a confession of his divinity; similarly, gold is seen as a confession of his kingship and myrrh a confession of his crucifixion and burial.) When used during the sacrifice of the Mass, incense represents the prayers of the faithful wafting up to God; the coal on which the incense burns signifies their hearts aglow with the Holy Spirit; and the thurible or censer from which it burns may be seen as a symbol of the Church, guided by the firm hand of Christ (represented by the priest or acolyte swinging the censer). Indeed, a link between incense and the Holy Sacrifice may be found in Psalm 140:2, "Let me prayer be directed as incense in thy sight; the lifting up of my hands, as an evening sacrifice." The evening sacrifice of the Levitical priesthood took place at around 3:00 P.M., the hour in which Christ, his hands lifted up and outstretched on the cross, completed the ultimate sacrifice.

The world is treated to another use of smoke at the election of a new pope. Ever since the Middle Ages, the pope has been elected by a vote of the

College of Cardinals. The ballot is taken in utmost secrecy, so much so that the cardinals are quarantined in the Sistine Chapel until they can agree on a new Supreme Pontiff. (Before, they were literally confined to the chapel; now, they are free to rest in an adjacent hostel that is swept for electronic devices and stripped of all means of communication with the outside world.) To let the people assembled in St. Peter's Square know how the votes were faring as well as to destroy the evidence of who voted for whom, there arose a custom of burning the ballot cards after they had been counted. If the ballot was unsuccessful, the cards were mixed with wet straw to produce **black smoke**; if successful, the cards were mixed with dry straw to produce **white smoke**. In practice, however, the straw did not always produce the desired color of smoke, and so chemicals were eventually included in the mixture. In April 2005 a new custom was added during the election of Pope Benedict XVI to eliminate any residual ambiguity: in addition to the white smoke, the bells of all the churches in Rome pealed simultaneously, making a gladsome noise for both the city and the world to hear.

**Mea Culpa.** One expression with an indisputably Catholic origin is the Latin *mea culpa,* meaning "my fault." The phrase is taken from the Tridentine or traditional Latin Mass, which was celebrated prior to Vatican II and continues to be celebrated in select churches around the world: "I confess . . . that I have sinned exceedingly in thought, word, and deed, through my fault, through my fault, through my most grievous fault"—*mea culpa, mea culpa, mea maxima culpa.* This frank, even brutal, acknowledgment of one's sinfulness brooks no rationalizations, excuses, or self-justification, and thus it serves as a model for critical self-evaluation and for taking complete responsibility for one's actions. (This same kind of honesty is also an important part of the sacrament of confession, in which a person confesses his sins to a priest and receives forgiveness from God. See John 20:21–23.) As a result, the phrase *mea culpa* has come to signify any public act of contrition or confession of wrongdoing. Incidentally, this powerful phrase is technically still in the Mass, but due to a mistranslation in the current English version, its presence is more difficult to discern.

**Silver Spoon.** The Mass is not the only celebration of a sacrament to have impacted our lexicon of expressions. The Roman Rite of Baptism consists of many memorable ceremonies, such as the anointing with chrism, the giving of a lit candle and a white garment, and, in its most traditional form, the three dramatic exorcisms performed over the candidate. These rituals evoke the awesome mystery of dying and being born again in Christ, a mystery that is recalled and renewed long after one's baptism through such simple acts as reciting the Creed and blessing oneself with holy water. But as we shall soon see with the word *gossip,* the customs surrounding baptism have also influenced the world on the other side of the church walls. An *apostle spoon* is a delicate spoon, usually silver, silver-plated, or pewter, with an image of Christ or one of his apostles at the end of the handle. It was customary for the godparents to present one of these spoons to the newly baptized infant as a gift, possibly because of an early tradition, long since defunct in the West, of giving the infant his or her first Holy Communion on a spoon immediately after he or she had been baptized. In any event, it was the conferral of these spoons that gave rise to the expression, "to be born with a silver spoon in one's mouth."

**Not One Iota.** Our expression for not yielding in the slightest amount may be based on Christ's promise that not one jot (*iota*) of the Law will pass away (see p. 172), but it may also come from the Council of Nicea in A.D. 325. The Council was convened to determine what Christians really believed about Jesus Christ: was he truly God, or was he merely godlike? The entire debate hinged on the Greek letter *iota* (comparable to our letter *i*): Christ was either of the selfsame substance as God (*homoousios*), or he was of a similar but distinct substance (*homoiousios*). After much deliberation, the Council professed Christ to be of the same substance (*homoousios*) as God the Father, enshrining their definition in the Nicene Creed that is now recited at Mass every Sunday. Thus, there is literally one iota of difference between orthodoxy and heresy, a fact which illustrates how the smallest deviation from the truth can lead to the greatest error.

## ANTI-CATHOLIC—
## OR AT LEAST A BIT IRREVERENT

*Whoever takes delight in the religion and worship of popery will be eternally lost in the world to come.*

—Martin Luther

*Down with Popery, Down with the Cross.*

—Banners carried by the mob that
burned down the Ursuline convent in
Charlestown, Massachusetts, 1834

In addition to inspiring generations of saints and sinners, Catholicism has also aroused a good deal of animosity, and this too has affected our linguistic world. Neologisms such as *popery* and *priestcraft* became a focal point of anti-Catholic hatred early on, equating Catholicism with conniving foreign autocracy or benighted superstition. On the other hand, there are a number of terms that can *barely* be labeled anti-Catholic, for they were either coined tongue-in-cheek or were developed with no intention of detracting from the Catholic faith *per se*. Both the playful and the pernicious are included here.

**Mackerel-Snapper.** Given that younger Catholics have no memories of the Friday abstinence from flesh meat (see p. 29), they would probably not know they were being insulted were someone to call them a "mackerel-snapper." A couple of generations ago, however, this American epithet for a Catholic would have elicited a much different reaction, for it was not meant as a compliment.

**Inquisition.** The formal definition of an inquisition is "the action or process of inquiring or searching into matters, especially for the purpose of finding out the truth or the facts concerning something." It is common, however, for the term to be used in a disparaging sense, as "an investigation that violates the privacy or rights of individuals" or "a rigorous, harsh interrogation."[19] This latter meaning comes from a common perception about the Spanish Inquisition, the institutional prosecution and punishment of heretics in Spain that lasted from 1478 to 1834. Though this troubled period is certainly not above reproach, riddled as it sometimes is with corruption and cruelty, the notoriety it has achieved is as much the result of myth as it is of history. This myth, known by historians today as the "Black Legend of Spain," was fueled by anti-Catholic and even racial bigotry as part of a British polemic against the dark-skinned "papists" of the Mediterranean.[20]

**Flat-Earther.** Our term for "one who stubbornly adheres to outmoded or discredited ideas"[21] similarly derives from a falsification of history that was indirectly anti-Catholic. Though the scenario of Christopher Columbus bravely defending his radical ideas of a spherical earth before the Spanish court and Inquisition was taught in American elementary schools for decades, the entire thing was invented out of whole cloth by the novelist Washington Irving in 1828. Not only did every educated Westerner know for centuries that the world was round, but ironically, Columbus was wrong about the earth's size, which he vastly underestimated. The calculations of the king's geographical advisors were much more accurate, which is why they correctly informed the king that Columbus would never reach Asia in the manner he proposed. Nonetheless, Irving's fiction about medieval belief in a flat earth proved quite useful to the polemic of anti-Catholic Americans like John William Draper and Andrew Dickson White, who used it as proof that clerical religion was inherently hostile to rationality.[22] (See pp. 15 and 124 for more on the Catholic use of Columbus).

**Legend.** And since we have mentioned the "Black Legend of Spain," it is appropriate also to mention that the word *legend* is another Catholic word that has now taken on somewhat negative overtones, at least if one considers the characterization of a story as inauthentic or historically unreliable negative.[23] *Legenda,* which in Latin simply means "what is to be read," was used in the Middle Ages to designate the stories of the lives of the saints that were read either the during the second nocturne at Matins (as part of the nocturnes, or nightly readings) or during the monks' "collation" (see pp. 55 and 25). The term was also popularized by the Dominican friar Jacobus de Voragine's collection of folklore about Mary and the saints called *The Golden Legend.* As some of these hagiographic accounts stretched credulity, a certain skepticism must have emerged that gradually changed the meaning of the term. This change, it should be noted, was not necessarily initiated by forces outside or antithetical to the Church. French clerics, for example, had an old saying for describing a fantastic prevaricator: "He lies like a second nocturne."

**Maudlin.** *Maudlin* is a variant of *Magdalen* (British spelling): in fact, as can be seen in the case of Oxford's Magdalen College, the English pronounce *magdalen* as *maudlin.* St. Mary Magdalene was the penitent former prostitute in the New Testament who was the first to see the risen Lord (John 20:1–18). Because she is traditionally believed to be the woman who washed Christ's feet with her tears and dried them with her hair (Luke 7:37–50, John 12:3) and because her crying is an important component of the Resurrection account in St. John's Gospel, Mary was portrayed in medieval art as weeping effusively. Despite the pathos of such scenes, the genre was probably overdone after a while, thus breeding a certain amount of cynicism. It was in this way that *magdalen* or *maudlin* became synonymous with "mawkish sentiment."[24]

**Macabre.** Our word for the gruesome, grim, and horrific also finds its origin in the art and life of the Middle Ages. A common subject in medieval art was the Dance of Death, or Danse Macabre, "an allegorical representation of Death leading men of all ranks and conditions in the dance to the grave."[25] The word *macabre* is most likely a corruption of *Maccabees,* two of the seven books of the Old Testament considered canonical by Catholics and Eastern Orthodox. The Books of the Maccabees may have been the inspiration for the grim pageant because II Maccabees 7 contains a vivid description of the gruesome torture and martyrdom of seven sons and their mother.[26]

**Gaudy.** Our adjective for tasteless ostentation comes from the rosary. Not unlike many rosaries today, the *Our Father* beads of the rosary in the Middle Ages were bigger and more extravagant than the *Hail Mary* beads. These large beads were called *gauds* or *gaudies* after the five Joyful Mysteries of the rosary, the Latin word for joy being *gaudium.* Chaucer, for example, describes the Prioress' rosary as a "peire of bedes, gauded al with grene," that is, a set of beads, with the gaudies in green.[27] Though the word also came to signify votive candles for Our Lady, it was the "gaudy's" association with brightly colored ornaments that helped give it its current meaning. For more on the rosary and rosary beads, see p. 80.

**Tawdry**. Another appellation for questionable taste that stems from the world of the sacred is tawdry. Ethelreda, or Audrey, was the daughter of King Anna of East Anglia who lived in the seventh century and who died from a growth in her throat which she claimed was punishment for wearing necklaces in her frivolous youth. To commemorate her feast on October 17, the people of Ely, East Anglia, held a fair which sold, among other things, a fine lace ribbon in honor of her death. Over time, the ribbon came to be known as "St. Audrey's lace," or tawdry lace for short. The lace was eventually deemed unfashionable, giving tawdry its current connotations.

**Cretin**. Putting this intriguing term for a moron or idiot in the anti-Catholic section of this chapter is only *prima facie* accurate. True, the word literally means "Christian," and true, the only Christians in Western Europe at the time were Catholic. But the moniker was meant as a positive affirmation rather than a slur. *Cretinism* refers to a species of mental and physical deficiencies that produce dwarflike deformities. Since the condition is caused by a lack of iodine, it was common in the "goiter belts" of the Alps, which are far removed from any natural iodine source. Thus, until that region began to receive regular shipments of iodine salt in the late nineteenth century, it had a disproportionately large number of dwarfs. Other Europeans called these hapless inhabitants *creitins,* which is Swiss patois for "Christians," in order to remind themselves that, appearances notwithstanding, these were fellow human beings made in the image and likeness of God. As the *Oxford English Dictionary* explains, "Christian" in the modern Romance languages (and sometimes in colloquial English) can mean "'human creature' as distinguished from the brutes, the sense being here that these beings are really human, though so deformed physically and mentally."[28]

**Dunce**. There is, however, another English word for a fool or dunderhead that has a genuine, if partial, anti-Catholic pedigree. The word *dunce* comes from one of medieval Catholicism's most influential and ostensibly erudite thinkers. Blessed John Duns Scotus (d. 1308) was a Franciscan priest and scholastic theologian whose textbooks on theology, philosophy, and logic were widely used throughout Europe, including Oxford University, where he had taught. Beginning in the sixteenth century, however, the works of the "Subtle Doctor" (as he was called) came under violent attack by Renaissance humanists as the embodiment of all that was wrong with medieval scholasticism. Again as the *Oxford English Dictionary* puts it, the philosophy of the "Dunsmen" came to be ridiculed as "a farrago of needless entities and useless distinctions," while their resistance to the new modes of scholarship gave them the reputation for being "dull and obstinate" and "impervious to new learning."[29] The early modern attack on Scotus's thought was no doubt unfair, though as a fan of Thomas Aquinas' work (which was in many ways eclipsed historically by Scotus's less impressive corpus), we cannot say that it was entirely unwarranted.

**The Gossip and the Godparent.** Not too many people today want to be known as a gossip, and rightly so. There was a time, however, when it was once an honor to be called a gossip, for the word originally referred to a godparent. *Gossip* is a contraction of the Middle English *god-sib* or *god-sibling* and was used to designate a child's sponsor at baptism. From this formal spiritual affinity the word was extended to any close friendship, especially to a woman's female friends who assisted her at childbirth. Once, however, the word came to be largely associated with a group of women, it came to take on—no doubt thanks to some rather chauvinist male logic—the prattling and rumor-mongering connotations that it has today.[30]

**Patter.** One English verb for chattering or jabbering is *patter.* The word derives from *Pater,* the first word of the *Our Father* in Latin, and refers to the "rapid and mechanical way" in which some Catholics are unfortunately wont to mumble their prayers.[31]

**Propaganda.** In 1622 Pope Gregory XV formed a special congregation to coordinate the vast missionary work that was taking place in the New World as well as the Church's efforts to regain the lands lost to Protestantism and the Great Schism. The congregation was officially entitled the Sacred Congregation for the Spread of the Christian Name, though it was better known as the Congregation for the Propagation of the Faith. The perfectly innocent Latin word used for *spread* and *propagation* in these titles is the Latin *propagando* or *propaganda,* meaning extension or enlargement. Over the next two centuries, however, *propaganda* became synonymous with the polemics of a dissident political sect, usually one disdained by the government. The politicizing trend continued in the twentieth century, when *propaganda* was often used to designate the brainwashing efforts of totalitarian (or, conversely, democratic capitalist, imperialist) regimes. Thus, a perfectly good word for evangelization has been tarred as a dirty word for tendentious political proselytizing.[32]

**Cavalier.** Though the English word *chivalrous* continues to have positive connotations (even if the idea itself is now subject to all sorts of criticism), there is one linguistic byproduct of medieval chivalry that has not fared so well. In today's parlance, a "cavalier" attitude suggests a posture that is flippant, disdainful, or haughty. Originally, however, the word—coming as it does from the Latin *caballarius,* or horseman—denoted the virtuous qualities of a Christian knight. Thus, to be cavalier was to be gallant and courtly and brave with perhaps just a bit of swagger.[33]

**Bloody Mary.** The name for a cocktail with vodka and tomato juice also happens to be the unflattering epithet for Mary Tudor, Queen of England from 1553 to 1558. After succeeding her Anglican brother Edward VI, Mary aggressively attempted to return England to the Catholic faith. Mary was well liked at the time, and her laws were generally merciful, but after a year on the throne, she and her advisors were convinced that the only way to restore peace to the realm was by persecuting its most powerful Protestant agitators. Thus, in four years, she ordered 277 people to be burned at the stake. In doing so Mary was enforcing not her own laws but those that had been enacted by Henry VIII years before, and she was living in a time when political sedition and religious heresy were virtually interchangeable terms.[34] Still, Mary can be rightly criticized for exceeding the limits of both canon law and justice then as well as now.[35] Whether it is fair to single her out among all of Britain's bloody monarchs in this manner, however, is another matter altogether.

**Bloody.** Since we are on the topic, one possible origin of this vulgar exclamation preferred by the British is "by Our Lady," an invocation of the Virgin Mary. The common contraction of this phrase, which we see in Shakespeare, is "byrlady," and in a letter from Jonathan Swift we see it used as an adjective: "it grows by'r Lady cold."[36] Other etymologists, however, prefer the theory that "bloody" refers to the noble blood of the aristocracy, and hence the phrase "bloody drunk" really means "as drunk as a lord."[37]

**Drat!** A word with a more certain religious origin is the once popular exclamation for "Confound it!" "Drat" is an abbreviation for "God rot" it, the English having first omitted the *G* and then the *o* in their haste to curse whatever it was they were cursing.[38]

**Lazy Laurence.** The nickname for one of the characters in Louisa May Alcott's *Little Women* has an older and more interesting derivation than is initially apparent. In English a "lazy Laurence" came to designate an indolent person, while the expression "Laurence bids wages" became a proverb for how idleness is an attractive temptation. Besides its alliterative qualities, the association of Laurence with laziness probably came about because the Feast of St. Lawrence falls on August 10, in the midst of the dog days of August, when industriousness is the last thing on anyone's mind (see p. 94 for another Laurentian link to the dog days). There may be, however, a more morbid reason for the unflattering designation. St. Laurence was the great Roman deacon who was martyred by being slowly roasted alive on a gridiron. Laurence not only bore his torment manfully, he is even said to have told his torturers, "You can turn me over. I am done on this side." According to a rather tasteless joke that once made the rounds in England, Laurence purportedly said this because he was too lazy to turn the grid himself.[39]

**Bedlam.** Our word for lunacy, uproar, and confusion is actually a contraction of the city of our Savior's birth. St. Mary of Bethlehem was a priory founded in 1247 near Bishopsgate, London, as the residence for the titular bishop of Bethlehem. In the fourteenth century, however, it became a hospital for the mentally ill, most likely the first of its kind. Following the English penchant for verbal abridgment, "Bethlehem" was shortened to "Bedlam," while "Bedlam" came to be synonymous with madness. The etymological identity of bedlam and Bethlehem has, in turn, provided rich fodder for preachers and journalists commenting on the current state of the Holy Land.[40]

**Hocus Pocus.** One theory about the origin of this popular phrase for magic acts is that it is a disparaging reference to the Catholic doctrine of transubstantiation. The Church teaches that when the priest pronounces the words of institution during the Mass, the bread and wine become the body, blood, soul, and divinity of Jesus Christ. In Latin, the words of institution for the sacred Host are *Hoc est enim corpus meum*—or in its corrupted form, "hocus pocus."[41]

**Sanctimonious.** *Sanctimonious* once described genuine holiness or sanctity, though today it betokens a hypocritical display of piety or a holier-than-thou attitude. One can see the transition from one meaning to the other in Shakespeare's plays, which use the word both ways. In *The Tempest*, for example, Prospero describes the ceremonies of the "full and holy rite" of matrimony as sanctimonious (IV.i.16); in *Measure for Measure*, on the other hand, Lucio says to another gentleman: "Thou conclud'st like the Sanctimonious Pirat, that went to sea with the ten Commandements, but scrap'd one out of the Table" (I.ii.7).[42] Perhaps the almost exclusively negative use of the word today reveals something about our current assumptions about the possibility of genuine holiness.

**The Bellarmine or Greybeard Jug.** A bellarmine is an earthenware or stoneware jug with a large belly and a narrow neck on which is featured the relief of a bearded man's face. Though early examples of this jug were made in the Germanic areas of Europe since the early 1500s, they were most likely redesigned and renamed in reaction to Robert Cardinal Bellarmine, S.J. (1542–1621), a Catholic saint and doctor of the Church. Bellarmine, a vigorous defender of the Catholic faith against the Protestant Reformers, became a professor at the University of Louvain in the Flemish region of Belgium in 1569. Flanders is a part of the Low Countries and was heavily influenced by the Reformation, and so Dutch and Flemish Protestants were not pleased to find such a formidable adversary on their own turf. To ridicule their opponent, they made jugs in Bellarmine's "burlesque likeness."[43]

**Jesuitical.** Given his reputation as a conniving Odysseus in a Roman collar, the Jesuit priest has long been the object of suspicion, accused of calamities ranging from the Fire of London in 1666 to the assassination of Abraham Lincoln. The clever *modus operandi* and brilliant proselytizing strategies of yesteryear's Society of Jesus have led to some interesting expressions: Germans, for example, occasionally refer to a poker face as a *Jesuit face*. In English this historic ill-regard has given us the word *Jesuitical,* defined as "deceitful, dissembling; practising equivocation, prevarication, or mental reservation of truth."[44]

**The Papacy.** Much of the hostility against or suspicion about Catholicism is concentrated on one man and one office: the pope and the papacy. The Petrine ministry, as the papacy is sometimes called, is frequently misunderstood by Catholics and non-Catholics. To give but one example, the doctrine of papal infallibility is often seen as a command that Catholics must take every single thing that the pope says as Gospel truth. In fact, papal infallibility only applies to the rare case when a pope solemnly defines a doctrine pertaining to faith or morals "from the seat" (*ex cathedra*) of St. Peter. Hence, the Catholic understanding of papal infallibility actually places a restraint on what the pope can say, subordinating his solemn, dogmatic statements to the fulfillment of several specific conditions, to the guidance of the Holy Spirit, and to the tradition that he is charged with defending.

The pope derives his important role of protecting the deposit of faith from Jesus Christ himself. During his earthly ministry, Christ not only established a hierarchy for his Church (notice that he treated the disciples differently from the crowds, the apostles differently from the disciples, and Peter, James, and John differently from the rest of the apostles), but he told St. Peter: "Thou art Peter, and upon this rock I will build my Church, and the gates of hell shall not prevail against it. And I will give to thee the keys of the kingdom of heaven. And whatsoever thou shalt bind upon earth, it shall be bound also in heaven: and whatsoever thou shalt loose on earth, it shall be loosed in heaven" (Matthew 16:18–19). This divine promise ensures the flourishing of both the Church and the papacy until the end of time, though it does not imply that every pope will make the best use of the keys entrusted to him. Consequently, the abuse of power by unscrupulous pontiffs during the Middle Ages and the Renaissance prompted not only a backlash against papal excesses, but an outright rejection of the Holy Father's authority. These reactions had a linguistic as well as a religious impact. Ever since William Tyndale coined **popery** to condemn the Roman Church,[45] the word has been a favorite slander against Catholics, along with **papist**, **popish**, and the like. Fortunately, the newest papologism in the English language, the **Popemobile**, has a positive if campy ring to it. Other terms, such as the following, were coined in a less benevolent spirit.

**Pontificate.** Pontificating literally refers to the act of fulfilling the office of a pope or bishop (the word *pontiff,* technically speaking, is not restricted to the pope, which is why the pope is often distinguished from his fellow bishops with the title, *Supreme Pontiff*). However, over time, the verb has also come to mean, "to behave or speak in a pompous or dogmatic manner,"[46] the assumption being, of course, that this is how a pontiff customarily acts.

**Papal Parts.** Various unflattering parts of animal bodies have also been christened with papal names. A **pope's eye** is the fat, round lymphotic gland in a leg of mutton, while a **pope's nose** is the plucked tail of a cooked turkey or other bird. The latter, however, may also be called a parson's nose—perhaps in the interest of ecumenical fairness.[47]

## POST-CATHOLIC

*Every important change in language goes back to a profound change in thought.*

—Allan Bloom[48]

By "post-Catholic" I am referring to those terms or concepts that were once essentially Catholic and that over time were subject to a modification of their meaning. Like many of the entries in this book, this devolution can be the product of time's erosive power or of the happenstance of history. On the other hand, grafting an alien meaning onto familiar Christian words *was* a deliberate strategy used by the intellectual architects of modernity and postmodernity, usually to cloak the novelty of their ideas and to displace the old religion from daily life. And by and large their strategy worked, so much so that even most Christians today are unaware of the silent revisions that were made to their self-understanding. Here are a few examples of our denuded latter-day diction.

**Charity.** One of the clearest examples of our contemporary loss of transcendence is the constriction of the Christian concept of *agape* or *caritas*—"charity." Today the word primarily refers to philanthropy, good deeds, or social work, and indeed someone who has charity is someone who also helps his or her neighbor. But the word once meant far more than that. St. Paul indicates that there is an important distinction between charity and altruism in his famous excursus on the former: "And if I should distribute all my goods to feed the poor, and if I should deliver my body to be burned, and have not charity, it profiteth me nothing" (I Corinthians 13:3). Clearly, if the two things—charity and giving to the poor—were synonymous, one would not be able to do one without the other, as Paul says one can.

What, then, is charity? Again St. Paul tells us that it "is poured forth in our hearts, by the Holy Ghost, who is given to us" (Romans 5:5). It is a divine gift from above, a virtue infused into our souls that enables us to love in a way that is not humanly possible. It is, among other things, the love that prompted Christ to forgive the men who crucified him (Luke 23:34), that enabled St. Stephen to forgive the men who stoned him (Acts 7:59), and that led St. Thomas More to tell his condemners how he hoped they would all meet "merrily together" one day in heaven. It animates but can never be reduced to a Christian's social outreach and altruistic activity. Starting in the early modern period, however, that is precisely what happened: the more that the transcendent and the vertical were eclipsed by secular, immanent, and horizontal norms of social progress, the more charity was relegated to the sphere of philanthropy.

**Compassion.** Another Catholic concept that has undergone a similar metamorphosis is compassion. *Compassio,* which literally means "suffering with," was used occasionally by Latin authors to signify fellow-feeling. With Christianity, however, the term was imbued with a new importance. One of the effects of the Incarnation was that for the first time God was entering into human suffering and experiencing it as a man. Not only does this transform the nature of suffering by binding God to our frail nature, it provides the ground for God's having true "compassion on our infirmities" (Hebrews 4:15).

Moreover, just as "the passion" came to signify the suffering of Christ at Golgotha, so too did "compassion" come to be closely associated with the Blessed Virgin Mary. Simeon the prophet had predicted that a sword would pierce Mary's soul (Luke 2:35), and that prediction came true as she watched her son tortured and killed on Good Friday. Mary has been subsequently viewed as a martyr for the pain she endured that day, a pain that is rightly and properly called her com-passion, for as St. Bernard of Clairvaux notes, she clearly shared her Son's suffering simply by seeing it.[49] That compassion is significant for us because Simeon had also predicted that from her pierced soul thoughts "out of many hearts" would be revealed (Luke 2:35). Hence in the traditional Roman calendar there were held two different feasts for the Seven Sorrows of the Blessed Virgin Mary, once on the Friday before Good Friday (known in some places as the Compassion of Our Lady) and once on the day after the Feast of the Holy Cross (September 15). Though the focus of each feast varied slightly, a common theme was the importance of aligning our feelings and dispositions with that of the Sorrowful Mother in order to enter more perfectly into the mystery of her Son's death and resurrection.

The main culprit behind the modern retooling of the concept is Jean-Jacques Rousseau. Rather than see compassion as a selfless, even painful habit of goodness, Rousseau praised it as a sweet and essentially onanistic feeling or emotion. Compassion for Rousseau brings with it a sense of elation that we are not the ones who are suffering. Those of us who have been properly reared in the sublimation of our emotions can then demonstrate our own superiority by helping the suffering person, an act that gives us even more pleasure and satisfaction and verifies our natural goodness. According to Rousseau, this is a very good thing: compassion is a selfish passion that counteracts other, more dangerous passions such as greed, cruelty, and avarice, which are particularly rampant in capitalist democracies.[50] Fellow-suffering becomes self-satisfaction, but a self-satisfaction that keeps us from cold-blooded acts of evil.

As Allan Bloom notes, "Rousseau's teaching on compassion fostered a revolution in democratic politics, one with which we live today."[51] Whether, for example, they are "feeling our pain" or qualifying their conservatism with that gentle adjective "compassionate," American politicians feel perpetually compelled to speak of their compassion in front of voters. Similarly, primary and secondary education have as one of their principal missions the fostering of a self-esteem (that is, self-satisfaction) that will produce compassionate human beings and tomorrow's community activists. Almost single-handedly Rousseau was able to make his retooled understanding of compassion the benchmark of what it means to be decent. Even Catholics seem to have lost the original sense of Christian compassion, at least if the liturgy is a reliable gauge. One of the Feasts of the Compassion of Our Lady was dropped from the calendar and the other truncated.

**Confession.** Rousseau has been behind more than one sea change in our self-understanding. *Confessio* in classical Latin referred to a somewhat reluctant acknowledgment of something, but this term took on new life in the mouths of Christian authors where, as see in St. Augustine's *Confessions,* it came to signify at least three things: 1) praise of God, 2) accusation of self, and 3) profession of faith.[52] Catholics themselves have been complicitous in the subsequent reduction of this word from its polyvalent richness by using it primarily in reference to the sacrament of penance. But it was Rousseau who added the voyeuristic, tell-all connotation to the word with his autobiography, the *Confessions.* Almost a parody of Augustine's eponymous work, Rousseau's *Confessions* unapologetically parades his life, warts and all (see p. 45 for more on the confession genre). The effect of Rousseau's masterful work was to further strip the concept of confession of its divine transcendence and infuse it with a titillating and unrepentant self-disclosure. It was such a change in meaning that led one scholar to remark: "it is obvious that our modern authors have deflowered a very great Christian word."[53]

**Hierarchy.** A canvassing of Rousseau's influence would be incomplete without a brief rumination on the shift in the meaning of *hierarchy.* The word, which in Greek literally means a holy order or ranking, was coined by the great Christian mystic Pseudo-Dionysius (fl. A.D. 500) to denote the differentiated panoply of celestial beings in heaven and the pecking order of God's ordained ministers on earth. Hierarchy, in other words, was a good thing, a great and sacred chain of being that linked all of us together, lifting up the downtrodden and compelling the mighty to be responsive to them. When animated by love, a hierarchy becomes the conduit for "a unifying and co-mingling power which moves the superior to provide for the subordinate, peer to be in communion with peer, and subordinate to return to the superior and the outstanding."[54] "The goal of a hierarchy," Pseudo-Dionysius concludes, "is to enable beings to be as like as possible to God and to be at one with him."[55] True hierarchy is a ladder to, rather than a ceiling obstructing, human excellence, holiness, and happiness.

It was Rousseau who most forcibly reduced our capacity to consider the value of a diverse symphony of unequal talent or rank by introducing the notion that *all* inequality is by its very nature unjust, the result being that virtually the only sins that are still recognized today are sins against equality (such as racism and sexism).[56] Because of this Rousseauian revolution, once innocent words designating structures of inequality are now used as accusations or epithets of contempt. **Hegemony**, which originally meant that the rule of those who *ought* to rule, is now used as a synonym for systemic oppression.[57] **Despot**, which simply meant "master," now means "tyrant," and even the word **master** is being slowly purged from the thesaurus of morally neutral words, a fact that can be seen from the recent reluctance of some realtors to call the main bedroom of a house the "master." Finally, the word *hierarchy* was secularized and then more or less vilified. When used today in reference to clerical ranks, it is more often than not with a note of suspicion and indignation.

**Charismatic.** Rousseau is not alone in manipulating Christian terminology. It was Max Weber, the father of modern social science, who turned an important Christian concept into a synonym for dynamic personal leadership. *Charisma,* which in Greek means "gift" or "grace," was used by St. Paul to designate such divinely endowed qualities as faith, healing, speaking in tongues, and interpretation of tongues.[58] Needless to say, as a gift that can only come from God, this was not something to be taken lightly. In Weber's parlance, however, charisma is one of three justifications for the legitimate exercise of power and violence, tradition and "rationality" being the other two. Men and women, Weber held, submitted to authority either because this was the way it had always been (traditional) or because the established rules seem reasonably ordained (rational) or because of the personal charm and draw of an individual leader (charismatic). By labeling this third kind of justification the way he did, Weber took the idea of God-given grace and turned it into a mesmerizing cult of personality. This not only enabled the likes of Adolf Hitler, John F. Kennedy, and Pope John Paul II to be lumped into the same category, it created "one of the most tiresome buzzwords in America."[59]

**Iconoclast.** From a vile and violent heretic to a celebrated rejector of the "Establishment," the iconoclast has made quite a journey. As noted above (see p. 49), iconoclasm was a fanatical heresy that led to the vandalism of churches, the destruction of priceless art, the suppression of monasteries, and the torture and death of priests, bishops, and layfolk. Now, however, thanks to the modern dichotomy between culture and counterculture and the association of iconoclasm with the latter, calling someone an iconoclast is generally seen as an edgy compliment.

**Cult.** It would no doubt raise more than a few eyebrows if the line from the first Eucharistic Prayer of the Mass, currently translated as "all those who hold and teach the Catholic faith,"[60] were instead rendered, "all cult-members of the orthodox, Catholic, and Apostolic Faith." Such a reaction would illustrate how far the operative word here, *cultor* or *cultus,* has fallen from its original meaning. *Cultus* in ecclesiastical Latin can either mean the worship that is due to God alone (as it does here in the canon of the Mass) or it can signify a more generic respect owed to someone else. Hence one occasionally hears of the "cult" of the Virgin Mary or of the saints, a harmless and age-old way of designating devotions to a specific saint, but one which confuses modern audiences nonetheless. The more flexible use of *cultus* in Church parlance, incidentally, is no different from "worship" in Elizabethan English, where "worship" can mean either divine worship in the strict sense or any kind of respect. Renaissance translations of the Bible, for example, include passages of non-idolatrous men "worshipping" their visitors,[61] and even today, the British still address certain dignitaries as "your worship."

*Cult* most likely took on its unflattering connotations as a result of the early modern period, which viewed all religion as the agent of intolerance, backwardness, and civil strife. The once meaningful distinction between a true divine *cultus,* which is founded by God and facilitates genuine human happiness, and the occult, which is steeped in superstition and warps the human mind and heart, was thus eliminated. *All* religion was now to be deemed "cultish." Thomas Hobbes, for instance, contends that all religion stems from an ignorance of natural causes and a fear of the invisible; the only difference between religion and superstition is that one is legal while the other is not.[62] From this crude nominalist paradigm, incapable as it is of making qualitative, objective distinctions between say, the Franciscans and al-Qaeda, it is not difficult to see how *cult* has arrived at its current meaning.

**Dogmatic.** Hobbes, a principal architect of modern political philosophy, also played a role in turning "dogma," a revealed truth defined by the Church, into a dirty word. In a letter to the Earl of Newcastle, Hobbes delineates two kinds of learning: "mathematical" learning, which proceeds from reason and is thus "free from controversy and dispute," and "dogmatical" learning, which proceeds from human passion and is contradictory and contentious.[63] The seemingly harmlessly distinction between the two belies Hobbes's breathless presupposition: dogma is by its nature opposed to reason and comes not from a source above us but from our lower drives and ambitions. From this dismissal of the very possibility that dogma can stem from a liberating and enlightening revelation from God, it is easy to see how the word *dogmatic* came to signify a narrow-minded will to power, the assertion of one's subjective opinion "in an authoritative, imperious, or arrogant manner."[64]

**Orientation.** If today you were to ask someone at a party about his or her orientation, you would most likely be committing a faux pas. The term originally, however, had nothing to do with sexual proclivities but stemmed from Christian dogmas about the Second Coming. All three of the great Western religions have a tradition of praying in a particular direction. The orthodox Jew faces Jerusalem and the Muslim faces Mecca, while the traditional Christian, rather than point himself toward any earthly city, faces eastward. This difference reflects Our Lord's statement that his kingdom is not of this world and cannot be associated with any particular regime or geographical territory (John 18:36), but it also underscores the eschatological hope in Christ's triumphant return to judge the living and the dead, a return that will come from the East (Matthew 24:27). And needless to say, the rising sun is an appropriate symbol of Christ, who is called in the New Testament the Dawn from on high (Luke 1:78). The early Church took its eastward praying quite seriously, which is why most traditional churches are built on an east-west axis: in the days when both the priest and the congregation prayed in the same direction, it enabled them both to be ready for the Lord's coming as they expectantly celebrated the sacrifice of the altar. In fact, some churches were not only aligned along an east-west axis, but they were built in such a way that the sanctuary pointed to that part of the horizon where the sun rises on the feast day of the church's titular saint. (This may also explain, incidentally, why a corpse was sometimes buried with its feet toward the east.) From this hallowed tradition of facing the East, or Orient, comes our term for a person's good bearing or position in life.

**Creativity.** *Creare* in classical Latin means to bring into being or give birth to, but in ecclesiastical Latin it signifies the ability of God to create something from nothing, that is, the doctrine of *creatio ex nihilo*. This ability, it must be stressed, is unique to God: while humans can *make* all sorts of things from preexistent materials, only God can truly *create* something out of nothing. That is, until Friedrich Nietzsche said otherwise. Nietzsche was horrified by the fact that modern society had "killed" God, and he wondered with dread what could ever replace the Divine Horizon that had given the West so much of its intellectual and cultural dynamism. His answer to the question came with his concept of the *Übermensch* or Overman, the superior human being who was above all conventional notions of morality and who would *create* his own set of values to replace those that had died along with the Christian God. The Overman, in other words, would be the new Creator of meaning for the world.[65]

Nietzsche, who was a radical critic of Rousseauian egalitarianism, depicted the Overman as an elite individual who would transcend the mindless herd. In one of the most bizarre twists in intellectual history, however, the "mindless herd" appropriated all of Nietzsche's language about the Overman and applied it to themselves, thanks in large part to the leftist populism of the 1960s. Now, not only God and the Overman, but everyone, from the brilliant artist to the thumb-sucking kindergartener, is encouraged to exercise his or her "creativity," for humanity's uniqueness is now seen not to lie in its ability to grasp reality as a rational animal nor in its ability to achieve moral excellence but in its ability to "create."[66] And in an even more bizarre twist, this New Left–Nietzschean language has been embraced (with due modifications, of course) by Pope John Paul II, who sometimes portrayed man as a co-creator with God.[67]

**Victim.** From a creature offered in sacrifice to a veritably privileged social status, the idea of victimhood has undergone substantial transformations. *Victim* first entered the English language as the term for an animal that was slain in solemn sacrifices and holocausts (whole burnt offerings) to God, chiefly in the Old Testament. The first time it appears in the Bible is in the mouth of Isaac on his way, the reader is led to think, to being sacrificed by Abraham: "My father. . . . behold fire and wood: where is the victim for the holocaust?" (Genesis 22:7). Abraham's riveting reply, "God will provide himself a victim for a holocaust, my son," foreshadows an additional and more specific sense of the term. God would not ultimately ask Abraham to sacrifice his son, but out of love for the world he would allow his own son to be sacrificed on the cross. God himself, in other words, provided the ultimate Victim, and thus "victim" was applied especially to Christ, the Lamb of God who was offered up on behalf of mankind.

"Victim" was first secularized, as far as we can tell, by Roger Coke when describing the plight of King Charles I (1600–1649), beheaded during the English civil war.[68] Now loosed from its religious mooring, a victim can be anyone who is treated unjustly or who has been the object of deception. Incidentally, this co-opting of a sacrificial concept is paralleled by similar changes to the meanings of **sacrifice** and **holocaust**, the former now applying to even the most banal selfless act while the latter now referring to the Third Reich's nefarious extermination campaign against the Jewish people.

It was Hegel, however, who not only continued the secularization of victimhood but elevated its position. In his Master-Slave dialectic, Hegel describes the Master as alienated from himself while the Slave, *because* he lives with the twin burdens of fear and work, is in a paradoxically better position of attaining "the truth of self-certainty": all that is required for the Slave's liberation is his becoming conscious of himself through his own fear and work.[69] Victimhood, in other words, establishes the conditions for a whole new self-actualization. Hegel's Master-Slave dialectic influenced both **Communist** and **Nazi** self-understanding (the former focusing on work as the means of liberation, the latter fear), but it also affected strains of democratic society. The **feminist** debt to Hegelian philosophy, for example, may be seen in the prominent place victimhood occupies in feminist theory, as does the emphasis placed on consciousness raising.[70]

**Epiphany.** Though *epiphany* in Greek simply means "manifestation," in the Catholic tradition it refers primarily to the manifestation of Christ's divinity to the Gentiles (as represented by the Magi, who came to adore him) and to the annual feast on January 6 commemorating this event. Though the term was on occasion used figuratively to describe any kind of disclosure or revelation, it was not until James Joyce introduced the notion into contemporary aesthetic discourse that its secular use became more common.[71] For Joyce, a cradle Catholic who left the Church in college, epiphany was not the manifestation of God to man but a sudden moment of spiritual insight that an artist experiences and then meticulously portrays. The artist, then, is "a priest of the eternal imagination, a revealer" who faithfully conveys what is there, no matter how humble or unpleasant.[72] Though Joyce's theory bears interesting resemblances to the Christian notion of epiphany, its essential displacement of God in the act of manifestation puts it at odds with an orthodox understanding of human cognition and art. It also led, ironically, to the vulgarization of the term so that it is no longer unusual to hear someone who has suddenly had an idea describe it as an epiphany. We say ironic because Joyce believed in a merit-based elitism of art; not everyone could be a high priest of the imagination. Indeed, the Catholic Church's inclusiviseness was one of the reasons why Joyce loathed it: he is reputed to have defined disdainfully Catholicism as, "Here comes everybody!"

**Talent.** A *talanton* in Greek or *talentum* in Latin was a weight or sum of money, much like a pound in Great Britain. Hence, in the Gospel of Matthew's Parable of the Talents (25:14–30), Our Lord speaks of a man who gave various talents to three servants, "every one according to his proper ability" (25:15). The first two servants took their talents—each one being worth fifteen years of a laborer's wages—and made them profitable while the third servant did nothing with the talent he received. The moral of the story—making good use of what God has given us—was so powerful that it influenced the meaning of "talent," which came to signify "a power or ability of mind body viewed as something divinely entrusted to a person for use and improvement."[73] After time, however, the sense of divine gratitude and stewardship was dropped, leading to the current sense of the word as any kind of native aptitude.

# BIBLICAL NAMES
# AND EXPRESSIONS

✠

The Bible is obviously something to which all Christians lay equal claim, and the profound impact of the majestic King James translation on our language is well-documented.[1] Even the errors of the "Authorized Version," as it is known by many Protestant Christians, have had a charming effect on the English tongue: the phrase, "by the skin of one's teeth," for example, comes from a mistranslation of Job 19:20.

Nonetheless, a section on biblical names and expressions in a book on Catholic origins should be included for two reasons. First, it may be reasonably argued that the canon of Sacred Scripture exists through the instrumentality of the Catholic Church. There would have been no Bible for William Tyndale or Martin Luther to translate into the vernacular had not the Church recognized early on which books were divinely inspired and which were not. Hence St. Augustine of Hippo (354–430), who cherished every syllable of Holy Writ and who lovingly referred to the Scriptures as "all honeyed with the honey of heaven," nevertheless writes, "I would not believe in the Gospel if the authority of the Catholic Church did not determine me to."[2]

Second, and more specifically, though the traditional Catholic English translation of the Bible, the so-called Douay-Rheims, tends to be compared unfavorably with the more mellifluous Protestant King James version, there is a possibility that much of the King James was actually influenced by the

Douay-Rheims. As church historian Reverend Samuel McComb notes, despite all the stylistic deficiencies of the first edition of the Douay-Rheims, "King James's translators found in it a rich mine from which they drew abundantly, to the great betterment of their own work—and this though it was not specified in the Rules drawn up for their guidance." McComb goes on to conclude that "there is scarcely a page of the Revised New Testament that, through the Authorised Version [the King James], does not bear the marks of Roman Catholic scholarship."[3]

Below, then, are a sampling of the biblical idioms that have found their way into everyday English. The historic popularity of these expressions is astonishing. But the influence of the Bible on our daily discourse is even more surprising when we consider the enormous resistance to these humble texts from the classically educated men and women of antiquity. St. Jerome and St. Augustine, for example, were initially repulsed by Christianity because the direct and simple prose of its Bible lacked the syntactical and rhetorical sophistication of ancient Greek and Roman literature. As Augustine confesses: "When I first read those Scriptures . . . they seemed to me unworthy to be compared with the majesty of Cicero. My conceit was repelled by their simplicity."[4] Once eloquence could be recognized in modesty as well as verbal ornament, however, the Bible went from being perceived as a churlish and unlettered set of writings to the high watermark of poetic beauty.

**Apple of the Eye.** This charming expression for the eye's pupil that appears several times in the Renaissance translations of the Bible is actually the product of English idiom rather than the original biblical languages, which do not use the word *apple* to designate a pupil. Moreover, when the phrase is used in the Old Testament, it is almost always meant to signify something precious that requires careful attention and protection. Over time, however, the "apple of my eye" has also come to signify something or someone that is supremely important or dear, as in Stevie Wonder's "You Are the Sunshine of My Life."[5]

**Blind Leading the Blind.** "Let them alone: they are blind, and leaders of the blind. And if the blind lead the blind, both will fall into the pit" (Matthew 15:14, Luke 6:39). Christ's unflattering description of the Pharisees and their disciples has been applied to any number of inept leaders and their hapless subjects.[6] The expression has also given rise to clever variations, sometimes unintentionally. We once heard a lector at a Mass mispronounce the phrase from the pulpit, with the result that the congregation was warned of the perils of the "bland leading the bland." The liturgical planners had made that Mass as trendy as possible, but to many of us in the pews, the lector's slip was providentially accurate.

**Breaking Bread.** Though "breaking bread" is often used today for dining together, it takes on a far more special meaning in the New Testament, where it functions as a synonym for the celebration of the Eucharist (Acts 20:7, I Corinthians 10:16). Aside from the Miracle of the Loaves (Matthew 14:19) and the Last Supper accounts which mention Our Lord breaking the bread that he blessed (Matthew 26:26, Mark 14:22, Luke 22:19), the first time we see the expression come into its own is the evening after the Resurrection, when the two disciples on the road to Emmaus recognize the stranger accompanying them as the risen Lord only after he breaks bread. Upon returning to Jerusalem they told the apostles "what things were done in the way; and how they knew [Jesus] in the breaking of the bread" (Luke 24:35). The scene is an important one, as it also suggests that it is primarily through the Eucharist that we encounter the resurrected Christ.

Incidentally, one wonders if the association between bread and Jesus Christ explains the origins of a euphemism for pregnancy. Because Christ is the Bread of Life (John 6:35), his mother's womb was sometimes likened to an oven, as in the old English poem which begins, "In virgyne Mary this brede was bake."[7] From here it would be a short leap to thinking of the "blessed state of expectancy," as the Carmelite sisters call it in their prayers for pregnant mothers, as having "**a bun in the oven**."

**Bricks without Straw.** Straw is an essential element in the traditional brick-making process, and so when the Pharoah commanded the Hebrew slaves to make bricks without straw (Exodus 5:6–19), he was effectively punishing them with an impossible task. Making bricks without straw has gone on to become a proverb either for a ruler's sadistic policy-making or for successfully doing the impossible.[8]

**A Camel Through the Eye of a Needle.** No discussion of the moral danger of wealth would be complete without Christ's declaration, "And again I say to you: It is easier for a camel to pass through the eye of a needle, than for a rich man to enter into the kingdom of heaven" (Matthew 19:24, Mark 10:25, Luke 18:25). The meaning of the needle's eye has been the subject of some debate. One theory is that the eye in question was really a low gate in one of the walls of Jerusalem: for a camel laden with goods to pass through, it had to be stripped of the cargo on its back, just as we must strip ourselves of materialism to enter Heaven. Though this exegesis continues to be popular among preachers and homilists, it unfortunately has no grounding in historical fact. As with other passages from the Sermon on the Mount, Christ no doubt intended the outrageous impossibility of the scenario to shock his listeners, which is exactly what it did (see Matthew 19:25). The expression continues to hold the same arresting value then as it did now, though recent usages can cleverly invert its original meaning. In Margaret Mitchell's *Gone*

*With the Wind,* Rhett Butler responds to Scarlett's assurances about the social power of money by saying, "Not [with] Southerners. It's harder for speculators' money to get into the best parlours than for the camel to go through the needle's eye."[9]

**My Cup Runneth Over.** This beautiful line of gratitude in response to God's abundant generosity comes from the King James translation of Psalm 23:5. In general it signifies any kind of bounty, though it has also been used playfully for athletic competitions which have a cup as their prize and lubriciously for a woman's frontal endowment. Perhaps such a titillating use of the Good Book is what Izaak Walton, the pious author of *The Compleat Angler,* had in mind when he said he did not like fellows who used "Scripture jests."[10]

**Deep Calleth unto Deep.** According to St. Augustine, in this fetching phrase from Psalm 41:8 (or in the King James, 42:7), "deep" refers to the human heart—"for what," he opines, "is more profound than that abyss?" The entire phrase would then mean, "man calls to man." Elsewhere in his writings, however, Augustine likens the two deeps to the waters that are above the firmament in Genesis 1:6–7 and the waters that are below it: thus, the waters above the firmament allegorically represent the gifts of the Holy Spirit that "call" to the waters below, the present age groaning and thirsting for completion.[11] The phrase is currently used in several different ways, the idea of like attracting like perhaps being the most common.

**East of Eden.** Admirers of John Steinbeck—or for that matter, James Dean—will recognize this phrase as the title of the popular book and movie that loosely recapitulate the theme of miserable wandering that lies at the root of original biblical verse. When Adam and Eve were expelled from Paradise and a Cherub with a flaming sword was placed at its entrance (Genesis 3:24), no mention was made in which direction they went. After Cain murdered his brother, however, God commanded him to be a wanderer and a vagabond, with the result that he went forth into the land of Nod, east of Eden (Genesis 4:16).[12] The phrase has since come to signify, to quote the prayer, "Haily, Holy Queen," our lives as "poor banished children of Eve . . . mourning and weeping in this valley of tears."

**Every Jot and Tittle.** A catchy term for minute thoroughness was coined by Our Lord in the Sermon on the Mount: "For amen I say unto you, till heaven and earth pass, one jot, or one tittle shall not pass of the law, till all be fulfilled." (Matthew 5:18; cf. Luke 16:17). A jot (*yod*) is the smallest letter of the Hebrew alphabet, while a tittle is a tiny diacritical mark placed above a letter, similar to the point placed over a lowercase "i."[13] The biblical reference emphasizes the New Covenant's fulfillment not just of the letter of the Law but of the smallest letter of the Law.

**An Eye for an Eye.** A popular expression for vengeance and retribution is taken from the Law given by God to Moses: "Eye for eye, tooth for tooth, hand for hand, foot for foot, burning for burning, wound for wound, stripe for stripe" (Exodus 21:24).[14] A closer examination of the sacred text, however, reveals a somewhat counterintuitive teaching, namely, that retributive justice requires a *curbing* of the desire for vengeance rather than a satiation of it. As St. Augustine notes, when we are wronged, our desire is not simply to get back what was taken back from us, but to get back more than what was taken; thus, getting only one eye in return for an eye taken imposes a restraint on our impulse for revenge.[15] St. John Chrysostom makes a similar observation when he notes that the *lex talionis,* as it is sometimes called, "drops a seed of great restraint," and that anyone who accuses the Old Law of being retaliatory is "very unskillful in the wisdom that becomes a legislator." As Chrysostom cleverly remarks, God "commanded this, not that we might strike out one another's eyes, but that we might keep our hands to ourselves."[16] The Church Fathers' exegesis is confirmed when one compares the one-to-one ratio of the Mosaic law with the earlier Song of Lamech, which records that within a few generations after the Fall, vendettas had multiplied from seven lives taken in exchange for one to seventy lives (Genesis 4:24). Seen in this light, the Sermon on the Mount's call to replace "an eye for an eye" with "turning the other cheek" is not a condemnation of the restraining principles of justice as they are articulated in the Mosaic law but an admonition for mercy and forgiveness to take greater precedence in one's life (see p. 180).

**Fatted Calf.** In what is arguably the most powerful parable of repentance and forgiveness in the Gospels, the father of the Prodigal Son who has come home instructs his servants: "Bring forth quickly the first robe, and put it on him, and put a ring on his hand, and shoes on his feet: And bring hither the fatted calf, and kill it, and let us eat and make merry: Because this my son was dead, and is come to life again: was lost, and is found" (Luke 15:22–24). Aside from the immediate meaning of eternal reward in exchange for genuine contrition and repentance, "killing the fatted calf" has come to signify the unleashing of merriment on a rare and special occasion.

**Feet of Clay.** The English expression, *feet of clay,* is based on a dream recorded in the Book of Daniel of a giant statue with a head made out of gold, a chest and arms made out of silver, a torso made out of brass, legs made out of iron, and feet made "part of iron and part of clay" (2:33). Because of this unstable combination, the statue is toppled and destroyed by a stone thrown at its feet. Daniel goes on to interpret the dream as referring to the various empires during and after the reign of King Nebuchadnezzar. Later commentators have speculated the gold represents Nebuchadnezzar's Babylonian Empire, the silver the Mede Empire, the brass the Persian Empire, and the iron and clay the Hellenistic Empire of Alexander the Great, which quickly broke apart after his death into smaller polities (for example, the Syrian and Egyptian).[17] Another political interpretation of the feet of iron and clay is the Roman Empire with its bloody civil wars. Regardless of the historical referent Daniel had in mind, the term *feet of clay* today betokens vulnerability despite the appearance of overwhelming strength. It is reputed to have been used first by Lord Byron in his "Ode to Napoleon Bonaparte."

**Fire and Brimstone.** "Brimstone" is an old word for sulfur, which along with fire fell from heaven onto the nefarious twin cities of Sodom and Gomorrah for their crimes against nature (Genesis 19:24). The phrase is also used to terrifying effect in the Book of the Apocalypse to describe the "second death" that evildoers will suffer at the Last Judgment when they are cast into a fiery lask of burning sulfur (Revelation 19:20, 20:9, 21:8). Over time, however, the phrase has been co-opted to designate, usually in an unflattering way, any preaching that lays heavy emphasis on damnation and judgment.[18]

**Flesh Pots of Egypt.** Not long after God's dramatic liberation of the Hebrews from the yoke of Egyptian slavery, "all the congregation of the children of Israel murmured against Moses and Aaron in the wilderness. And the children of Israel said to them: 'Would to God we had died by the hand of the Lord in the land of Egypt, when we sat over the flesh pots, and ate bread to the full'" (Exodus 16:2–3). That piquant term, *flesh pots,* was first used in William Coverdale's translation and later appeared in the King James and Douay-Rheims Bibles. Since meat was a rarity among the poor, the former slaves' murmuring for flesh pots amounts to a desire for self-indulgence and luxury. The phrase *flesh pots* has thus come to betoken living high on the hog, usually in a somewhat squalid way. After all, preferring well-fed bondage to a lean freedom won by the hand of God is not exactly the mark of a grateful or noble spirit.

**Fly in the Ointment.** Our expression for "a drawback, especially one that was not at first apparent," most likely comes from a curious verse in the Book of Ecclesiastes.[19] In the Douay-Rheims we read, "Dying flies spoil the sweetness of the ointment"; in the King James it is translated, "Dead flies cause the ointment of the apothecary to send forth a stinking savour" (10:1). The meaning of the original verse is somewhat obscure, but the context suggests that a comparison is being made between "small and short-lived folly," which ruins "wisdom and glory," and flies, which ruin a fragrant ointment (see Ecclesiastes 10:2).

**Forbidden Fruit.** The popular term for desiring what we cannot have simply because we cannot have it is not found in the Bible but is inspired by the Genesis account of the Fall. After the serpent told Eve that she would be like a god if she ate the fruit proscribed by God, she "saw that the tree was good to eat, and fair to the eyes, and delightful to behold," and so she ate it (Genesis 3:6). Though the forbidden fruit concept is certainly valid and though the Bible evinces a keen awareness of this disordered psychology, correlating this notion with the tree of knowledge of good and evil is a some-what misleading characterization of the Fall. According to the sacred text, Eve was motivated either by the devil's promise of divinity (which she be-lieved [I Timothy 2:14]) or by the fair appearance of the fruit, but not, it would seem, by the simple fact that it was forbidden. The Book of Proverbs provides a better and more vivid illustration of the phenomenon in question:

> A foolish woman and clamorous, and full of allurements, and knowing nothing at all, sat at the door of her house, upon a seat, in a high place of the city, to call them that pass by the way . . . And to the fool she said: "Stolen waters are sweeter, and hidden bread is more pleasant." And he did not know that giants are there, and that her guests are in the depths of hell (9:13–18).

Needless to say, it is difficult to imagine a more vigorous condemnation of the foolish woman's line of thought, especially given the company she keeps: the damned souls of Hell along with the giants, the wicked race doomed to die in the Flood (Genesis 6:4). Perhaps the new tagword for forbidden fruit should be the *stolen waters* or *hidden bread* syndrome.

**Gird Up Thy Loins.** In the Old Testament, girding up one's loins refers to the practice of cinching up one's long and flowing garments so that they will not hinder one's movement or become soiled when walking, working, or fighting. Metaphorically the expression signifies a state of readiness to do battle and was used as such by Our Lord, St. Paul, and St. Peter.[20]

**How Are the Mighty Fallen.** An exclamation that today is more often than not used ironically or playfully was originally made with heartwrench-ing sincerity. Despite being persecuted by Saul, David could only weep over the defeat of Israel's first king and of his virtuous son Jonathan: "Ye daugh-ters of Israel, weep over Saul, who clothed you in scarlet, with other delights, who put on ornaments of gold upon your apparel. How are the mighty fallen in the midst of the battle! O Jonathan, thou wast slain in thine high places" (II Samuel 1:25, KJV). The Douay-Rheims translation is similar, using the word *valiant* instead of *mighty,* and it records a similar lament over the death of Judas Maccabeus, "How is the mighty man fallen, that saved the people of Is-rael!" (I Maccabees 9:21). In the Latin the David passage inspired one of the most poignant and best examples of Gregorian chant: the "Montes Gelboe." The antiphon for the First Vespers of the fifth Sunday after Pentecost, the "Montes Gelboe" consists of David's lament as it is recorded in II Samuel (II

Kings in the Vulgate/Douay-Rheims). The biblical text is beautifully enhanced and expanded by the sweet sorrow of the chant.

**House Divided.** When the Pharisees accused Jesus of exorcizing demons "by Beelzebub," Jesus refuted the accusation by reminding them that a "city or house divided against itself shall not stand" (Matthew 12:25, Mark 3:25). The political image Christ employed has, appropriately enough, been popular in political disputation. The most famous example in American politics is Abraham Lincoln's "House Divided" Speech, in which he declared that "this government cannot endure permanently half slave and half free."[21] When Judge Stephen Douglas challenged his position, Lincoln wryly responded, "I would like to know if it is his opinion that a house divided against itself *can stand.* If he does, then there is a question of veracity, not between him and me, but between [Judge Douglas] and an authority of a somewhat higher character."[22]

**Jeremiad.** In the book bearing his name, the prophet Jeremiah gloomily predicts that the remnants of Jeuralem will be "a reproach, and a byword, and a proverb" for what happens when one forsakes the Lord God (24:9). Not inappropriately, Jeremiah has in turn become a byword in his own right. A *Jeremiah* denotes "a person given to lamentation or woeful complaining," while a *jeremiad* refers to any speech or lament evocative of Jeremiah's doleful tones and dismal forecasts.[23] Both terms are generally employed more as a complaint than a compliment, thus obliquely confirming another famous biblical verse, that a prophet is never welcome in his own country.

**Jezebel.** Another biblical figure whose name has become proverbial is Jezebel—the wife of King Ahab, the monarch who effectively introduced idolatry into the Kingdom of Israel, the bitter enemy of the prophet Elijah, and the shrewd murderer of Naboth. As a result of her wickedness, God foretold through Elijah that "the dogs shall eat Jezabel [*sic*] in the field of Jezrahel" (III Kings 21:23). After her husband's forces were defeated, the prophecy was fulfilled. Jezebel was thrown from the window of a tower, and by the time the Israelites arrived to bury her, nothing was left but "but the skull, and the feet, and the extremities of her hands" (IV Kings 9:35; see p. 63 for how the Jesuits portrayed this on stage.) Jezebel's name was already a byword before the end of the biblical age: the Book of the Apocalypse, or Revelation, uses the name to signify a seductress who leads the faithful away from the true God to the adulterous bed of idols (2:20). Today the name is used allusively to designate an evil woman or a woman who "paints her face."[24]

**Job.** "I am turned into the song" of foolish and base men," Job laments; "I am become their byword" (Job 30:9, 8). The tribulations and patience of Job, already renowned during the biblical period,[25] went on to help and inspire countless believers wrestle with the enigma of suffering and evil. Job's misery has also inspired a number of additions to our daily discourse. *Job* has become a byword for either extreme destitution or patience, while phrases like *Job's cat* or *Job's turkey* are jocular references to poverty.[26]

**Kick against the Pricks.** When Saul/Paul is thrown off his horse on the road to Damascus, he hears a voice tell him, "I am Jesus whom thou persecutest: it is hard for thee to kick against the pricks" (Acts 9:4–5, KJV; cf. 28:14). A prick is a sharp stick used to motivate unwilling animals, and thus "kicking against the goads or spurs is figurative for an unruly horse or beast of burden doomed to painfully unsuccessful rebellion."[27] In modern times the expression is thus used to signify fatalistic resignation or stoic surrender. The vulgar meaning that the word *prick* has taken on in recent decades may, however, account for a decline in the expression's use. In order to reverse this trend, perhaps we should instead start using the Douay-Rheims translation, "It is hard for thee to kick against the goad."[28]

**A Leopard's Spots.** When the word of the Lord came to the prophet Jeremiah, it asked him: "Can the Ethiopian change his skin, or the leopard his spots? Then may ye also do good, that are accustomed to do evil" (Jeremiah 13:23, KJV). In the early Church the spots were taken to be symbolic of sins, indelibly inscribed on our souls. (That God *does* nevertheless remove our spots through grace attests to his miraculous ability to change the unchangeable.) It is because of this allegorical interpretation that medieval art often portrayed a leopard in the Garden of Eden along with Adam and Eve.[29]

**The Letter Killeth, but the Spirit Quickeneth.** One of St. Paul's most famous lines, immortalized in English in the King James translation, "the letter killeth, but the spirit giveth life" (II Corinthians 3:6), has been subject to a number of misinterpretations and abuses. It is common to hear the verse quoted in support of the idea that it is not necessary to obey the law as long as one is following its "spirit": indeed, according to this line of thought, any attempt to follow civil or ecclesiastical law assiduously is viewed as Pharisaicism. Besides involving a misleading assessment of the Pharisees (who were hypocritical innovators, not authentic lovers of tradition),[30] this antinomian reading of the verse belies a more fascinating possibility. According to St. Augustine and many others, the letter in question is the tendency to read Scripture in a narrow or fundamentalist manner while the spirit betokens the "typological" or allegorical method of reading everything in the Bible as a "type" or symbol of a deeper, spiritual reality. Thus, the "letter" of the sacred text is good, true, and worthy of close study, but its real value is only disclosed in light of the greater things to which it points. Abraham's sacrifice of Isaac, for example, can and should be studied in its own right, but its full significance becomes apparent only when it is seen as a foreshadowing of the passion of God's only-begotten Son.[31] Paul's contrast between letter and spirit is not so much a contrast between scrupulous and lackadaisical as it is a hermeneutical foundation for reading the Bible in a nuanced, polysemous or multi-leveled manner.

**Man of Sorrows.** Fans of the movie *O Brother, Where Art Thou?* will recognize this epithet in the Soggy Bottom Boys' hit, "Man of Constant Sorrow." Given that the movie is a loose adaptation of Homer's *Odyssey,* it is appropriate that this song be the jewel of the group's repertoire, since the name Odysseus means, "man of pain or suffering." The expression itself, however, comes not from classical literature but from the Bible. The prophet Isaiah describes the Suffering Servant, the Messiah who will be offered up for the sins of the people, as "despised, and the most abject of men, a man of sorrows, and acquainted with infirmity" (53:3). Christians have traditionally seen these passages to be a poignant prediction of the passion of the Christ.

**My Brother's Keeper.** In one of the most blatant acts of insolence against God recorded in the Bible, when God asks Cain where Abel is, Cain retorts, "I know not: am I my brother's keeper?" (Genesis 4:9). The irony, of course, is that Cain should have acted as his brother's keeper rather than as his murderer. Cain's remark is thus used ironically to underscore our responsibility for each other or to criticize those who act in a mercenary manner.

**No Respecter of Persons.** When St. Peter declared to Cornelius that "God is not a respecter of persons" (Acts 10:34), he was invoking one of the key foundational principles of justice in the Judeo-Christian tradition. The Mosaic Law is the first to make this explicit: "Thou shalt not do that which is unjust, nor judge unjustly. Respect not the person of the poor, nor honour the countenance of the mighty. But judge thy neighbour according to justice."[32] Since *respecting* means looking upon (and being influenced by what one sees) and *person* the rank or position of an individual, the basic idea is that neither God nor Justice takes into account matters extraneous or detrimental to making a fair and equitable judgment. The concept is enshrined in the legal principle of "equality under the law" and is allegorized in our images of a blindfolded Lady Justice, which did not originate until the sixteenth century and may thus be the result of a Christian influence.[33] It is also a useful biblical corrective to Marxist misreadings of Catholic social justice teachings about what is often called the preferential option for the poor. For another juridical image from the Bible, see p. 181.

**The Noonday Devil.** One of the few conspicuous examples of the Douay-Rheims Bible directly affecting English idiom is the fetching phrase, *noonday devil.* When the psalmist addresses the man who abides "under the protection of the God of Jacob" (Psalm 90:1), he mentions four things that he will not fear: "Thou shalt not be afraid of the terror of the night, of the arrow that flieth in the day, of the business that walketh about in the dark, of invasion, or of the noonday devil" (90:5–6). In these verses, the Douay-Rheims is merely remaining faithful to the Latin Vulgate, which in turn is remaining faithful to the Greek Septuagint, the translation of the Old Testament made during the second and third centuries before the birth of Christ. (The King James Bible, on the other hand, was based on the Masoretic Hebrew text.) But what exactly is a "noonday devil"? According to one traditional interpretation, it is an allegory for sloth or *acedia:* just as one grows sluggish under the hot midday sun and yearns for a siesta, so too does the vice of sloth make one grow apathetic to a lively love of the Good. The concept was featured prominently in medieval literature but faded after the introduction of the King James Bible in 1611. It did, however, continue to be used by English Catholics such as Alexander Pope,[34] and, as can be seen by recent articles such as "Fighting the Noonday Devil," it still inspires some Catholic reflection.[35] Incidentally, in France the phrase *le démon de midi* has taken on an additional meaning; it is the equivalent of our "midlife crisis."

**Out of the Mouth of Babes.** Our phrase for children who "speak the truth which adults or the most sophisticated either do not see or lack the candor to state" is based on the King James translation of Psalm 8:2, "Out of the mouth of babes and suckling thou hast ordained strength."[36] Ironically, the Douay-Rheims translation puts a strong emphasis on speech and thus better evokes the popular use of the verse: "Out of the mouth of infants and of sucklings thou hast perfected praise" (Psalm 8:3). The psalmist's remark is often juxtaposed with Christ's words in Matthew 11:25: "I confess to thee, O Father, Lord of heaven and earth, because thou hast hid these things from the wise and prudent, and hast revealed them to the little ones."

**Pearls Before Swine.** "Give not that which is holy to dogs; neither cast ye your pearls before swine, lest perhaps they trample them under their feet, and turning upon you, they tear you" (Matthew 7:6). Christ's admonition in the Sermon on the Mount is traditionally interpreted to refer to the caution that must be exercised in communicating sacred truths that not every listener is necessarily ready to hear and in safeguarding those truths from a hostile audience.[37] The phrase has since become synonymous with wasting something precious on an unworthy recipient, though it has also been used in more creative ways. According to a popular story, the devilishly witty essayist Dorothy Parker (1893–1967) and Clare Boothe Luce—another literary luminary with whom Parker did not get along—met in front of a door at the same time. Luce stepped aside, murmuring, "Age before beauty." Parker then went in, riposting as she went by, "Pearls before swine."

**Pearl of Great Price.** One of Christ's parables likens the Kingdom of Heaven to a merchant who, "when he had found one pearl of great price, went his way, and sold all that he had, and bought it" (Matthew 13:46). The image nicely illustrates how possessing eternal happiness in the Beatific Vision is that for which all else should be done, though the pearl has also come to take on additional associations. For St. Augustine, the pearl represents either Christ himself or the virtue of charity, while St. Jerome treats the pearl as a symbol of the monastic or contemplative life. The latter interpretation went on to inspire medieval poetry's portrayal of the pearl as representative of purity or chastity, a motif that continued into modern literature. When, for example, Hester Prynne in *The Scarlet Letter* names her bastard daughter "Pearl," it is with a note of bitter irony.[38]

**The Spirit Is Willing.** When Christ catches Peter napping in the Garden of Gethsemane after he had asked him to watch and pray, he says to him: "Watch ye, and pray that ye enter not into temptation. The spirit indeed is willing, but the flesh weak" (Matthew 26:41, Mark 14:38). Our Lord's contrast between spirit and flesh has been used ever since to justify the failure of good intentions to materialize into something actual. The distinction has also been subject to all sorts of distortions that equate the spirit with goodness and the body with evil, with the result that Christianity is unfairly accused of being dualistic or hostile to the body. The text, however, refers not to the body but to the "flesh," which in the New Testament generally signifies our physical natures made frail and vulnerable by original or personal sin. And sin, of course, is a product not of the body but of the soul.

**Turn the Other Cheek.** Another famous verse prone to misinterpretation is Christ's famous injuction to turn the other cheek (Luke 6:29). Naïve commentators, for example, often invoke the passgage as proof of a disjunction between an angry, vengeful Old Testament God and a kind, forgiving New Testament God. Yet just as the "eye for an eye" principle is not as vengeful as one might initially think (p. 173), so too are Christ's remarks here not as "pacifist" as they seem at first blush. A careful look at the actual wording of the verse as it is found in the Gospel according to St. Matthew reveals the complexity behind Christ's teaching. "You have heard that it hath been said, 'an eye for an eye, and a tooth for a tooth.' But I say to you not to resist evil: but if one strike thee on thy right cheek, turn to him also the other" (Matthew 5:38, 39). The complexity of this seemingly straightforward teaching is revealed in the fact that in Matthew's Gospel, Christ admonishes his listeners to turn only when they are struck on the right cheek. Given the fact that almost everyone in Jesus' world was raised right-handed, the chances of being punched in the right cheek would have been rare (a right-handed blow usually lands on the opponent's left cheek). Several Church Fathers took this peculiarity to indicate that a deeper figurative meaning lay underneath the ostensible blanket rejection of self-defense. That deeper meaning would in no way contradict the essential message of responding to evil with love, but it would militate against a narrowly literal interpretation.[39]

**Wailing and Gnashing of Teeth.** An image that Christ uses to great effect in Matthew's Gospel to describe the fate of the damned is "weeping and gnashing of teeth" ("wailing" in the King James translation).[40] Now used to signify in a playful way any kind of conspicuous or dramatic lamentation, the phrase is particularly popular among religion and theology teachers to describe their students after grades have been handed out.

**Weighed in the Balance.** A vivid biblical image for judicial verdicts is being "weighed in the balance" (see Job 6:2, Ecclesiasticus [Sirach] 21:28). When, for example, King Belshazzar asks Daniel to interpret some handwriting on the wall (see below), Daniel rightly sees one of the words as meaning, "Thou are weighed in the balances, and art found wanting"; as a result, the wicked king was smitten by God that night (Daniel 5:27). The metaphor of being weighed is echoed today in our images of a blindfolded Lady Justice holding a scale in her hand, though the image itself likely predates Christianity.

**Wheels within Wheels.** When the prophet Ezekiel is describing his vision of four-faced, four-winged spiritual beings, he remarks, "and their appearance and their work was, as it were, a wheel in the midst of a wheel" (Ezekiel 1:16). In Judaism, Ezekiel's account inspired a tradition known as Merkabah mysticism and in Byzantine Christianity it became the foundation for artistic portrayals of Seraphim and Cherubim, the two highest angelic orders. In Latin Christianity, the passage was revered as an allegory of the life of the Law within the life of grace. Everyday English, however, assigns a more pedestrian and potentially misleading meaning, using "a wheel within a wheel" to denote a complicated set of forces or influences or a complication of motives or plans.[41]

**Wolf in Sheep's Clothing.** One of Christ's commands in the Sermon on the Mount is to "beware of false prophets, who come to you in the clothing of sheep, but inwardly they are ravening wolves" (Matthew 7:15). Christ's warning was against heretics within the Church, men and women who pretend to be faithful Christians but who poison their co-religionists with false teachings. The Church Fathers would later take the warning to apply especially to corrupt priests and other members of the clergy.[42] Today, however, the expression is used to designate any person whose treachery is belied by an innocent appearance.

**Writing on the Wall.** After Babylonian King Belshazzar and his friends had had too much to drink at a party, the king decided to serve his guests and his concubines with the sacred vessels that had been taken from the Holy Temple during the sack of Jerusalem. As they continued to drink away the night, the laughter and merriment suddenly stopped and their blood ran cold: next to a wall there had appeared a spidery hand, silently writing three words in Hebrew. The king summoned the prophet Daniel, who correctly interpreted the miraculous graffiti as a sign that God was displeased with Belshazzar's idolatry and that his empire was subsequently doomed. That very night Belshazzar was slain (Daniel 5:1–32).

By itself the story is a chilling reminder of the importance that God attaches to the distinction between the sacred and the profane, between rituals and objects consecrated for divine use on the one hand and the things of everyday life on the other. (Vessels used for the sacrifice of the Mass, for example, are supposed to be utterly different than those used at a Tupperware party or a barbecue.) The story's central image, on the other hand, has come to be used as a metaphor for the importance of properly reading the "signs of the times" (another biblical expression—see Matthew 16:3) before it is too late.

# Notes

NOTES FOR INTRODUCTION

1. *The Catholic Imagination* (Berkeley: University of California Press, 2000), p. 1.

NOTES FOR CHAPTER ONE

1. All biblical passages, unless otherwise indicated, are taken from the Douay-Rheims translation, *The Holy Bible* (Baltimore: John Murphy Co., 1914). The numbering of the Psalms likewise follows that of the Douay-Rheims translation.
2. *Encyclopædia Britannica Online,* s.v. "Chronology," http://search.eb.com/eb/article?tocId=58756.
3. *The Origins of Everyday Things,* ed. Ruth Binney (Pleasantville, New York: Readers' Digest Association, 1999), pp. 206–207.
4. Joseph Cardinal Ratzinger, *A New Song for the Lord: Faith in Christ and Liturgy Today,* trans. Martha M. Matesich (New York: Crossroad Publishing, 1996), p. 60.
5. Francis X. Weiser, S.J., *Handbook of Christian Feasts and Customs: The Year of the Lord in Liturgy and Folklore* (New York: Harcourt, Brace & World, Inc., 1958), p. 9.
6. Valérie-Anne Giscard d'Estaing, *Second World Almanac Book of Inventions* (New York: World Almanac, 1986), p. 284; *Catholic Encyclopedia,* s.v. "Pope Sylvester II" (by J. P. Kirsch), http://www.newadvent.org/cathen/14371a.htm.
7. *Paradiso* X.139–141, 143–144. Translation by Allen Mandelbaum in *The Divine Comedy* (New York: Everyman's Library, 1995), p. 427.

NOTES FOR CHAPTER TWO

1. George William Douglas, *The American Book of Days,* revised by Helen Douglas Compton (New York: The H.W. Wilson Company, 1948), p. 584.
2. Weiser, *Handbook,* p. 165.
3. Douglas, *American Book,* p. 78.

4.   Weiser, *Handbook,* pp. 318–319.

5.   Weiser, *Handbook,* p. 220.

6.   Weiser, *Handbook,* pp. 220–221.

7.   Douglas, *American Book,* pp. 279–280.

8.   Weiser, *Handbook,* pp. 295, 178.

9.   Catholic News Service, "Knights' leader says corporate success comes from ethics, not profits," October 4, 2004, http://www.catholicnews.com/data/stories/cns/0405427.htm; John B. Kennedy, "The Knights of Columbus," in *Catholic Builders of the Nation,* ed. C. E. McGuire (Boston: Continental Press, 1923), vol. 2, p. 337.

10.   Douglas, *American Book,* pp. 530–531.

11.   Lesley Pratt Bannatyne, *Halloween: An American Holiday, an American History* (Gretna, Louisiana: Pelican Publishing Company, 1998), pp. 2–4, 9–11, 15–16, 142–143.

12.   Weiser, *Handbook,* p. 271. Though the goose tale is not reliable, it is true that Martin did not want to become a bishop. Apparently he was tricked into leaving his monastery on the ruse that a dying person needed his help, only to be dragged to the cathedral and forcibly ordained. See *Butler's Lives of the Fathers, Martyrs, and Other Saints,* ed. Rev. F. C. Husenbeth, vol. 4 (Great Falls, Montana: St. Bonaventure Publications, 1997), p. 189.

13.   Weiser, *Handbook,* pp. 66–67, pp. 96–100.

14.   Weiser, *Religious Customs in the Family* (Collegeville, Minnesota: The Liturgical Press, 1956), pp. 56–57.

## NOTES TO CHAPTER THREE

1.   Emily Post, *Etiquette* (New York: Funk and Wagnalls, 1945), p. 587.

2.   Cf. Charles Panati, *Extraordinary Origins of Everyday Things* (New York: Perennial Library, 1987), p. 83.

3.   "The Young Children's Book," found in *Manners and Morals in Olden Time,* ed. Frederick J. Furnivall (London: Early English Text Society, 1868), p. 17. I have updated the spelling and diction of the passage.

4.   *Pontificale Romanum,* Pars Prima (Rome: Mechliniae, 1845), p. 257, translation mine.

5.   Chrétien de Troyes, *Arthurian Romances,* trans. William W. Kibler (London: Penguin Books, 1991), p. 387.

6.   *Catholic Encyclopedia,* s.v. "Truce of God" (by C. Moeller), http://www.newadvent.org/cathen/15068a.htm, and "Chivalry" (by C. Moeller), http://www.newadvent.org/cathen/03691a.htm.

7.   *Dictionary of Superstitions,* eds. Iona Opie and Moira Tatem (Oxford: Oxford University Press, 1989), pp. 364, 454.

8.   See Binney, *Origins,* p. 61.

9.   Furnivall, *Manners,* pp. 6, 20, 23, 18.

10.   Geoffrey Chaucer, *The Canterbury Tales,* trans. Nevill Coghill (New York: Penguin Books, 2003), ll. 127–135, p. 6.

11. Furnivall, *Manners,* pp. 14, 15, 29, 13.

12. See Furnivall, *Manners,* pp. 3, 15, 29; Erasmus, *De Civilitate Morum Puerilium* (1534).

13. "Our Lady, n.," 4a, *The Oxford English Dictionary,* 2nd ed., henceforth *OED.*

14. *Rules of Civility: The 110 Precepts That Guided Our First President in War and Peace,* ed. Richard Brookhiser (New York: The Free Press, 1997), pp. 1–2, 4.

15. "Dinner, n.," *OED.*

16. Weiser, *Handbook,* p. 170.

17. Weiser, *Handbook,* p. 171.

18. See "Beg," "Beghard," and "Beguine," *OED.*


NOTES FOR CHAPTER FOUR

1. See "French Cheese," *On Gourmet,* http://www.ongourmet.com/eshop/store946/3-cat.html; "Munster, Munster Géromé," *Frencheese: Any Meal, Any Time,* http://www.frencheese.co.uk/glossary/cheese.cfm/cheeseID/108.

2. "Port Salut," *Frencheese: Any Meal, Any Time,* http://www.frencheese.co.uk/glossary/cheese.cfm/cheeseID/121.

3. Cooking.com, http://www.cooking.com/advice/adfeatu2.asp?Alias=AR_bw_ottawa&Step=1.

4. Nino Lo Bello, *The Incredible Book of Facts and Papal Curiosities: A Treasury of Trivia* (New York: Gramercy Books, 1998), p. 27; *Catholic Encyclopedia,* s.v. "Pope Benedict XIII" (by Patrick J. Healy), http://www.newadvent.org/cathen/02431a.htm.

5. http://www.st-ignatius-loyola.com/trivia/trivia2.html.

6. See canons 1250–1253 of the 1983 Code of Canon Law.

7. Evelyn Vitz, *A Continual Feast: A Cookbook to Celebrate the Joys of Family and Faith Throughout the Christian Year* (San Francisco: Ignatius Press, 1985), pp. 190–191.

8. Vitz, *A Continual Feast,* p. 153.

9. Ann Ball, *Catholic Traditions in Cooking* (Huntington, Indiana: Our Sunday Visitor, 1993), p. 87; cf. "Mexican Cuisine," http://gourmet.sympatico.ca/countries/mexico/mexico.htm.

10. Bryan Gruley, "Who Put the Paunch In Paczki and Droves In Shrove Tuesday?" *Wall Street Journal,* Eastern Edition, 3/01/2000, vol. 235, issue 43, p. A1.

11. Gill Donovan, "World—Current Events," National Catholic Reporter, February 23, 2001, http://www.findarticles.com/p/articles/mi_m1141/is_17_37/ai_77435018.

12. Weiser, *Handbook,* p. 183.

13. Vitz, *A Continual Feast,* p. 114.

14. Cf. RecipeSource.com, http://www.recipesource.com/ethnic/asia/japanese/00/rec0095.html. For more on the Ember Days, see http://www.holytrinitygerman.org/Ember-Days.html.

15. Giscard d'Estaing, *Book of Inventions,* p. 160.

16. See Williiam Younger, *Gods, Men, and Wine* (London: The Wine and Food Society, 1966), pp. 232–233; *Alexis Lichine's New Encyclopedia of Wines & Spirits* (New York: Alfred A. Knopf, 1985), pp. 129, 149, 394, 465, 562; Vincent P. Carosso, *The California Wine Industry, 1830–1895* (Berkeley: University of California Press, 1951), p. 2.

17. *Alexis Lichine's New Encyclopedia,* p. 164.

18. *Alexis Lichine's New Encyclopedia,* pp. 153–154.

19. *Alexis Lichine's New Encyclopedia,* pp. 500–501.

20. See E. Frank Henriques, *The Signet Encyclopedia of Whiskey, Brandy, & All Other Spirits* (New York: Signet Library, 1979), p. 45; *Alexis Lichine's New Encyclopedia,* pp. 162–163.

21. *Alexis Lichine's New Encyclopedia,* p. 106.

22. Henriques, *Signet Encyclopedia,* p. 44.

23. Scott Stavrou, "Disrobing the Monk: Frangelico," *Wine X Magazine,* winexwired.com/3point3/ss33.htm.

24. Cited in Jim Murray, *Classic Irish Whiskey* (London: Prion Boooks Ltd., 1997), p. 16; see E. B. McGuire, *Irish Whiskey: A History of Distilling, the Spirit Trade and Excise Controls in Ireland* (New York: Barnes & Noble, 1973), p. 91.

25. David Daiches, *Scotch Whiskey: Its Past and Present* (Edinburgh: Birlinn Ltd., 1995), p. 11.

26. *Faith & Family* (Winter 2002), "Nov. 3," p. 42.

27. Cf. The Paulaner Brewery website, http://www.paulaner.de. Many thanks to Prof. Thomas Prügl at Notre Dame for sharing his knowledge of Bavarian beer.

28. "Mark of Aviano (1631–1699)," Homily of John Paul II, April 27, 2003, http://www.vatican.va/news_services/liturgy/saints/ns_lit_doc_20030427_d-aviano_en.html.

29. "Pope beatifies 'father of cappuccino,'" BBC News World Edition, April 27, 2003, http://news.bbc.co.uk/2/hi/europe/2979993.stm.

30. Simon Caldwell, "Never Too Latte for a Blessed Cappucchino," in *The Catholic Herald,* No. 6109, May 2, 2003.

NOTES FOR CHAPTER FIVE

1. Josef Pieper, *Only the Lover Sings: Art and Contemplation,* trans. Lothar Krauth (San Francisco: Ignatius Press, 1990), p. 27.

2. Pieper, *Only the Lover Sings,* Preface. See pp. 25, 74, 26.

3. Don Andrés de Salas Y Gilavert, *The Influence of Catholicism on the Sciences and on the Arts,* trans. Mariana Monteiro (London: Sands & Co., 1900), pp. 153–154.

4. *Encyclopædia Britannica Online,* s.v. "Architecture, History of Western," http://search.eb.com/eb/article?tocId=47324.

5. Gustave Thibon, *Des Pierres, Un Chant* (1991). The translation is taken from an unpublished essay by Dom de Feydeau entitled, "The New Clear Creek Monastery."

6. *The Hunchback of Notre Dame,* chapter 23.

7. See Thomas E. Woods, Jr., *How the Catholic Church Built Western Civilization* (Washington, D.C.: Regnery, 2005), pp. 119–124.

8. *Encyclopædia Britannica Online,* s.v. "Baroque Period," http://search.eb.com/eb/article?tocId=9013445.

9. *Catholic Encyclopedia,* s.v. "Barocco Style" (by Thomas H. Poole), http://www.newadvent.org/cathen/02303b.htm.

10. Weiser, *Handbook,* 258.

11. "Storey," *OED.*

12. "Catherine," 2, *OED.*

13. "Lobby, n.," "Lodge," *OED.* Cf. http://www.st-ignatius-loyola.com/trivia/trivia10.html.

14. *Catholic Encyclopedia,* s.v "English Literature" (by K. M. Warren), http://www.newadvent.org/cathen/05458a.htm.

15. See Ann Hartle, *The Modern Self in Rousseau's* Confessions: *A Reply to St. Augustine* (South Bend, Indiana: University of Notre Dame Press, 1983).

16. "The Holiness of the Ordinary," in *Signposts in a Strange Land,* ed. Patrick Samway (New York: Farrar, Straus, and Giroux, 1991), p. 369.

17. Quoted in Regis Martin, "Brideshead Revisited: The Catholic Novel Manqué?," *Center Journal,* Fall 1982, p. 60.

18. *Encyclopædia Britannica Online,* s.v. "Tolkien, J. R. R.," http://search.eb.com/eb/article?tocId=9072803.

19. *Encyclopædia Britannica Online,* s.v. "Kagame, Alexis," http://search.eb.com/eb/article?tocId=9044304.

20. There is a fair amount of information about this debate on the Internet. See Michael J. Cummings, "Was Shakespeare Catholic?" http://sites.micro-link.net/zekscrab/Catholic.html; Glen Cascino, "Shakespeare and the Catholic Question," http://www.theuniversityconcourse.com/V,8,5–4–2000/Cascino.htm; Julie Sachs, "Was Shakespeare a Closet Catholic?," http://www.oread.ku.edu/Oread00/OreadJuly14/shakespeare.html.

21. De Salas, *The Influence of Catholicism,* p. 138.

22. For an excellent study, for example, of the early Anglican destruction of Catholic churches, see Eamon Duffy, *The Stripping of the Altars: Traditional Religion in England, 1400–1580,* 2nd ed. (New Haven: Yale University Press, 2005).

23. See Michael P. Foley, "What's In a Name," *Homiletic & Pastoral Review* (November 2001), pp. 8–16, available at http://www.catholic.net/rcc/Periodicals/Homiletic/2001–11/foley.html. Another consideration is that the Levitical prohibition against graven images was never interpreted as a ban against all images. See *Catholic Encyclopedia,* s.v. "Images, Veneration of" (by Adrian Fortescue), http://www.newadvent.org/cathen/07664a.htm.

24. Epistle CV, translation mine.

25. De Salas, *The Influence of Catholicism,* pp. 135–136.

26. See *Catholic Encyclopedia,* s.v. "Iconoclasm" (by Adrian Fortescue), http://www.newadvent.org/cathen/07620a.htm; De Salas, *The Influence of Catholicism,* pp. 136–137.

27. Ep. 1.33, cited and translated by Adrian Fortescue, "Iconoclasm," *Catholic Encyclopedia.*

28. *Encyclopædia Britannica Online,* s.v. "Baroque Period," http://search.eb.com/eb/article?tocId=9013445.

29. *The End of the Affair* (New York: Viking, 1951), pp. 132–133.

30. See *Catholic Encyclopedia,* s.v. "Sculpture" (by George Kriehn and Beda Kleinschmidt), http://www.newadvent.org/cathen/13641b.htm.

31. De Salas, *The Influence of Catholicism,* pp. 144–146.

32. *Encyclopædia Britannica Online,* s.v. "Gargoyle," http://search.eb.com/eb/article?tocId=9036079.

33. *Apologia ad Guillelmum Sancti-Theoderici Abbatem* 12.29, translation mine.

## NOTES FOR CHAPTER SIX

1. *Sacrosanctum Concilium,* 116, found in *The Documents of Vatican II,* ed. Walter M. Abbott, S.J. (New York: Guild Press, 1966), p. 172.

2. "Take Five with Christ," *Faith & Family* (February 2002), p. 55. For an excellent article on this topic, see Michael Sherwin, O.P., "Jazz Goes Back to Church: Dave Brubeck's Religious Music," *America* (August 4–11, 2003), pp. 12–15.

3. *Catholic Encyclopedia,* s.v. "Dies Irae" (by H.T. Henry), http://www.newadvent.org/cathen/04787a.htm.

4. "Anthem," *OED.*

5. Karp, *Dictionary,* pp. 270, 416.

6. Weiser, *Handbook,* pp. 191, 203–204.

7. Jonathan Dunsby, "Polyphony," *The New Oxford Companion to Music,* vol. 2, ed. Denis Arnold (Oxford: Oxford University Press, 1983), p. 1465.

8. Karp, *Dictionary,* p. 275.

9. *Catholic Encyclopedia,* s.v. "Oratorio" (by Joseph Otten), http://www.newadvent.org/cathen/11270a.htm

10. Lassels, *Voyage to Italy* II.227. The Oratorio genre continues today thanks to the religious music of Dave Brubeck (see Michael Sherwin, O.P., "Jazz Goes Back to Church: Dave Brubeck's Religious Music," *America* (August 4–11, 2003), pp. 12–15).

11. *The Oxford Dictionary of Nursery Rhymes,* eds. Iona and Peter Opie (Oxford: Oxford University Press, 1997), p. 358.

12. *Oxford Dictionary of Nursery Rhymes,* pp. 113, 267, 355.

13. Ted Gioia, *The History of Jazz* (New York: Oxford University Press, 1997), pp. 3–6.

14. Perhaps another factor in the preservation of African music in New Orleans was the *Code Noir*'s statute against an owner breaking up a family, a statute that may have enabled music to be passed on more easily from one generation to the next. Since Catholic doctrine teaches that marriage is a sacrament, selling off a slave's spouse or even preventing slaves from marrying was considered by the Church an impious act. See Fred Stopsky, *Catholicism and Slavery* (New York: The Catholic League, 1999).

15. http://www.tobaccoheritage.com/completehistoryofauctionsystem1.htm; see Carl Charlson, "Search for a Safe Cigarette," NOVA, PBS, October 2, 2001. Cf. http://www.pbs.org/wgbh/nova/transcripts/2810cigarette.html.

16. Dom Guéranger, O.S.B., *The Liturgical Year,* trans. Dom Laurence Shepherd, O.S.B., vol. 6 (Great Falls, Montana: St. Bonaventure Publications, 2000), p. 249.

17. "Dirge," *OED.*

18. Karp, *Dictionary,* pp. 264–265.

19. Marie Pierik, *The Spirit of Gregorian Chant* (Boston: Bruce Humphries, Inc., 1939), p. 54.

20. *Catholic Encyclopedia,* s.v. "Passion Plays" (by Adam Salzer), http://www. newadvent.org/cathen/11531a.htm, and see "Theatre" (by Herbert Thurston), http://www.newadvent.org/cathen/14559a.htm.

21. *Catholic Encyclopedia,* s.v. "Miracle Plays and Mysteries" (by Georges Bertrin and Arthur F. J. Remy), http://www.newadvent.org/cathen/10348a.htm.

22. *Catholic Encyclopedia,* s.v. "Miracle Plays and Mysteries" (by Georges Bertrin and Arthur F. J. Remy), http://www.newadvent.org/cathen/10348a.htm.

23. *Catholic Encyclopedia,* s.v. "Theatre" (by Herbert Thurston), http://www. newadvent.org/cathen/14559a.htm.

24. William H. McCabe, S.J., *An Introduction to the Jesuit Theater: A Posthumous Work,* ed. Louis J. Oldani, S.J. (St. Louis, Missouri: The Institute of Jesuit Sources, 1983), pp. 9–10.

25. M. Elizabeth C. Bartlet and Thomas Bauman, "Jesuit Drama," in *The New Grove Dictionary of Opera,* vol. 2, ed. Stanley Sadie (London: Macmillan, 1992), p. 897.

26. http://www.passion-play.com/pp_history.html (the play's official website).

27. http://www.blackhills.com/bhpp/pp_index.htm (the play's official website).

28. John Warrack and Ewan West, *The Oxford Dictionary of Opera* (Oxford: Oxford University Press, 1992), p. 362.

29. *Germany Present and Past* (London: C. K. Paul & Co., 1879), 9.249.

30. "Pageant," *OED.*

31. "Transforming the Culture," *Faith & Family* (April 2002), p. 61.

32. Weiser, *Handbook,* p. 150.

33. "Out-Herod," *OED.*

34. "Old Nick," *OED.*

35. Weiser, *Handbook,* pp. 63, 126–127, 132–133.

36. "Zany, n. (a.)," *OED; Encyclopædia Britannica Online,* s.v. "Commedia dell'arte," http://search.eb.com/eb/article?tocId=1433,

## NOTES FOR CHAPTER SEVEN

1. Chaucer, "The Knight's Tale," *The Canterbury Tales,* trans. Nevill Coghill (Baltimore: Penguin Books, 1952), p. 71, lines 1679–1681, 1682–1684.

2. See Benny Peiser, "Thou Shalt Not Kill! The Judaeo-Christian Basis of The Civilizing Process," *The Sports Historian* 17:1 (May 1997), pp. 93–108.

3.  Michaela Lochmann, "Les fondements pédagogiques de la devise olympique 'citius, altius, fortius'," http://www.coubertin.ch/pdf/PDF-Dateien/115-Lochmann.pdf.

4.  Jean Durry, "Pierre de Coubertin: The Visionary," trans. John Sinnbard-Murphy and Nick Growse, Comité Français Pierre de Coubertin, pp. 10, 35, available on http://www.coubertin.ch/pdf/MEP%20Angl.%20Cou%202%20%2B%208p.%20%2B%206%20.pdf.

5.  *Official Encyclopedia of Tennis,* staff of U.S. Lawn Tennis Association (New York: Harper and Row, 1972), p. 1; Binney, *Origins,* p. 267.

6.  Giscard d'Estaing, *Book of Inventions,* p. 57.

7.  *Encyclopædia Britannica Online,* s.v. "Golf," http://search.eb.com/eb/article?tocId=222219.

8.  Raymond R. Camp, *Family Circle's Guide to Trout Flies* (Newark, New Jersey: Family Circle, 1954), p. 4.

9.  See "Rev. Josef Murgas: the Forgotten Radio Genius," Botany, http://205.160.127.253/Murgas/botany.htm; Dictionary.LaborLawTalk.com, http://encyclopedia.laborlawtalk.com/List_of_Slovaks.

10. "Dumb-bell, n.," 1a, *OED.*

11. Examples include *The Innocent Morality,* attributed to Franciscan friar John of Waleys, and the *Liber de moribus hominum et officiis nobilium* of Dominican friar Jacobus de Cessolis, which was later translated into English by William Caxton in 1475. See *The Encyclopedia of Chess,* compiled by Anne Sunnucks (New York: St. Martin's Press, 1970), pp. 398–399.

12. W. Gurney Benham, *Playing Cards: History of the Pack and Explanations of Its Many Secrets* (London: Ward, Lock & Co., 1931), pp. 10–11.

13. "Steeplechase," *Wikipedia,* http://en.wikipedia.org/wiki/Steeplechase.

14. See Wendy Devlin, "History of the Piñata," Mexico Connect, http://www.mexconnect.com/mex_/travel/wdevlin/wdpinatahistory.html; Olga Rosino, Belinda Mendoza, and Christine Castro, "Piñatas!" http://www.epcc.edu/ftp/Homes/monicaw/borderlands/10_pi%C3%B1atas.htm.

15. "Nicknames—Pro Football Hall of Fame," http://www.profootballhof.com/history/nicknames.jsp.

16. "Hail Mary Pass," *Wikipedia,* http://en.wikipedia.org/wiki/Hail_Mary_pass.

17. "The Mavens' Word of the Day," February 1, 1999, http://www.randomhouse.com/wotd/index.pperl?date=19990201.

18. "Crosse," "Lacrosse," *OED.*

19. Leopold Wagner, *Manners, Customs, and Observances: Their Origin and Signification* (London: William Heinemann, 1894), p. 151; "Domino," Probert Encyclopedia, Costume (D), http://www.probertencyclopaedia.com/PD.HTM; "Domino," *OED.*

NOTES FOR CHAPTER EIGHT

1.  "Mary's Gardens Home Page," http://www.mgardens.org/index.html.

2. John S. Stokes, Jr., "Flower and Human Symbols of the Trinity," http://www. mgardens.org/JS-FAHSOTT-MG.html.

3. See Vincenzina Krymow, *Mary's Flowers: Gardens, Legends, and Meditations* (Cincinnati: St. Anthony Messenger Press, 1999), p. 56.

4. "Christ," 5, *OED;* cf. "MARIANA 1," http://www.mgardens.org/OLG-MARIANA–1-MG.html.

5. Margaret B. Downing, "Catholic Contributions to Botanical Science," *Catholic Builders,* vol. 4, p. 362.

6. See "Passion Flower," The Hangarter Lab, Department of Biology, Indiana University, http://sunflower.bio.indiana.edu/~rhangart/plantmotion/flowers/passionflower/passion.html; John Stokes, Jr., "The Passion Flower," http://www.mgardens.org/JS-TPF-MG.html.

7. See *Encyclopædia Britannica Online,* s.v. "Water Lily," http://search.eb.com/eb/article?tocId=9076222; "MARIANA 1," http://www.mgardens.org/OLG-MARIANA–1-MG.html; "Selaginella," http://www.botany.com/selaginella.html.

8. See the hymn "Veni Creator Spiritus"; "Avocado" and "Holy Ghost," 4, *OED.*

9. Weiser, *Handbook,* p. 162.

10. Cited in Krymow, *Mary's Flowers,* p. 28.

11. Krymow, *Mary's Flowers,* p. 40.

12. Krymow, *Mary's Flowers,* p. 15.

13. Cited in Krymow, *Mary's Flowers,* p. 12.

14. Krymow, *Mary's Flowers,* p. 124.

15. See Krymow, *Mary's Flowers,* p. 76. There is some etymological uncertainty as to whether *Marinus* refers to Mary or to the Latin word for the sea. See "Rosemary," *OED.*

16. Krymow, *Mary's Flowers,* pp. 80, 72.

17. Krymow, *Mary's Flowers,* pp. 60–61.

18. Krymow, *Mary's Flowers,* p. 100.

19. Krymow, *Mary's Flowers,* p. 112.

20. Krymow, *Mary's Flowers,* p. 116.

21. Krymow, *Mary's Flowers,* p. 128.

22. See "MARIANA1," http://www.mgardens.org/OLG-MARIANA–1-MG. html, and "Angel," B.2., *OED,* 1997 Appendix.

23. "Jacob's Ladder," 1 and 2, *OED;* "Jacob's Ladder," in *A Dictionary of Biblical Tradition in English Literature,* ed. David Lyle Jeffrey (Grand Rapids, MI: Eerdmans, 1992), pp. 388–390.

24. "Joseph," 3, *OED.*

25. See "Aaron's-beard," *OED;* "MARIANA 1," http://www.mgardens.org/OLG-MARIANA–1-MG.html.

26. "Aaron's-rod," 1, *OED.*

27. 2:8, in the Septuagint, Vulgate, and, by extension, Douay-Rheims translations of the Bible. For the biblical uses of Job, see Tobias 2:12, 2:15, James 5:11. For Job's tears, see "Job," n. 4, *OED.*

28. "Peter, n. 1," 8b, and 8c, *OED.*

29. See "St. John's Wort," http://www.wala.de/english/pflanze/archiv/johannis. htm and T. F. Thiselton Dyer, *The Folk-Lore of Plants* (London: Chatto and Windus, 1889), pp. 72–73, available online at lithead.com.

30. See *Catholic Encyclopedia,* s.v. "St. Barnabas" (by John F. Fenlon), http://www.newadvent.org/cathen/02300a.htm; Dyer, *Folk-Lore of Plants,* p. 65; and http://onlinedictionary.datasegment.com/word/Saint.

31. Dyer, *Folk-Lore of Plants,* p. 67.

32. Dyer, *Folk-Lore of Plants,* p. 76.

33. Weiser, *Handbook,* p. 106.

34. Charles Panati, *Extraordinary Origins of Almost Anything* (New York: Perennial Library, 1987), p. 393.

35. Dyer, *Folk-Lore of Plants,* pp. 65–66.

36. Guéranger, *Liturgical Year,* vol. 4, p. 304. St. Margaret's body may now be seen over the high altar of Santa Margherita Church in Cortona, Italy.

37. See http://onlinedictionary.datasegment.com/word/Saint and http://www.herbs2000.com/herbs/herbs_ignatius_bean.htm.

38. "Christmas," 4, *OED.*

39. Krymow, *Mary's Flowers,* p. 48.

40. See Weiser, *Handbook,* p. 104; Magnificat antiphon for December 18 in *Breviarum Romanum,* Pars Hiemalis (Ratisbona, 1939), p. 350; third antiphon for January 1 in *Breviarum Romanum,* Pars Hiemalis, p. 440.

41. Krymow, *Mary's Flowers,* p. 64.

42. Joanna Bogle, *A Book of Feasts and Seasons,* 3rd ed. (Leominster: Gracewing Books, 1992), p. 90; "Simnel," def. #2, *OED,* 2nd ed.

43. Weiser, *Handbook,* p. 190.

44. "Easter Lily," http://aggie-horticulture.tamu.edu/plantanswers/publications/lily/lily.html.

45. Dyer, *Folk-Lore of Plants,* p. 64.

46. Margaret B. Downing, "Catholic Contributions to Botanical Science," *Catholic Builders,* vol. 4, p. 362.

47. "Monk's-Head," "Monkshood," *OED.*

48. See "Monk's Rhubarb," *OED;* Christopher Hobbs L.Ac., A.H.G., "The Chaste Tree—Vitex agnus-castus," http://www.healthy.net/scr/article.asp?ID=430.

49. "Bishop, n. 1," 10b, *OED.*

50. "Cardinal-Flower," *OED.*

51. "Pope's head," *OED.*

## NOTES FOR CHAPTER NINE

1. "Lady-bug," http://dictionary.reference.com/search?q=lady-bug.

2. "Lady-bird," *OED.*

3. "Cardinal, n.," III.7, *OED.*

4. Mary Ann Sweeters, "Breed Profile: Chartreux," Cat Fanciers' Association, http://www.cfainc.org/breeds/profiles/chartreux.html; "Cat Breeds, Types,

Variants, and Hybrids," The Messybeast.com, http://www.messybeast.com/breeds.htm.

5. *Catholic Encyclopedia,* s.v. "St. Bernard of Menthon" (by Barnabas Dieringer), http://www.newadvent.org/cathen/02503b.htm.

6. *Encyclopædia Britannica Online,* s.v. "Saint Bernard," http://search.eb.com/eb/article?tocId=9064811; "Saint Bernard," Dog Breed Info Center, http://www.dogbreedinfo.com/saintbernard.htm; John Schwartz, "History of two *large dogs*—Saint Bernards and Great Danes," Puppies-Dog-Supplies.com, http://www.puppies-dogs-supplies.com/5271-large-dogs.html.

7. Cf. Arizona Pigeon Club Website, http://www.azpigeons.org/; "Priest," 9, *OED.*

8. "Blue Rockfish," http://hmsc.oregonstate.edu/odfw/finfish/sp/bluerf.html.

9. "Guadalupe Bass," *Wikipedia,* http://en.wikipedia.org/wiki/Guadalupe_bass; "Alonso De León," http://www.its-my-website.com/Texasdocs/alonso-de-leon.htm.

10. "Requiem," n. 1 and n. 2, *OED;* http://www.fact-index.com/r/re/requiem_shark.html.

11. "Monkfish," *OED.*

12. *Encyclopædia Britannica Online,* s.v. "Monkfish,"http://search.eb.com/eb/article?tocId=9053376.

13. "John Dory," *OED.* It should be noted that the editors of the dictionary reject the possibility that John Dory is derived from *Janitor,* despite the linguistic evidence mentioned.

14. "Petrel, n." *OED.*

15. Patrick Ching, "Hawaii's Native Seal," http://www.aloha-hawaii.com/hawaii/monk+seal/; *Encyclopædia Britannica Online,* s.v. "Monk Seal," http://search.eb.com/eb/article?tocId=9053370.

16. *Wikipedia,* s.v. "Monk Parakeet," http://en.wikipedia.org/wiki/Monk_Parakeet.

17. *Encyclopædia Britannica Online,* s.v. "Bishop," http://search.eb.com/eb/article?tocId=9015409.

18. "Dictionary of Animals—Scallop," http://www.tiscali.co.uk/reference/dictionaries/animals/data/m0008640.html.

19. *Encyclopædia Britannica Online,* s.v. "Sydenham Chorea," http://search.eb.com/eb/article?eu=2503, and "Dance, Western," http://search.eb.com/eb/article?eu=117768; "Chorea, n." *OED.*

20. *Catholic Encyclopedia,* s.v. "Orders of St. Anthony" (by F. M. Rudge), http://www.newadvent.org/cathen/01555a.htm; *Butler's Lives of the Saints,* vol. 1 (Great Falls, Montana: St. Bonaventure Publications, 1997), p. 74.

21. "St. Elmo, n.," *OED.*

22. Guéranger, *Liturgical Year,* vol. 13, pp. 299–301.

23. Binney, *Origins,* p. 149.

24. Panati, *Extraordinary Things,* pp. 400–401. According to the *OED,* however, the true origin of the word is uncertain.

25. "Angelite," http://mineral.galleries.com/minerals/sulfates/anhydrit/anhydrit.htm; "Angelite," *OED.*

26. Evelyn Waugh, *Sword of Honour* (Boston: Little Brown & Company, 1961), p. 395.

27. Charles Mackay, "Basil Valentine," *Memoirs of Popular Delusions,* vol. 3, http://www.worldwideschool.org/library/books/relg/socialecchtheology/MemoirsofPopularDelusionsV3/chap17.html.

28. *Catholic Encyclopedia,* s.v. "Franz Xaver Freiherr von Wulfen" (by Joseph H. Rompel), http://www.newadvent.org/cathen/15715d.htm.


NOTES FOR CHAPTER TEN

1. "Why I'm a Christian," in *G. K. Chesterton: Essential Writings,* ed. William Griffin (New York: Orbis Books, 2003), p. 122.

2. See Woods, *How the Catholic Church Built Western Civilization,* pp. 75–85; Stanley L. Jaki, *Science and Creation: From Eternal Cycles to an Oscillating Universe* (Edinburgh: Scottish Academic Press, 1986). Nothing of this is to suggest, however, that the theoretical foundations of modern science are without their problems.

3. A. F. Zahm, "Catholic Contributions in the Field of Aeronautics," *Catholic Builders,* vol. 3, p. 225.

4. James J.Walsh, "Catholic Achievements in Science," *Catholic Builders,* vol. 3, pp. 365–367.

5. *Catholic Encyclopedia,* s.v. "Nicholaus Copernicus" (by J. G. Hagen), http://www.newadvent.org/cathen/11060b.htm.

6. See "Scheiner, n.," *OED.*

7. *Catholic Encyclopedia,* s.v. "Christopher Steiner" (by H. M. Brock), http://www.newadvent.org/cathen/ 02078a.htm.

8. *Encyclopædia Britannica Online,* s.v. "Secchi, Pietro Angelo," http://search.eb.com/eb/article?tocId=9066512.

9. James J. Walsh, "Catholic Achievements in Science," *Catholic Builders,* vol. 3, p. 361.

10. Woods, *How the Catholic Church,* p. 4.

11. *Encyclopædia Britannica Online,* s.v. "Pasteur, Louis," http://search.eb.com/eb/article?tocId=12562; *Catholic Encyclopedia,* s.v. "Louis Pasteur" (by James J. Walsh), http://www.newadvent.org/cathen/11536a.htm.

12. Margaret B. Downing, "Catholic Contributions to Botanical Science," *Catholic Builders,* vol. 4, p. 362.

13. *Catholic Encyclopedia,* s.v. "Franz von Paula Hladnik" (by Joseph H. Rompel), http://www.newadvent.org/cathen/07380b.htm, and "Franz Xaver Freiherr von Wulfen" (by Joseph H. Rompel), http://www.newadvent.org/cathen/15715d.htm.

14. *Encyclopædia Britannica Online,* s.v. "Lemaître, Georges," http://search.eb.com/eb/article?tocId=9047718.

15. *Catholic Encyclopedia,* s.v. "René-Just Haüy" (by Henry M. Brock), http://www.newadvent.org/cathen/07152a.htm.

16. *Catholic Encyclopedia,* s.v. "Pierre-André Latreille" (by Joseph H. Rompel), http://www.newadvent.org/cathen/09035b.htm.

17. John L. Heilbron, *Electricity in the 17th and 18th Centuries: A Study of Early Modern Physics* (Berkeley: University of California Press, 1979), p. 2.

18. See Woods, *How the Catholic Church,* p. 107.

19. *Catholic Encyclopedia,* s.v. "Jean-Antoine Nollet" (by William Fox), http://www.newadvent.org/cathen/11090b.htm;"Procopius Divisch" (by William Fox), http://www.newadvent.org/cathen/05054b.htm; "Giuseppe Toaldo" (by Brother Potamian), http://www.newadvent.org/cathen/14749a.htm; and "Andrew Gordon" (by Brother Potamian), http://www.newadvent.org/cathen/06649b.htm.

20. *Catholic Encyclopedia,* s.v. "Mendel, Mendelism" (by B. C. A. Windle), http://www.newadvent.org/cathen/10180b.htm.

21. See Woods, *How the Catholic Church,* p. 109; Erik Iverson, *The Myth of Egypt and its Hieroglyphs* (Copenhagen, 1961), pp. 97–98.

22. *Catholic Encyclopedia,* s.v. "Giovanni Battista Morgagni" (by James J. Walsh), http://www.newadvent.org/cathen/10567c.htm.

23. See Woods, *How the Catholic Church,* p. 110.

24. "32.–Benedictio Seismographi," in *Rituale Romanum* (Rome: Desclee, 1943), p. 626.

25. *Catholic Encyclopedia,* s.v. "Lawrence Hengler" (by F. L. Odenbach), http://www.newadvent.org/cathen/07215b.htm.

26. See Giscard d'Estaing, *Book of Inventions,* p. 254.

27. Alan Cutler, *The Seashell on the Mountaintop* (New York: Dutton, 2003), pp. 106–114.

28. *Catholic Encyclopedia,* s.v. "Nicolaus Steno" (by Niels Hansen), http://www.newadvent.org/cathen/14286a.htm.

29. Giscard d'Estaing, *Book of Inventions,* p. 189.

30. *Catholic Encyclopedia,* s.v. "Jean de Hautefeuille" (by Henry M. Brock), http://www.newadvent.org/cathen/07151b.htm.

NOTES FOR CHAPTER ELEVEN

1. "Why I'm a Christian," in *G. K. Chesterton: Essential Writings,* ed. William Griffin (New York: Orbis Books, 2003), p. 119.

2. Allyn Freeman and Bob Golden, *Why Didn't I Think of That? Bizarre Origins of Ingenious Inventions We Couldn't Live Without* (New York: John Wiley & Sons, Inc., 1997), p. 176; Joel Levy, *Really Useful: the Origins of Everyday Things* (New York: Firefly Books, 2002), p. 161.

3. "November 16," *Faith & Family* (December 2001), p. 38.

4. http://www.st-ignatius-loyola.com/trivia/trivia10.html; Dom Gaspar Lefebvre, O.S.B., *Saint Andrew Daily Missal* (St. Paul, Minnesota: E. M. Lohmann Co., 1952), pp. 1462, 1464; "Pantaloon, n.," *OED.*

5. "Cardinal, n.," III.7, *OED.*

6. "Monk, n.," IV.8.c, *OED.*

7. 5.2; cf. "Bride's Clothes: 'something blue,'" in *Dictionary of Superstitions*, p. 42.

8. Lo Bello, *Papal Curiosities*, p. 153.

9. Vitz, *A Continual Feast*, p. 231.

10. Joel Levy, *Really Useful*, p. 146.

11. Giscard d'Estaing, *Book of Inventions*, p. 99. For a differing point of view, see http://www.luikerwaal.com/newframe_uk.htm?/huygens_uk.htm.

12. See "Josef Murgas: The Real Radio Genius," http://205.160.127.253/Murgas/index.html, run by the students of Wyoming Valley West High School.

13. Binney, *Origins*, p. 252.

14. *Catholic Encyclopedia*, s.v. "Evangelista Torricelli" (by William Fox), http://www.newadvent.org/cathen/14784a.htm.

15. *Encyclopædia Britannica Online*, s.v. "Secchi, Pietro Angelo," http://search.eb.com/eb/article?tocId=9066512.

16. The Mercedes-Benz website, http://www.mercedes-benz.com/com/e/home/heritage/history/index.html.

17. *Saint Andrew Daily Missal*, p. 1578.

18. "Priest," 8, *OED*. Cf. Duane Vigue, "Priest," Fly Patterns, http://globalflyfisher.com/patterns/bigvig/priest.php.

19. "Catherine Wheel, n.," no. 4 and 2, *OED*.

20. "Cemetery," *OED*. Cf. http://www.st-ignatius-loyola.com/trivia/trivia4.html.

NOTES FOR CHAPTER TWELVE

1. *The Essential G. K. Chesterton*, introduced by P.J. Kavanaugh (Oxford University Press, 1987), p. 316.

2. Ernest L. Fortin, A.A., "Gladly to Learn and Gladly to Teach: Why Christians Invented the University," in *Ernest L. Fortin: Collected Essays*, vol. 1, ed. J. Brian Benestad (Lanham, Maryland: Rowman and Littlefield, 1996), p. 226.

3. Charles Homer Haskins, *The Rise of Universities*, intro. by Lionel S. Lewis (London: Transaction Publishers, 2002; New York: Henry Holt & Co., 1923), pp. xi, 9.

4. *Catholic Encyclopedia*, s.v. "Universities" (by Edward A. Pace), http://www.newadvent.org/cathen/15188a.htm, and "College" (by Robert Schwickerath), http://www.newadvent.org/cathen/04107b.htm.

5. *Catholic Encyclopedia*, s.v. "Biretta" (by Herbert Thurston), http://www.newadvent.org/cathen/02577a.htm; "The Ballad of the Caps," in *Illustrations of Early English Poetry*, ed. J. Payne Collier, vol. 5, no. 3 (London, 1866–70), p. 40.

6. See Helen Walters, *The Story of Caps and Gowns* (Chicago: E. R. Moore Company, 1939), pp. 5–10, 15; Msgr. A. S. Barnes, *Catholic Oxford* (London: Catholic Truth Society, 1933), p. 10.

7. *Catholic Encyclopedia*, s.v. "Universities" (by Edward A. Pace), http://www.newadvent.org/cathen/15188a.htm.

8. "Primer, n. 1," 1 and 2, *OED*.

9. See Augustine, *Confessions*, trans. Frank Sheed (Indianapolis, Indiana: Hackett, 1993), p. 10.

10. Thomas Morley, *A plaine and easie introduction to practicall musicke* I.36.

11. See *Romanum Breviarum,* Pars Aestiva, p. 724; *Encyclopædia Britannica Online,* s.v. "Alphabet," http://search.eb.com/eb/article?query=alphabet&ct=&eu=119413, "Cyrillic," http://search.eb.com/eb/article?eu=28889.

12. *Encyclopædia Britannica Online,* s.v. "Special Education," http://search.eb.com/eb/article?tocId=6807.

13. Binney, *Origins,* p. 219; *Encyclopædia Britannica Online,* s.v. "Sicard, Roch-Ambroise Cucurron, Abbé,"http://search.eb.com/eb/article?tocId=9067616.

14. *De corona militis,* iii, translation taken from *Catholic Encyclopedia,* s.v. "Sign of the Cross" (by Herbert Thurston), http://www.newadvent.org/cathen/13785a.htm.

15. *Dictionary of Superstitions,* pp. 107, 109.

16. Don Lewis, *Religious Superstition Through the Ages* (London: Mowbrays, 1975), p. 35.

17. Lewis, *Religious Superstition,* pp. 167–169.

18. See Lewis, *Religious Superstition,* p. 95; Michael P. Foley, *Wedding Rites: The Complete Guide to Traditional Weddings* (South Bend, Indiana: St. Augustine's Press, 2005), p. 200.

19. Butler's Lives of the Saints, vol. 2, p. 190; Panati, Extraordinary Origins, p. 4.

## NOTES FOR CHAPTER THIRTEEN

1. Weiser, *Handbook,* p. 191.

2. Benjamin F. Shearer and Barbara S. Shearer, *State Names, Seals, Flags, and Symbols: An Historical Guide* (New York: Greenwood Press, 1987), p. 12.

3. All of the information for the section on counties, unless otherwise noted, has been taken from Michael A. Beatty, *County Name Origins of the United States* (Jefferson, NC: McFarland & Company, Inc., 2001).

4. *Catholic Encyclopedia,* s.v. "Charles Carroll of Carollton" (by J. E. Hagerty), http://www.newadvent.org/cathen/03379c.htm.

5. *Catholic Encyclopedia,* s.v. "Jacques Marquette, S.J." (by Henry S. Spalding), http://www.newadvent.org/cathen/09690a.htm.

6. Chittenden and Richardson, *Life, Letters, and Trials of Father Pierre Jean de Smet* (4 vols., 1905), cited in *Catholic Encyclopedia,* s.v "Antonio Ravalli" (by James Mooney), http://www.newadvent.org/cathen/12662a.htm.

7. The other counties are: Albany County in Wyoming, Dukes County in Massachusetts, New York County in New York, Ulster County in New York, and possibly York County in Maine, Nebraska, Pennsylvania, South Carolina, and Virginia.

8. For more on St. Botolph, see D. F. Wilkinson, "The Life of St. Botolph," *Studia Patristica,* vol. IV, pt. II, *Texte und Untersuchungen zur Geschichte der Altchristlichen Literatur,* Baud 79 (Berlin: Akademie-Verlag, 1961).

9. Weiser, *Handbook,* p. 266.

10. George R. Stewart, *American Place-Names: A Concise and Selective Dictionary for the Continental United States of America* (New York: Oxford University Press, 1970), p. 134.

11. Douglas, *American Book,* p. 467.

12. Douglas, *American Book,* p. 499.

13. Guéranger, *Liturgical Year,* vol. 12, p. 127.

14. http://www.infoplease.com/spot/spanishnames.html.

15. *Catholic Encyclopedia,* s.v. "St. Didacus" (by Stephen M. Donovan), http://www.newadvent.org/cathen/04781a.htm.

16. http://www.infoplease.com/ipa/A0108600.html.

17. Barbara and Rudy Marinacci, *California's Spanish Place-Names: What They Mean and How They Got There* (Houston, Texas: Gulf Publishing Co., 1997), p. 83.

18. Douglas, *American Book,* p. 462.

19. Douglas, *American Book,* p. 454.

20. E. Lee North, *The 55 West Virginias: A Guide to the State's Counties* (Morgantown: West Virginia Proess, 1985), p. 76.

21. Douglas, *American Book,* p. 451.

22. Stewart, *American Place-Names,* p. 418.

23. Thomas F. Meehan, "Catholic Pioneer Captains of Industry," *Catholic Builders,* vol. 3, p. 162.

24. Cf. EWTN Church News, "Istanbul Names Street in Honor of Pope John XXIII," October 16, 2000; ZENIT.org, "Street in Bethlehem Named After John Paul II," March 14, 2000.

25. Philip Tucker, "Confederate Secret Agent in Ireland: Father John B. Bannon and his Irish Mission, 1863–1864," *Journal of Confederate History,* vol. 5, 1990, pp. 55–85.

26. Cf. http://www.nps.gov/wamo/memorial/setbacks.htm.

27. Stewart, *American Place-Names,* pp. 418–419.

28. Stewart, *American Place-Names,* pp. 418–419, 209.

NOTES FOR CHAPTER FOURTEEN

1. http://www.caribbeanflags.com/flag_info.cfm.

2. Pierre Gay, "Kingdom of France," *Flags of the World,* http://www.crwflags.com/fotw/flags/fr_mon.html#thr.

3. Pierre Gay, "France," *Flags of the World,* http://www.crwflags.com/fotw/flags/fr.html#col.

4. Vincent Morley, "Ireland," *Flags of the World,* http://www.crwflags.com/fotw/flags/ie.html.

5. Zeljko Heimer, "Lebanon," *Flags of the World,* http://www.crwflags.com/fotw/flags/lb.html.

6. Marc Junele Hoyos, "Mexico," *Flags of the World,* http://www.crwflags.com/fotw/flags/mx.html.

7. Juan Manuel Gabino Villascan, "Mexico—Army of the Three-Guarantees (1821–1823)," *Flags of the World,* http://www.crwflags.com/fotw/flags/mx^tri.html.

8.  Steve Kramer, "Montserrat," *Flags of the World,* http://www.crwflags.com/fotw/flags/ms.html#island.

9.  T. F. Mills, "Switzerland," *Flags of the World,* http://www.crwflags.com/fotw/flags/ch.html#symb.

10. http://www.crwflags.com/fotw/flags/va.html#flag.

11. U.S. Department of State, *The Seal of the United States,* Department and Foreign Service Series 64 (Washington, D.C.: 1957), pp. 1, 2; Weiser, *Handbook,* p. 257.

12. Greg Briggs, "Florida (U.S.)," *Flags of the World,* http://www.crwflags.com/fotw/flags/us-fl.html; William M. Grimes-Wyatt, "Confederate Flags (U.S.)," *Flags of the World,* http://www.crwflags.com/fotw/flags/us-csa.html; Shearer, *State Names,* p. 36.

13. Shearer, *State Names,* pp. 66 and 78.

14. Greg Briggs, "Florida (U.S.)," *Flags of the World,* http://www.crwflags.com/fotw/flags/us-fl.html.

15. David Harley, "Ideas in Society, 1500–1700," www.nd.edu/~dharley/HistIdeas/Sarpi.html; "Idaho's State Motto," *Idaho State Historical Society Reference Series,* No. 134 (revised March 1970), http://www.idahohistory.net/Reference%20Series/0134.doc.

16. The line begins the sixth quatrain of the *Adore Te Devote.* See *Catholic Encyclopedia,* s.v. "Pie Pelicane, Jesu, Domine," http://www.newadvent.org/cathen/12079b.htm.

17. Shearer, *State Names,* pp. 25–26.

18. Cf. *The Maryland Manual, 1959–1960,* vol. 168, p. 728, http://www.mdarchives.state.md.us/megafile/msa/speccol/sc2900/sc2908/000001/000168/html/am168—728.html.

19. "History of Our State Flag," *State of Rhode Island and Providence Plantations, Office of the Secretary of State,* http://www.state.ri.us/rihist/riemb.htm.

20. *Catholic Encyclopedia,* s.v. "The Anchor (as Symbol)" (by Maurice M. Hassett), http://www.newadvent.org/cathen/01462a.htm.

## NOTES FOR CHAPTER FIFTEEN

1.  St. Thomas Aquinas, *Summa Theologiae* I–11.92.1. The quotation is borrowed by St. Thomas from Aristotle's *Nicomachean Ethics.*

2.  Harold J. Berman, "Religious Foundations of Law in the West: An Historical Perspective," *The Journal of Law and Religion* 1:1 (Summer 1983), pp. 5–11.

3.  Guéranger, *Liturgical Year,* vol. 15, p. 350.

4.  Harold J. Berman, *Law and Revolution: The Formation of the Western Legal Tradition* (Cambridge: Harvard University Press, 1983), p. 228.

5.  Berman, "Influence of Christianity Upon the Development of Law," *Oklahoma Law Review* 12 (1959), p. 93.

6.  Herbert W. Titus, "God's Revelation: Foundation for the Common Law," *Regent University Law Review* 4 (Spring 1994), pp. 1, 5–9, 3, 17.

7. Quoted by Stuart Banner, "When Christianity Was Part of the Common Law," *Law and History Review* 27 (Spring 1998), p. 54.

8. Charles Donahue, Jr., "The Interaction of Law and Religion in the Middle Ages," *Mercer Law Review* 31:2 (Winter 1980), p. 475.

9. Jack Moser, "The Secularization of Equity: Ancient Religious Origins, Feudal Christian Influences, and Medieval Authoritarian Impacts on the Evolution of Legal Equitable Remedies," *Capital University Law Review* (1997), pp. 485, 489–492, 538; *Encyclopædia Britannica Online,* s.v. "Equity," http://search.eb.com/eb/article?tocId=9032851.

10. See Woods, *How the Catholic Church,* pp. 193–194; Berman, *Law and Revolution,* p. 188.

11. Woods, *How the Catholic Church,* pp. 133–138.

12. See Woods, *How the Catholic Church,* p. 187; Berman, *Law and Revolution,* p. 166.

13. Panati, *Extraordinary Origins,* pp. 52–53.

14. Paul Scalia, "Courting Reverence: Why Has the Courtroom Retained the Reverence the Mass has Lost?" *Adoremus Bulletin* 7:6 (September 2001), p. 3, available online at http://www.adoremus.org/0901Scalia.html.

15. Leopold Wagner, *Manners, Customs, and Observances: Their Origin and Signification* (London: William Heinemann, 1894), pp. 44, 46. Only a bishop is permitted to wear gloves during the sacrifice of the Mass, but he must take his hat (miter) off at certain times.

16. *Catholic Encyclopedia,* s.v. "Biretta" (by Herbert Thurston), http://www.newadvent.org/cathen/02577a.htm.

17. Wagner, *Manners,* p. 43.

18. I am indebted to Michael Marcucci, Esq., for his assistance with these distinctions.

19. "Clerk, n.," *OED.*

## NOTES FOR CHAPTER SIXTEEN

1. Etymology is a Greek word used also by several Latin authors, but Isidore's *Etymologies* was the first work in which the word appeared in its Latinized form. See *A Latin Dictionary,* eds. Charlton T. Lewis and Charles Short (Oxford: Clarendon Press, 1951), p. 663.

2. *De natura deorum,* 1.17.44, translation mine.

3. "Integrity, n.," 1 and 3b, *OED.*

4. Thomas More, *Utopia,* trans. Clarence H. Miller (New Haven: Yale University Press, 2001), p. 1.

5. David Wootton, *Thomas More: Utopia* (Indianapolis, Indiana: Hackett, 1999), p. 6.

6. Lewis and Short, *A Latin Dictionary,* p. 77.

7. See Pierre Barbet, M.D., *A Doctor at Calvary: The Passion of Our Lord Jesus Christ As Described by a Surgeon* (Fort Collins, CO: Roman Catholic Books, 1993), p. 160.

8. Though Cicero had used *rumination* in a metaphorical sense before the advent of Christianity, it was the Church Fathers who permanently wedding this meaning to the term.

9. *Enarratio in Psalmum* 66.3.

10. *Confessions* 10.14.21–22.

11. That said, Augustine is often wrongly accused of the so-called turn to the subject which led to an ultimately nihilistic schizophrenia in modern epistemology and metaphysics. That distinction rightly goes to René Descartes, a philosopher who paradoxically borrowed from Augustine *in order to* depart from Augustinian realism. See Michael Hanby, *Augustine and Modernity* (New York: Routledge, 2003).

12. *Confessions* 8.3.7.

13. Professor Khrostenko made this remark in a course he taught on the Latin of Augustine's *Confessions*.

14. "Rubric, a. and n.," *OED*.

15. "Red letter," 1b, 2a, *OED*.

16. John Stuart Mill, *On Liberty,* ed. Alburey Castell, ch. 2, ll. 198–203 (Arlington Heights: Crofts Classics, 1947), p. 27; see *Catholic Encyclopedia,* s.v. "Advocatus Diaboli" (by R. L. Burtsell), http://www.newadvent.org/cathen/01168b.htm.

17. Binney, *Origins,* pp. 309–310.

18. *Butler's Lives of the Saints,* vol. 2, p. 414.

19. See "Inquisition, n." 1, *OED;* "Inquisition, n." 3, dictionary.com.

20. See the entire see the November/December 1996 issue of *Catholic Dossier* as well as *Catholic Encyclopedia,* s.v. "Inquisition" (by Joseph Blötzer), http://www.newadvent.org/cathen/08026a.htm.

21. "Flat-Earther," dictionary.com.

22. For the fascinating history of this myth, see Burton Russell, *Inventing the Flat Earth: Columbus and Modern Historians* (New York: Praeger, 1991).

23. See "Legend," 6a, *OED*.

24. "Maudlin, a. and n." *OED*.

25. "Dance," 6c, *OED*.

26. "Macabre, n. 1," *OED*.

27. "Prologue," l.159. See Geoffrey Chaucer, *The Canterbury Tales,* trans. Nevill Coghill (Baltimore: Penguin Books, 1952), p. 507.

28. "Cretin," and "Cretinism," *OED*.

29. "Dunce," *OED*.

30. "Gossip," *OED*.

31. "Patter, v. 1," *OED*.

32. *Catholic Encyclopedia,* s.v. "Sacred Congregation of Propaganda" (by U. Benigni), http://www.newadvent.org/cathen/12456a.htm.

33. "Cavalier, n. and a.," *OED*.

34. *Catholic Encyclopedia,* s.v. "Mary Tudor" (by Herbert Thurston), http://www.newadvent.org/cathen/09766a.htm. Thurston is quoting a Dr. Gairdner.

35. D. G. M. Jackson, "Mary Tudor and the Protestants," http://web.archive.org/web/20010801231144/cts.bvm.com.au/australia/acts1198.html. For a more

recent assessment of Mary Tudor and English Catholicism, see Duffy's *Stripping of the Altars.*

36. Eric Partridge, *Words, Words, Words* (Freeport, New York: Books for Libraries Press, 1970), pp. 79–90.

37. "Bloody, a. and adv.," B.2, *OED.*

38. "Drat," *OED.*

39. "Laurence, n. 2," *OED.*

40. See "Bedlam," *OED,* and Manfred Siebald, "Bethlehem," in *A Dictionary of Biblical Tradition,* p. 85.

41. Don Lewis, *Religious Superstition,* p. 58.

42. "Sanctimonious, a.," *OED.*

43. "Bellarmine," *OED;* Anthony Thwaite, "The Chronology of the Bellarmine Jug," *The Connoisseur Magazine* (April 1973), available online at http://www1.bellarmine.edu/strobert/jugs/index.asp.

44. "Jesuitical, a.," no. 2, *OED;* David J. Endres, "The Legend of the Evil Jesuits: Reviving Catholicism in Elizabethan England," *The Gonzaga Catholic Studies Review,* vol. 1 (2003), p. 87.

45. *An exposicion vpon the v. vi. vii. chapters of Mathew (a* 1550) 64; cf. "Popery," *OED.*

46. "Pontificate, v.," def. 2a, *OED.*

47. "Pope's nose," dictionary.com, http://dictionary.reference.com/search?q=pope %27s%20nose.

48. Allan Bloom, "Commerce and 'Culture,'" in *Giants and Dwarfs: Essays 1960–1990* (New York: Simon and Schuster, 1990), p. 277.

49. *Sermon on the Twelve Stars,* cited in Guéranger, *Liturgical Year,* vol. 6, p. 172.

50. Rousseau's teaching on a sublimated human compassion is in *Emile,* which is different from depiction of the subpolitical animal compassion described in the *Second Discourse.* See Allan Bloom, "*Emile,*" in *Giants and Dwarfs,* pp. 194–198.

51. Bloom, "Emile," p. 196.

52. See Christine Mohrmann, *Liturgical Latin: Its Origins and Character* (Washington, D.C.: Catholic University of America Press, 1957), p. 36.

53. F. Cayré, "Le sens et l'unité des Confessions de saint Augustin," *L'Année Theologique Augustinienne* (45–46), 13, translation mine.

54. "The Divine Names," in *Pseudo-Dionysius: The Complete Works,* trans. Colm Luibheid (New York: Paulist Press, 1987), p. 83.

55. "The Celestial Hierarchy," 3.2, in *Pseudo-Dionysius,* p. 154.

56. See the *Second Discourse,* or *Discourse on Inequality.*

57. See Cicero, *De natura deorum* 2.11.29.

58. See Romans 12:6, I Corinthians 7:7, 12:30–31.

59. Allan Bloom, *The Closing of the American Mind* (New York: Simon and Schuster, 1987), p. 211. Bloom's entire discussion of Weber is noteworthy (pp. 208–214).

60. This is the approved translation currently used in most English-speaking countries for the Latin, *et omnibus orthodoxis atque catholicæ et apostolicæ*

*fidei cultoribus.* See *Handbook of Prayers,* ed. Charles Belmonte and James Socias (Manila: Aletheia Foundation, Inc., 1988), pp. 132–133.

61. See Genesis 19:1, Exodus 18:7, Numbers 22:31 in the Protestant King James Version and the Catholic Douay-Rheims translations.

62. *Leviathan,* Part I, chapter 6.

63. Thomas Hobbes, *De Hominis Natura,* Epistle Dedicatory. Hobbes goes on to indicate that his new mode of doing political science will be more mathematical than dogmatical. Such a retooling, however, did not render Hobbes's philosophy free from "controversy and dispute."

64. "Dogmatic, a. and n.," 4, *OED.*

65. See Friedrich Nietzsche, *Thus Spoke Zarathustra.*

66. See Bloom, *Closing,* pp. 180–184. Bloom locates the germ for the emphasis on creativity in Rousseau.

67. Though not found in any official papal documents, the word *co-creator* was used in the earlier writings of Karol Wojtyla (before he became Pope John Paul II), and it is generally seen as a faithful synopsis of the anthropology advanced by him after his elevation to the papacy. See Edward Vacek, "John Paul II and Cooperation with God," *The Annual of the Society of Christian Ethics* (Washington, D.C.: Georgetown University Press, 1990), p. 101, fn. 2. This by no means implies, of course, that the Holy Father was a Nietzschean.

68. *Justice vindicated from the false fucus put upon it by Tho. White* etc. *as also, Elements of power and subjection,* Ep. Ded. 5, quoted in "Victim, n.," 2a, *OED.*

69. G. W. F. Hegel, *Phenomenology of Spirit,* §§166–96. Hegel's logic is difficult to follow, but the basic argument is that the human subject becomes free through self-consciousness and he or she becomes self-conscious by negating, confronting, or overcoming fear and work, which is possible only when one has fear and work in one's life. Hence, fear and work are instrumental in the liberation of self-consciousness.

70. The crucial link between Hegel and feminism appears to be Simone de Beauvoir's *The Second Sex.* See Nancy Bauer, *Simone de Beauvoir, Philosophy, and Feminism* (New York: Columbia University Press, 2001), especially chapter six.

71. I am indebted to Dr. Daniel McInerny at Notre Dame for his insights into this topic.

72. See Francesa Valente, "Joyce's *Dubliners* as Epiphanies," http://www.themodernword.com/joyce/paper_valente.html.

73. "Talent," III.5, *OED.*

## NOTES FOR CHAPTER SEVENTEEN

1. For a recent example, see Alister McGrath, *In the Beginning: The Story of the King James Bible and How it Changed a Nation, a Language, and a Culture* (New York: Doubleday, 2001).

2. *Confessions* 9.4.11 (Sheed, p. 157), *Epistle Against Fundatus* 5.6, translation mine.

3. Samuel McComb, *The Making of the English Bible* (New York: Moffat, Yard, and Company, 1909), pp. 78–79.

4. *Confessions* 3.5.9 (Sheed, p. 39).

5. "Apple of the Eye," in *A Dictionary of Biblical Tradition*, p. 52.

6. "Blind Lead the Blind," in *A Dictionary of Biblical Tradition*, p. 93.

7. Quoted in David L. Jeffrey and I. Howard Marshall, "Eucharist," in *A Dictionary of Biblical Tradition*, p. 246.

8. "Bricks Without Straw," in *A Dictionary of Biblical Tradition*, p. 105.

9. Chapter 48; see Lenore Gussin and David L. Jeffrey, "Camel Through a Needle's Eye," in *A Dictionary of Biblical Tradition*, pp. 123–124.

10. Izaak Walton, *The Compleat Angler,* ed. Richard Le Gallienne (London: Senate, 1994), p. 69.

11. Augustine, *Enarratio in Psalmum 42* and Augustine, *Confessions* 13.13.14, cited in Richard Schell, "Deep Calleth unto Deep," in *A Dictionary of Biblical Tradition*, p. 190.

12. "East, East of Eden," in *A Dictionary of Biblical Tradition*, p. 220.

13. "Jot and Tittle," *OED.*

14. Cf. Leviticus 24:20, Deuteronomy 19:21.

15. Augustine, *De sermone Domini in Monte* 1.19.56; see "*Lex Talionis,*" in *Tradition*, p. 450.

16. "Homily XVIII," in *The Homilies of S. John Chrysostom, Archbishop of Constantinople, on the Gospel of St. Matthew,* Part I, Hom. I-XXV, trans. John Henry Parker (London: J. G. F. and J. Rivington, 1843), pp. 270–271.

17. Daniel himself does not tell us which empires correspond to which parts.

18. "Fire and Brimstone," in *A Dictionary of Biblical Tradition*, p. 280.

19. "Fly in the Ointment," The New Dictionary of Cultural Literacy, 3rd ed., 2002, http://www.bartleby.com/59/4/flyintheoint.html.

20. Luke 12:35, Ephesians 6:13–14, and I Peter 1:13.

21. Springfield, Illinois, June 16, 1858. An online copy of the speech may be found on the History Place website, http://www.historyplace.com/lincoln/divided.htm.

22. First joint Lincoln-Douglas debate, Ottawa, August 21, 1858. An online copy of the debate may be found at http://www.usconstitution.com/Lincoln-DouglasDebates1.htm.

23. "Jeremiah," "Jeremiad," *OED,* respectively.

24. "Jezebel," *OED.*

25. See Tobias 2:12, James 5:11.

26. "Job, n., 4," *OED.*

27. "Kick Against the Pricks," in *A Dictionary of Biblical Tradition,* p. 426.

28. Interestingly, the verse in question has been omitted from most modern biblical translations.

29. "Leopard Change His Spots," in *A Dictionary of Biblical Tradition,* p. 443.

30. See Matthew 15:3–9, where Christ criticizes the Pharisees, not for being rigid in their enforcement of the Mosaic law, but for *ignoring* it in favor of their own ancestral, nonscriptural innovations. See Michael P. Foley, "The Paradox

of Christian Tradition," in *Gladly to Learn and Gladly to Teach: Essays on Religion and Politial Philosophy in Honor of Ernest L. Fortin, A.A.,* eds. Michael P. Foley and Douglas Kries (Lanham, Maryland: Lexington Books, 2002), pp. 3–16.

31. Augustine, *De spiritu et littera,* 4; see "Letter and Spirit," in *A Dictionary of Biblical Tradition,* p. 445.

32. Leviticus 19:15; cf. Deuteronomy 1:17, 16:19, Numbers 15:15, James 2:1–9.

33. See "No Respecter of Persons," in *A Dictionary of Biblical Tradition,* p. 551. The personification of Justice as a woman holding scales goes back to ancient Greece and Rome, but "the blindfold with which Justice is now associated probably started in the 16th century" ("Ancient/Classical History," http://ancienthistory.about.com/cs/godsreligion/a/justicegoddess.htm).

34. Ernest K. Kaulbach, "Noonday Demon," in *A Dictionary of Biblical Tradition,* p. 554.

35. R. R. Reno, "Fighting the Noonday Devil," *First Things* 135 (August/September 2003), pp. 31–36, available at http://www.firstthings.com/ftissues/ft0308/articles/reno.html.

36. Phillip Rogers, "Out of the Mouth of Babes," in *A Dictionary of Biblical Tradition,* p. 580.

37. See St. Augustine, *De sermone Domini in Monte* 2.20.68–69; "Pearls Before Swine," in *A Dictionary of Biblical Tradition,* p. 595.

38. "Pearl of Great Price," in *A Dictionary of Biblical Tradition,* pp. 594–595.

39. See Origen, *De principiis* 4.3.1; Augustine, Letter 138.2.12; Cassian, *Conferences* 3.24. Indeed, the basic idea is that the same God who initiated restraint by imposing the *lex talionis,* or "eye for an eye," is now bringing the idea of restraint to its ultimate perfection with the command to turn the other cheek (see Chrysostom, *Homilies on the Gospel of Matthew* 18.1; Cassian, *Conferences* 8.3).

40. Matthew 8:12, 13:42, 13:50, 22:13, 24:51, and 25:30. Cf. Psalm 35:12, 110:10.

41. David Sten Herrstrom, "Wheels within Wheels," in *A Dictionary of Biblical Tradition,* p. 823.

42. "Wolves in Sheep's Clothing," in *A Dictionary of Biblical Tradition,* p. 844.

# Works Consulted

St. Augustine, *Confessions,* trans. Frank Sheed (Indianapolis, Indiana: Hackett, 1993)

Ball, Ann, *Catholic Traditions in Cooking* (Huntington, Indiana: Our Sunday Visitor, 1993)

Bannatyne, Lesley Pratt, *Halloween: An American Holiday, an American History* (Gretna, Louisiana: Pelican Publishing Company, 1998)

Barbet, Pierre, *A Doctor at Calvary: The Passion of Our Lord Jesus Christ As Described by a Surgeon* (Fort Collins, Colorado: Roman Catholic Books, 1993)

Baring-Gould, Sabine, *Germany Present and Past* (London: C. K. Paul & Co., 1879)

Barnes, A. S., *Catholic Oxford* (London: Catholic Truth Society, 1933)

Bauer, Nancy, *Simone de Beauvoir, Philosophy, and Feminism* (New York: Columbia University Press, 2001)

Beatty, Michael A., *County Name Origins of the United States* (Jefferson, North Carolina: McFarland & Company, Inc., 2001)

Camp, Raymond R., *Family Circle's Guide to Trout Flies* (Newark, New Jersey: Family Circle, 1954)

Benham, W. Gurney, *Playing Cards: History of the Pack and Explanations of Its Many Secrets* (London: Ward, Lock & Co., 1931)

Binney, Ruth, ed., *The Origins of Everyday Things* (Pleasantville, New York: Readers' Digest Association, 1999)

Bloom, Allan, *The Closing of the American Mind* (New York: Simon and Schuster, 1987)

———, *Giants and Dwarfs: Essays 1960–1990* (New York: Simon and Schuster, 1990)

Bogle, Joanna, *Book of Feasts and Seasons,* 3rd ed. (Leominster: Gracewing Books, 1992)

*Breviarum Romanum* (Ratisbona, 1939), 4 vols.

Brookhiser, Richard, ed., *Rules of Civility: The 110 Precepts That Guided Our First President in War and Peace* (New York: The Free Press, 1997),

*Butler's Lives of the Fathers, Martyrs, and Other Saints,* 4 vols., ed. Rev. F. C. Husenbeth, (Great Falls, Montana: St. Bonaventure Publications, 1997)

Cameron, Kenneth, *English Place Names,* new ed. (London: B. T. Batsford, 1997)

Carosso, Vincent P., *The California Wine Industry, 1830–1895* (Berkeley: University of California Press, 1951)

*Catholic Builders of the Nation,* 5 vols., ed. C. E. McGuire (Boston: Continental Press, 1923)

*Catholic Encyclopedia,* 25 vols. (New York: The Gilmary Society, 1907–1912), available online at http://www.newadvent.org/cathen/

Chaucer, Geoffrey, *The Canterbury Tales,* trans. Nevill Coghill (New York: Penguin Books, 2003)

Chesterton, G. K., *G. K. Chesterton: Essential Writings,* ed. William Griffin (New York: Orbis Books, 2003)

Chrétien de Troyes, *Arthurian Romances,* trans. William W. Kibler (London: Penguin Books, 1991)

Collier, J. Payne, ed., *Illustrations of Early English Poetry,* Vol. 5, No. 3 (London, 1866–70)

Daiches, David, *Scotch Whiskey: Its Past and Present* (Edinburgh: Birlinn Ltd., 1995)

Dante, *The Divine Comedy,* trans. Allen Mandelbaum (New York: Everyman's Library, 1995)

De Salas Y Gilavert, Don Andrés, *The Influence of Catholicism on the Sciences and on the Arts,* trans. Mariana Monteiro (London: Sands & Co., 1900)

*Dictionary of Superstitions,* eds. Iona Opie and Moira Tatem (Oxford: Oxford University Press, 1989)

*The Documents of Vatican II,* ed. Walter M. Abbott, S.J. (New York: Guild Press, 1966)

Douglas, George William, *The American Book of Days,* revised by Helen Douglas Compton (New York: The H.W. Wilson Company, 1948)

Duffy, Eamon, *The Stripping of the Altars: Traditional Religion in England, 1400–1580,* 2nd ed. (New Haven: Yale University Press, 2005)

Dunsby, Jonathan, "Polyphony," *The New Oxford Companion to Music,* Vol. 2, ed. Denis Arnold (Oxford: Oxford University Press, 1983)

Dyer, T. F. Thiselton, *The Folk-Lore of Plants* (London: Chatto & Windus, 1889)

*The Encyclopædia Britannica* from Encyclopædia Britannica Online, http://search.eb.com/.

*The Encyclopedia of Chess,* compiled by Anne Sunnucks (New York: St. Martin's Press, 1970)

Foley, Michael P., *Wedding Rites: The Complete Guide to Traditional Weddings* (South Bend, Indiana: St. Augustine's Press, 2005)

Fortin, Ernest L., *Ernest L. Fortin: Collected Essays,* Vol. 1, ed. J. Brian Benestad (Lanham, Maryland: Rowman and Littlefield, 1996)

Freeman, Allyn, and Golden, Bob, *Why Didn't I Think of That? Bizarre Origins of Ingenious Inventions We Couldn't Live Without* (New York: John Wiley & Sons, Inc., 1997)

Furnivall, Frederick J., ed., *Manners and Morals in Olden Time* (London: Early English Text Society, 1868)

Gioia, Ted, *The History of Jazz* (New York: Oxford University Press, 1997)

Giscard d'Estaing, Valérie-Anne, *Second World Almanac Book of Inventions* (New York: World Almanac, 1986)

Greene, Graham, *The End of the Affair* (New York: Viking, 1951)

Dom Guéranger, O.S.B., *The Liturgical Year,* trans. Dom Laurence Shepherd, O.S.B., 15 vols. (Great Falls, Montana: St. Bonaventure Publications, 2000)

*Handbook of Prayers,* eds. Charles Belmonte and James Socias (Manila: Aletheia Foundation, Inc., 1988)

Hartle, Ann, *The Modern Self in Rousseau's* Confessions: *A Reply to St. Augustine* (South Bend, Indiana: University of Notre Dame Press, 1983)

Haskins, Charles Homer, *The Rise of Universities,* intro by Lionel S. Lewis (London: Transaction Publishers, 2002; New York: Henry Holt & Co., 1923)

Henriques, E. Frank, *The Signet Encyclopedia of Whiskey, Brandy, & All Other Spirits* (New York: Signet Library, 1979)

*The Holy Bible* [Douay-Rheims] (Baltimore: John Murphy Co., 1914)

Jeffrey, David Lyle, ed., *A Dictionary of Biblical Tradition in English Literature* (Grand Rapids, Michigan: Eerdmans, 1992)

Levy, Joel, *Really Useful: The Origins of Everyday Things* (New York: Firefly Books, 2002)

St. John Chrysostom, *The Homilies of S. John Chrysostom, Archbishop of Constantinople, on the Gospel of St. Matthew,* trans. John Henry Parker (London: J. G. F. and J. Rivington, 1843)

Karp, Theodore, *Dictionary of Music* (Evanston, Illinois: Northwestern University Press, 1983)

Krymow, Vincenzina, *Mary's Flowers: Gardens, Legends, and Meditations* (Cincinnati: St. Anthony Messenger Press, 1999)

Lefebvre, Dom Gaspar, *Saint Andrew Daily Missal* (St. Paul, Minnesota: E. M. Lohmann Co., 1952)

Lewis, Don, *Religious Superstition Through the Ages* (London: Mowbrays, 1975)

Lichine, Alexis, *Alexis Lichine's New Encyclopedia of Wines & Spirits* (New York: Alfred A. Knopf, 1985)

Lo Bello, Nino, *The Incredible Book of Facts and Papal Curiosities: A Treasury of Trivia* (New York: Gramercy Books, 1998)

Marinacci, Barbara and Rudy, *California's Spanish Place-Names: What They Mean and How They Got There* (Houston, Texas: Gulf Publishing Co., 1997)

McCabe, William H., *An Introduction to the Jesuit Theater: A Posthumous Work,* ed. Louis J. Oldani, S.J. (St. Louis, Missouri: The Institute of Jesuit Sources, 1983)

McComb, Samuel, *The Making of the English Bible* (New York: Moffat, Yard, and Company, 1909)

McGuire, E. B., *Irish.Whiskey: A History of Distilling, the Spirit Trade and Excise Controls in Ireland* (New York: Barnes and Noble, 1973)

Meyer, Jr., Robert, *Festivals U.S.A.* (New York: Ive Washburn, Inc., 1950)

Mill, John Stuart, *On Liberty,* ed. Alburey Castell (Arlington Heights: Crofts Classics, 1947)

Mohrmann, Christine, *Liturgical Latin: Its Origins and Character* (Washington, D.C.: Catholic University of America Press, 1957)

More, Sir Thomas, *Utopia,* trans. Clarence H. Miller, (New Haven: Yale University Press, 2001)

Murray, Jim, *Classic Irish Whiskey* (London: Prion Boooks Ltd., 1997)

*The New Grove Dictionary of Opera,* Vol. 2, ed. Stanley Sadie (London: Macmillan Press, 1992)

*Official Encyclopedia of Tennis,* U.S. Lawn Tennis Association Staff (New York: Harper and Row, 1972)

*Oxford English Dictionary,* 2nd ed., available online at http://dictionary.oed.com/entrance.dtl

Opie, Iona and Peter, eds., *The Oxford Dictionary of Nursery Rhymes* (Oxford: Oxford University Press, 1997)

Panati, Charles, *Extraordinary Origins of Everyday Things* (New York: Perennial Library, 1987)

Partridge, Eric, *Words, Words, Words* (Freeport, New York: Books for Libraries Press, 1970)

Percy, Walker, *Signposts in a Strange Land,* ed. Patrick Samway (New York: Farrar, Straus, and Giroux, 1991)

Pieper, Josef, *Only the Lover Sings: Art and Contemplation,* trans. Lothar Krauth (San Francisco: Ignatius Press, 1990)

*Pontificale Romanum,* Pars Prima (Rome: Mechliniae, 1845)

Post, Emily, *Etiquette* (New York: Funk and Wagnalls, 1945)

*Pseudo-Dionysius: The Complete Works,* trans. Colm Luibheid (New York: Paulist Press, 1987)

*Rituale Romanum* (Rome: Desclee, 1943)

Ratzinger, Joseph Cardinal, *A New Song for the Lord: Faith in Christ and Liturgy Today,* trans. Martha M. Matesich (New York: Crossroad Publishing, 1996)

Russell, Burton, *Inventing the Flat Earth: Columbus and Modern Historians* (New York: Praeger, 1991)

Shearer, Benjamin F. and Barbara S., *State Names, Seals, Flags, and Symbols: An Historical Guide* (New York: Greenwood Press, 1987)

Stewart, George R., *American Place-Names: A Concise and Selective Dictionary for the Continental United States of America* (New York: Oxford University Press, 1970)

Stopsky, Fred, *Catholicism and Slavery* (New York: The Catholic League, 1999)

U.S. Department of State, *The Seal of the United States,* Department and Foreign Service Series 64 (Washington, D.C.: 1957)

Vitz, Evelyn Birge, *A Continual Feast: A Cookbook to Celebrate the Joys of Family and Faith Throughout the Christian Year* (San Francisco: Ignatius Press, 1985)

Walters, Helen, *The Story of Caps and Gowns* (Chicago: E. R. Moore Company, 1939)

Warrack, John, and West, Ewan, *The Oxford Dictionary of Opera* (Oxford: Oxford University Press, 1992)

Waugh, Evelyn, *Sword of Honour* (Boston: Little Brown & Company, 1961)

Weiser, Francis X., *Religious Customs in the Family: The Radiation of the Liturgy into Christian Homes* (Collegeville, Minnesota: The Liturgical Press, 1956)

———, *Handbook of Christian Feasts and Customs: The Year of the Lord in Liturgy and Folklore* (New York: Harcourt, Brace & World, Inc., 1958)

Thomas E. Woods, Jr., *How the Catholic Church Built Western Civilization* (Washington, D.C.: Regnery, 2005)

Younger, William, *Gods, Men, and Wine* (London: The Wine and Food Society, 1966)

# Index

Aaron, high priest, 81
*a capella,* 60
aeronautics, 97–98
agony, 146–147
agricultural science, 98
Alabama, symbols of,
    134–135
alphabet, 117
amps, volts, and coulombs,
    101
anchor, 136
angelite, 95
angels, 71, 80, 91
Anne polkas, 57–58
*anno Domini* (A.D.), 8
anthem, 56
'apple of the eye,' 170
architecture, 40–45
Arizona, state flag of, 135
art and leisure, 39–40
    *see under* individual
        arts
artificial fertilization, 111
astronomy, 98–99
autobiography, 45–46
*Ave Maria, see* 'Hail Mary'

bacteriology, 99–100
baptism, 14, 150–151, 155
barometer, 109
Baroque, 43, 50
bead, 80
bedlam, 157
beer, 35
'before Christ' (B.C.), 8

begging, 25
bellarmine jug, 157
Benedictine, 25, 28, 34, 90,
    114, 116
bishop, 70, 72, 87, 93, 106,
    141
black, 106, 107
Blessed Sacrament, 67, 126,
    136
'blind leading the blind,'
    170
Bloody Mary, 156
blue, 107, 119
Boston, 125–126
botany, 100
bowling, 69
Boxing Day, 18–19
brandy, 33
breakfast, 24
'breaking bread,' 171
'bricks without straw,' 171
'bun in the oven,' 171

calculator, 108
calendar, 8–9
'camel through the eye of a
    needle,' 171
Candlemas, 13, 85
cap and gown, 115
cappuccino, 35–36
cardinal, 87, 90, 107–108,
    150
cards, playing, 70
carnival, 12, 59
Catherine wheel, 44, 111

cavalier, 155
cemetery, 111–112
champagne, 33
charismatic, 162–163
charity, 159–160
Chartreuse, 33, 34, 90, 108
Châteauneuf-du-Pape,
    32–33
cheese, 28–29
chess, 69–70
chivalry, 22
Christmas, 17–18, 76, 78,
    84
city names, 125–129
clerking, 141–142
clock, 10
clothes, 105–107
    *see under* specific
        kinds of clothing
collation, 25
colors, 107–108
    *see under* different
        colors
Columbus, Christopher,
    124–125, 152
Columbus Day, 15
compassion, 160
confession, 45, 124, 140,
    141, 150, 161
contracts, 138
corporal punishment, 116
Corpus Christi, 67, 126
costmary, 82
courtroom, 140–141
creativity, 164–165

cretin, 154
crisscross, 116–117
croissant, 29
cross, 77, 118, 140
county names, 124–125
cult, 163
Cyrillic alphabet, 117

Dannebrog, 131
death penalty, 140
'deep calleth unto deep,' 172
devil, 80, 94–95
devil's advocate, 148
dinner, 24–25
dirge, 60–61
diseases, 93–94
Divine Office, 10, 55–56,
    58–59, 60–61, 72,
    116
dogmatic, 163–164
dollar bill, 134
Dominican Republic, 131
Dominicans, 58–59, 114
dominoes, 72
drat, 156
drinks, 32–36, 156
dumbbells, 69
dunce, 154–155

Easter, 14, 77, 86, 123
'east of Eden,' 172
education, 113–118
eggs benedict, 29
eighth day, 9
electricity, 101–102
elementary school, 115–116
Ember Days, 31–32
entomology, 101
epic, 47
epiphany, 166
equity, 139
etymology, 145
Eucharist, see Mass,
    Blessed Sacrament
'every jot and tittle,' 172
'eye for an eye,' 173

'fatted calf,' 173
'feet of clay,' 173–174

filberts, 83
Finnish flag, 131
'fire and brimstone,' 174
fishing, 46, 69, 109
fish on Friday, 29–30, 152
flags, 131–136
    see under individual
        states and nations
flat-earther, 152
'flesh pots of Egypt,' 174
fleur-de-lis, 132
Florida, 123, 135
flowers, 75–87
'fly in the ointment,' 174
food, 27–32, 148
    see under individual
        foods
forbidden fruit, 174–175
Franciscans, 44, 71, 114,
    126–128
frangelico, 34
French flags, 132
Friday, 29–30, 119

gargoyles, 51–52
gaudy, 153
genetics, 102
Georgia, state flag of, 135
'gird up thy loins,' 175
golf, 68–69
'goodbye,' 23
'God bless you,' 23
gossip, 155
Gothic, 42–43
Graham cracker, 27
Gregorian chant, 54, 59–60
greybeard jug, 157
Groundhog Day, 13
Guy Fawkes Day, 11–12, 17

'Hail Mary,' 56, 71–72, 80
Halloween, 16–17
Hawaiian state flag, 135
hearse, 110
Herod, 65
hierarchy, 161–162
high school, 115–116
hocus pocus, 157
holidays, 11–19

    see under individual
        holidays
holly, 84
holy orders, 141–142
holy smoke, 149–150
Holy Spirit flowers, 77
horseshoe, 119–120
hot cross buns, 30
'house divided,' 176
'how are the mighty fallen,'
    175–176
hydrostatics, 103

Icelandic flag, 131
iconoclasm, 49–50, 163
Idaho, state motto of, 135
Ignatius bean, 84
incense, 149–150
inquisition, 152
integrity, 146
inventions, 10, 105–112
    see under individual
        inventions
Iowan state flag, 135
Irish flag, 133

jack-o'-lantern, 16
Jacob's ladder, 80–81
Jägermeister, 34–35
jazz, 59
jeremiad, 176
Jesuitical, 157–158
Jesuits, 24, 32, 44, 63, 64,
    84, 87, 99, 103, 116
Jezebel, 176
Job, 81, 176–177
John Dory fish, 91–92
johnswort, 82
Joseph's coat, 81
judicial garb, 141
juniper, 79

Kellogg cornflake, 27
'kick against the pricks,' 177

lacrosse, 72
'ladies first,' 22
ladybug, 89–90
'lady' flowers, 79

*Laetare,* or Mothering, Sunday, 15, 85
lamentations, 56
last rites (anointing of the sick), 110–111
laurence, 94
lazy, 156
law, 137–142
Lebanese flag, 133
legend, 152–153
Lent, 12, 14, 22, 25, 31, 35, 59, 71, 85, 141
leopard's spots, 177
'the letter killeth,' 177–178
liability, 139
lightning rod, 101–102
lily of the valley, 79–80
linguistics, 102
literature, 45–48
    *see under* individual genres
Liturgy of the Hours, *see* Divine Office
lobby, 45
lodge, 45
Los Angeles, 126
Louisiana, state flag of, 135–136

macabre, 153
mackerel-snapper, 152
Madonna lily, 78
manners, 21–25
    *see under* individual manners
'man of sorrows,' 178
marguerite daisy, 83
marigolds, 78
marriage, 119, 138
Mary, Blessed Virgin, 13, 15, 31, 55, 56, 77–80, 85, 86, 89–90, 91, 107, 109–110, 126, 127, 128, 132, 160, 171
Maryland, symbols of, 136
Mass, 17, 40, 53–57, 58, 62, 106, 141, 150, 157, 163, 182

    *see also* Requiem, Blessed Sacrament
maudlin, 153
*mea culpa,* 150
Mercedes, 109–110
Mexican flag, 133
Michaelmas, 86–87, 141
midnight snack, 24
mincemeat pie, 30
minerals, 94–95
mission style, 44
Mississippi, state flag of, 135
mole, 30
monks, 87, 91, 92, 104, 107
    *see under* individual orders
Montserrat flag, 133
Moses in the bulrush, 81
Mother's Day, 14–15
music, 53–62
musical notation, 61
'my brother's keeper,' 178
'my cup runneth over,' 172

New Mexico, state flag of, 135
New York, name of, 124
nickel, 94
noon, 25
noonday devil, 178
'not one iota,' 151
Norwegian flag, 131
novel, 46–47
nursery rhymes, 58–59

Old Nick, 65
Olympics motto, 68
opera, 64
oratorio, 57
orientation, 164
'Our Father,' 153, 155
'out of the mouths of babes,' 179

p_czki, 30–31
Padres, San Diego, 71
pageantry, 64
painting, 48–50

Palm Sunday, 85, 123
pants, 106
papacy, 149–150, 158, 159
Passion (of Christ), 8, 56–57, 62–64, 76–77, 106, 160
pasta, 31
pathology, 102–103
patter, 155
'pearl of great price,' 179
'pearls before swine,' 179
pelican, 135–136
petrel, 92
physics, 101
pigeons, 91
piñata, 71
Pio Nono Avenue, 129–130
plants, 75–87
polyphony, 57
pontificate, 158–159
popery, 151, 158
pretzel, 31
priest, 31, 91, 106, 110–111, 115, 126, 141, *see also* holy orders
primer, 116
propaganda, 155
pseudo-Catholic names, 130
pumpernickel, 94
Purgatory, 16, 124

quarantine, 12
*Quo vadis?,* 149

radio, 109
red, 108
red-letter day, 148
Requiem Mass, 55, 91
'respecter of persons,' 178
Rhode Island, state flag of, 135
roadside shrines, 112
Rogation Days, 86
Romanesque, 41–42
rompope, 34
rosary, 80, 154
rosemary, 79
rubrics, 148
rule of law, 138–139

rumination, 147

sacramentality, 2, 27–28,
    75–76, 89
Sacramento, California, 126
sacraments,
    *see under* individual
      sacraments
sainfoin, 78
St. Anthony's fire, 93–94
St. Augustine grass, 83
St. Barbara's cress, 82–83
St. Barnaby's thistle, 82
St. Bernard dog, 90–91
St. Elmo's fire, 94
St. James shell, 93
St. Lawrence, 94, 156
St. Louis, Missouri, 128
St. Mary Magdalene, 82,
    153
St. Marys, West Virginia,
    128
St. Paul, Minnesota, 128
St. Peter, 82, 91–92
Saints, New Orleans, 71
Saint Tammany Parish,
    Louisiana, 130
St. Vitus' dance, 93
San Antonio, Texas,
    126–127
San Diego, California, 127
San Francisco, California,
    127
Santa Fe, New Mexico, 127
science, modern, 97–104
    *see under* individual
      sciences
sculpture, 50–51
season (theatrical), 64
seismology, 103

Seven Last Words, 56
Shakespeare, William, 48
sign language, 117–118
silver spoon, 150–151
simnel, 15, 85
slide projector, 108–109
snack food, 148
soliloquy, 147
solmization, 61–62
'something blue,' 119
'spirit is willing,' 180
statics, 103
steeplechase, 70
stollen, 31
story, 44
stratigraphy, 103–104
street names, 129–130
Sunday, 9, 39–40
superstition, 118–120
Swedish flag, 131
Swiss flag, 133

table knife, 23
talent, 166–167
tartan, 106
tawdry, 154
technology, 108–110
television, 109
tempura, 31–32
tennis, 68
Termagant, 64–65
Thanksgiving Day, 17
theater, 62–66
thirteen, 119
tide tables, 104
time, 7–10; *see also* noon
tobacco auctioneering,
    59–60
transubstantiation, 157
Trappists, 28, 35

trick or treat, 17
Trinity columns, 43–44
    plants, 76
'turn the other cheek,'
    180–181
Twelfth Night, 65
tying the knot, 119

Union Jack, 132
universities, 113–115
utopia, 146

Valentine's Day, 13
valentinite, 95
Vatican City flag, 134
veronica, 82
victim, 165–166

'wailing and gnashing of
    teeth,' 181
Washington, D.C., 129
Washington, George, 24
weekend, 9
'weighed in the balance,'
    181
'wheels within wheels,'
    181
'When in Rome,' 148–149
whiskey, 34
wine, 32–33
'wolf's in sheep's clothing,'
    181
wood, knocking on, 118
'writing on the wall,'
    181–182
wulfenite, 95

'X,' 140

zany, 65–66